Here and Away

Discovering Home on an Island in Maine

DEBORAH CUMMINS

Also by Deborah Cummins

Counting the Waves
Beyond the Reach
From The Road It Looks Like Paradise

Here and Away
©2012 Deborah Cummins
ISBN 978-1-936447-03-9

Cover image "House Island" is courtesy of artist Alison Goodwin,
www.alisongoodwin.com

Designed and Produced by
Maine Authors Publishing
558 Main Street, Rockland, Maine 04841
www.maineauthorspublishing.com

In Memory of

my brother,
Joseph Anton Bolda, Jr.

and

my mother,
Leona Helen Bolda

Contents

PROLOGUE • 5

HERE
HOW IT GOES • 13
NAMES • 21
OF TWO WORLDS • 35
EBB AND FLOW • 39
PROTECTING THE DREAMER • 55
OLD DOG • 71
WHAT THE BODY KNOWS • 89
A NECESSARY BALLAST • 101
IN CONCERT • 117
GUIDING ME HOME • 137

AWAY
TOUCHSTONE • 153
IN THEIR HANDS • 169
UNEARTHED • 185
EDGES • 193
MESSAGES • 207
WITH OPEN EYES • 211
THE LONG GOOD-BYE • 225

ACKNOWLEDGMENTS • 235

SELECTED BIBLIOGRAPHY • 237

ABOUT THE AUTHOR • 239

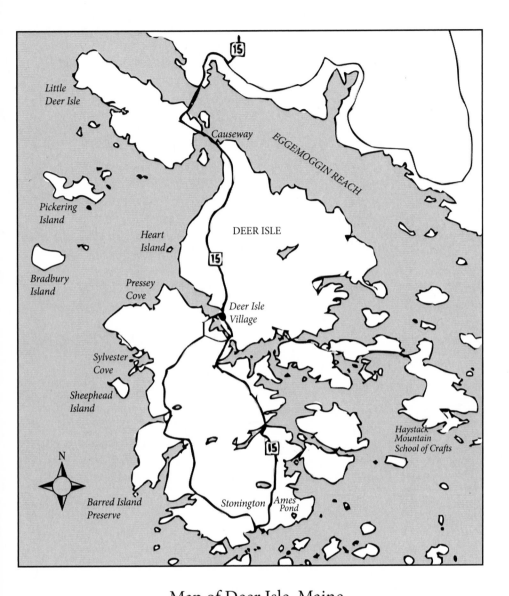

Map of Deer Isle, Maine,

highlighting some locations mentioned in the following pages.

"There is the place that happens,
and the place that happens to you."

Eavan Boland

PROLOGUE

*F*or several months each year, I live on an island in Downeast Maine.

A small island in the northeast Atlantic may seem a surprising choice for a lifelong Midwesterner who doesn't swim very well and is transformed into a welter of thumbs aboard a boat. Whose family never traveled to this part of the country. Who had no claims to it, no connections or ties.

But in the summer of 1995, well into middle age, I came home to a place where I'd never been. To a home I didn't know I'd lost.

*O*n a map of the United States, Deer Isle appears as no more than a speck at the northeastern corner of the vast North American continent. It lies off the southern tip of the Blue Hill Peninsula, across the Eggemoggin Reach, and extends into the eastern portion of Penobscot Bay, Maine's largest bay and home to more than 200 islands. Due in part to its rugged coastline, the Bay is often likened to the waterways of Finland or Norway, but less frigid—a comparison that offers small comfort even in mid-August when water temperatures stay so low it's long prompted the logic of local lobstermen who, confronting the potential danger of being pitched overboard into those icy waters, ask: Why bother to learn how to swim?

Measuring approximately 12 by 6 miles, Deer Isle is not particularly large but well exceeds what the U.S. Geological Survey reportedly requires: that to be counted among Maine's more than 4,000 islands, it must be at least one acre, or roughly the size of a Super Walmart parking lot. According to recent census figures, approximately 1,800 folks reside on Deer Isle, the demographics of which, as with most remote and rural communities, reflect an ongoing trend: the number of older residents is increasing as school populations decline. Here, you'll find not a single traffic light, fast-food restaurant, or shopping mall. But we do have two food stores. Also two town governments, two phone exchanges, two bank branches and two schools. Likewise, two volunteer fire departments and two transfer stations, or, as they're known elsewhere, town dumps. Given the recent cutbacks, I suspect the federal government has something up its sleeve about our three post offices—four if you count Little Deer's. And though there are multiple gas stations, art galleries, and churches, it's likely we'll stick with one shellfish warden.

Though discrete and surrounded by water, Deer Isle connects to the mainland by way of a vehicular suspension bridge. And though our bridge is nearly 2,500 feet long and possesses a main span of more than 1,000 feet, with an arcing drive deck soaring 100 feet above the Reach and taller cabled towers double that, it can't deflect the belief held by some folks that Deer Isle is a mere extension of the mainland.

But ask the residents here and, fiercely proud of it, they'll tell you Deer Isle is an island. As if the bridge didn't exist. Or that it was capable of being rolled up, a feat that, come late July when the tourist count is high, more than a few locals might wish were possible.

*A*s if I'd been meant to cross that bridge, the needles of my inner compass pointed me in this direction. True, I long harbored an amorphous and, I suspect, rather clichéd fantasy about living in a house by the sea. But that can't account for, nor can it explain how, living within walking distance of a Great Lake and an easy enough drive to lakefront cottages in nearby Michigan, I felt unmistakably pulled toward the distant Northeast, Maine specifically. As though I were a migrating bird that had been blown off course and landed for a time (more than forty years!) in the Midwest. Or as though I'd been drawn here by a memory older than me. Some deep-within, unclear-as-to-source urge that told me I must follow up on it.

Such were not the details, however, that I offered to the person responsible for suggesting this part of the state—a former Illinois neighbor originally from Massachusetts whose family had for many years spent part of each summer in Maine. As with many important discoveries, my route to this island began with serendipity and a simple question. "Where did you go in Maine?" I asked him.

On the cusp of a summer now nearly seventeen years ago, determined at last to make good on my desire, I heeded his recommendation to steer in the direction of the Blue Hill Peninsula, its many communities and nearby islands. In those pre-Google and quick Internet-search days, a phone call to the Blue Hill Chamber of Commerce put me in touch with a rental agent who had a handful of cottage rentals available on such short notice, including one on an island called Deer Isle.

As I pointed my car east along a route that was not yet physically inscribed, I had no quest, no purpose in mind. I was simply answering an urge, yielding to a transcontinental tug. I was not looking—at least I did not know I was looking—for anything in particular. Crossing over the bridge for the first time, a physical sensation that still exhilarates but also unmistakably announces "arrival," I'd come to a place I'd never seen, an island that had not yet offered me its stories, about which I had not yet learned any of its names. But a place that, I don't think it's inaccurate to say, from my first few weeks here claimed me.

Even before the end of that first two-week, too-brief, stay, I yearned to become an island inhabitant. To better understand what that meant. I became aware of the natural world in a way I'd never been before, of how it informs so much about the human lives lived here. I wanted to know it, better understand my connection within it, and how best to care for it. *Geography* and *landscape* began to take on new meaning. More slowly, the people I was coming to know increasingly gave shape to *community*. Though I was not aware of it at the time, I was creeping toward an understanding of how the knowledge of place—a small island shared in close proximity with people of different incomes, educations, experiences, and opinions—may define and limit possibilities but also encourage mutual concern and trust. And, maybe, the solutions for what, within such limiting borders, it's harder to turn away from or ignore. I found myself retrieving *neighborly* from my lexicon's back shelf and dusting it off after years of little use. None of which I found the least bit corny—nor do I still, even if, or maybe particularly because, the currency of our mobile, modern lives seems to favor *data base* and *social networking*. I knew at the end of that first stay I'd come back, stay longer, and one day perhaps, who knows?, go from cottage renter to house owner. If anything, the tug had intensified. An urge of unknown origin now had a specific place attached to it.

I did return to the island the following summer. And subsequent stays did grow longer until, after six years, I'd extended my stay to the entire summer. By then, the possibility of owning a home rather than renting one had become a serious pursuit. Nine years ago, my husband and I became island homeowners. Each year, in my recurring cyclical late-May-to-October journey of return and leave, I travel from the center of this country to one of its outer edges. But rather than teetering at the edge, I feel grounded. At an edge, I feel like I've found my center. Well past youth's outermost edge and yet to land squarely at the cusp of old age, I'd still like to think I'm dwelling in, though admittedly more than inching out of, middle age. Which is to say, I may have come late to the dance in recognizing my need for an identity rooted in a place where I feel the greatest affinity and strongest connection. To understanding the difference between being *from* somewhere and *of* a deeply-loved and intimately-known place.

Previously, I was not aware of being plagued by a sense of "placelessness." In fact, I've always considered home my locus. But even a notion of home-ness and what that meant to me I'd not previously examined in any depth. Now, from this island, with a perspective spanning many summer seasons, and, half the year, from a distance of 1,300 miles away as commitments to work and family still demand, I'm more convinced than ever that we each need a "belonging place."

This is mine.

*W*riting this book extended over nearly five years, commencing not long after my second volume of poetry was published and I shifted my writer's focus onto prose where I thought it might remain for only a short time, rummaging about in the closet of other possibilities, flexing its muscles into the more expansive terrain of long sentences and paragraphs. Writing what has found its way into this book took longer than I anticipated, given the number of fits and starts that, sadly, were too often due to sudden family emergencies of illness and loss. Likewise, my brief foray back into prose began to resemble less the temporary campsite I'd anticipated than a settlement with planted flag.

Years ago, I was an explorer who'd arrived on the island without guide, map, or compass, yet was eager to make discoveries. Over time I did, of course, and I continue to. Some of what's been discovered occurred in the writing itself. Venturing into the territory of the personal essay was new to me, although there I had numerous guides and maps by way of many fine essayists, some of whom—like Scott Russell Sanders and Wendell Berry—write masterfully about their home place where, over decades, they've lived the advice of poet Gary Snyder: "Find your place. Dig in…"

Michel de Montaigne, considered the "father" of the contemporary personal essay, called his prose "essais," derived from the Old French *assayer*, meaning to try, to attempt, to endeavor, test and try out. In his essays, the writer, by turns informative, discursive, reflective, and, yes, even self-absorbed, explores experiences, perceptions, philosophies. Unanswered questions often outweigh conclusions. Rather than clicking shut, a door stays ajar. Solving mysteries is not the aim. Nor, typically, is it to be exhaustive or definitive, whatever subject is tackled.

In much of the prose that follows, I've aspired to the personal essay, to what I believe is a fitting form for the woman and writer exploring her terrain, in a physical journey and in a journey to the interior, where I ask: What drew me to this place? What does my choice of putting down roots here and not someplace else say about me? How does what I come to know about it inform my experiences elsewhere? Can learning about where I live help teach me how to live? This is also, I've discovered, a journey to the past, that part of us we each carry along, and is, as I too often forget, not merely measured in time but is its own place.

Perhaps it's more appropriate to call what follows a series of meditations, or, more generally and label-eschewing, prose pieces. As opposed to a "collection," I prefer a "gathering." Of independent pieces that, juxtaposed, are each hopefully enriched by the others and become, either obliquely or directly, linked. And with enough connective tissue between them so that they become a cohesive whole—like the way shell and bone bits found in the wrack on a low-tide walk provide evidence of larger dramas played out at the tide's turn. Ultimately, of course, the only thing that can truly hold such a gathering together is the place itself.

Because this was written over a number of years, the incidents and experiences summoned may have occurred at different times than suggested or out of the chronological sequence depicted. In some cases, time and incident have been conflated or compressed. Wherever possible, I've attempted to use the actual names of island places, but to protect the privacy of people, I have in some instances changed their names. I have not attempted to write a historical portrait of the island. I leave that to the good folks at the Deer Isle–Stonington Historical Society. As for the scientific accuracy about the natural world which often takes center stage, allow me to use the words of Annie Dillard: "I am no scientist. I explore the neighborhood." In addition to personal observation, I have sought out facts, names, identifying characteristics, and habits by way of research, consultation, and reading, following Sanders' example of making "an amateur's raid into the domain of experts." Though I cannot vouch for scientific accuracy, I hope I do not mislead. As for my personal revelation in such matters, in what has astonished me but is no doubt common knowledge in other circles, I willingly accept any potential embarrassment.

On an island, you're often encountering edges. And though they may help tell you where you are, that doesn't mean you will subsequently know where you are. To acquire such knowledge, there's no quick or easy way, no single path. No arrows point or signs direct: Start here. It's a little like writing. You choose a spot, a beginning point. You set a few words down on the page and see where they lead, what discoveries are revealed, connections made. It's a long and irregular process to make of abstract space a particular loved place. Along the way, it's best to heed the navigational warning found in coastal sailing guides: "Local knowledge advised." And while I have sought local knowledge, the perceptions and opinions reflected in these pages are mine alone, even though they often derive, in addition to firsthand observation and experience, from what I've learned from others, often in casual non-research-based conversations or in what, second- or third-hand, has been passed on. It is my hope that any retelling here is a faithful rendition.

As acknowledged by Sanders, "The work of belonging to a place is never finished." There is always more to know. I'm still an explorer, eager to discover what this place has yet to reveal to me and further bind me to it. This island may have become increasingly familiar to me, but this is still both a new and an ongoing journey, as though I'm on the embarkation of a ship putting out from harbor, again and again. Or the way, as I drive over the bridge, whether on my annual return to the island in late May or just back from a quick trip to the mainland, I feel as though I'm crossing over, coming home again, for the first time.

HERE

*"Place becomes a question of time
and incident, not maps,
no matter how fine their scale."*

Verlyn Klinkenborg

HOW IT GOES

*I*t goes like this:

Near the end of this quiet, mile-and-a-half-long dead-end road on which nothing could pass as a curve and only a few gentle rises pose any challenge to the driver, a generally good road too for walking or biking except for the black flies wicked in early summer and the mosquitoes just about any other time, past the stretch of woods threatening to encroach upon the road, past the few cleared meadows that brighten with lupines in June, past the two art galleries, the chair caner's workshop, a lobsterman's dooryard of stacked traps and freshly painted buoys, past the rental house where a woman walked out on her husband and young son and past a tidy Cape's front-yard table where many summer mornings it's possible to buy cinnamon doughnuts and whoopee pies made by a retired island baker, the hum of pavement becomes the crunch of hard-packed gravel. By sound alone, I know I'm almost home.

Closing in, the gravel the tires kick up pings against the car. Overhead, chickadees and wrens natter among the spruce and balsam. Startled, a white-tail deer bolts. In the boggy stream bottom nudged deeper by an unusually wet spring, ferns uncoil and colonies of skunk cabbages throw back their cowls. Bunchberries carpeting the forest floor beam their small white stars among glacial erratics cloaked with moss. Beneath the branches of a few young maples, I follow the sun's late afternoon path of tossed gold coins and at last turn into a narrow lane that, making a small bend, ends at an expanse of water.

Here then is the island on an island. A small clearing of house, yard, an old wide-armed sheltering oak, a bordering garden. And just beyond, a wind-scoured bluff.

Here is where the land falls away.

At an edge at the edge of an island. A meeting place of earth, water, sky. Where sculpted cumuli balloon against the horizon's thin and seemingly porous rim. Where distant spruce-capped islands anchor and, closer in, granite ridges and outcroppings corset. Where rock has no plan to be sand.

The making of this island and this bluff spans a brain-synapse-busting number of years. Of cyclical heave and collapse. Of rocks extruded, thrust, heated and cooled. Pulverized by glacial weight, compressed by ice, drowned by ice melt, gnawed by lichen, pelted by rain. Scraped, polished, ground. Each residing within the energy of stillness and quietude. Of holding up, holding on.

Here is where I arrive. Or, perhaps more accurately, return.

*I*t also goes like this:

Because I believe as poet Amy Clampitt did upon returning after a decade to a familiar low-tide isthmus—"Nothing's certain. There's no knowing what the slamming/seas, the gale of another winter/may have done"—first, as soon as I'm out of the car, I walk around to the water side or western-facing side of the house.

Nothing, best I can tell, has shifted.

There's Heart Island, a quick dinghy ride away for neighbors down the road who own it. Farther out to the right and much beyond is the distant dark nubble of diminutive Scott Island framed by the southern shore of Little Deer. Straight ahead in the distance are sizable Bradbury, Pickering, and Butter Islands. Just barely visible, as though sneaking a peek over Butter's shoulder, is Great Spruce Head, the family island that famously inspired the paintings and photographs of the Porter brothers, Fairfield and Eliot. Closer in, Little Crow is a mere green button but dwarfs tiny Gull Ledge that just now is appropriately thick with gulls but at high tide nearly disappears. Tacking down the view to the far left is humped Eagle Island. For more than 200 years, it's been home to generations of the same family who've served as boat captains and keepers of Eagle Light that, now automated, still pricks the dark with a single pulse of light every ten seconds. Visible from my bedroom, it's the finest kind of nightlight. Beyond Eagle, miles out to sea, are glimpses of distant Vinalhaven and the open ocean, and though no oceanic horizon is in sight, I know that were I to head out the passage beyond Eagle and make for open seas, passing en route Isle au Haut, Samuel Champlain's "high island," I could eventually wind up in Spain.

Back-dropping all this, far opposite us at center and right, are the gentle contours of the distant Camden Hills, behind which, most of the summer, the sun in its transit sets, often in a prolonged cinematic show. Sunsets that, in the words of Scott Russell Sanders, "deliver no sermons."

This then is the view that in the months ahead will lure me from household chores, from ordered thought, a drafted essay, some necessary and overdue correspondence. It will halt me in my tracks as I pass from one room to another, will stay my hand as I stand at the kitchen sink peeling Kennebecs. Already I feel my eyes adjusting bit by bit to this unobstructed sweep, growing accustomed to the breadth, the stretch, like an athlete who, after a season of short sprints, needs to train for the marathon, attune the muscles, recalibrate the lungs.

I've arrived at the place that in the months ahead I'll look out from— this threshold where small finite things on the shore are back-dropped against expanse. A meeting place of the small and enormous, close and distant. The concise and ambiguous. The here. The there.

*A*nd it goes like this:

Be sure the pump is switched to the main well. Scour the cellar for spring leaks and dead mice. Raise the blinds, uncover furniture, check cupboards. Position the table and chairs on the deck, wheel the grill into its customary place, set binoculars on the windowsill.

As though reintroducing myself, I go from room to room, savoring, assessing. I finger the striped "wishing stones" heaped in a wooden trencher, stroke the top of our dining table, a formerly hinged door bearing all the nicks and scars of 150 years' of use. I screw on lamp shades, shelve new books, clear a spot among the refrigerator door's magnet-clamped photographs for this season's tide chart. Beneath my hand, the feel of the linen closet handle is unmistakable. Were I to wrap my fingers around a similar one anywhere else, I'd be transported here the way a chair's struts hitting me in a particular spot on my back returns me to long-ago Thanksgiving dinners at my grandmother's dining room table. In rituals that inscribe another chapter in what I hope is a long history here, I open more windows, make the beds.

"A house is not simply a building," Wendell Berry reminds us in *The Long-Legged House*, "it is an enactment. To ever arrive at what one would call home even for a few days, a decent, thoughtful approach must be made, a clarity, an opening." The mere fact of a house must somehow be turned into meaning. Necessity, he claims, must be made a little ceremonious. By opening, sweeping, cleaning and clearing, it's as if I'm earning the right to be back here. Necessities are met, order restored, but, as Berry notes, so, too, the old recognitions return. Familiar sights and sounds are slowly restored to their places.

Other people come to such seasonal places carting more family history. They make their annual pilgrimages to cottages and camps where, decades before them, previous generations learned to swim, sail, fish, experienced first kisses and marriage proposals, conceived babies, planted in gardens tilled by ancestral hands, mourned deaths, healed illnesses, overcame fears. When I stand before a closet in this house and pull bed sheets from shelves for the first time each summer, I'm almost able to imagine that for decades my family's hands preceded mine in this same gesture.

In doing so, I'm struck anew by the unlikeliness of my traveling here, many miles and years from my childhood realization that the privilege of owning or renting a summer place belonged to other families. No matter how bountiful I see my childhood now, with its simple and utterly essential pleasures of a public library, a backyard tree house, the nearby woods and river, my early lessons in class distinction were further reinforced in college when classmates "summered" (who knew there was such a word?) on the shore, or, with their parents' encouragement, backpacked in Europe. Here, back again on the island and in this house, I marvel at my journey to this place, at all the riches that, through a somewhat mysterious confluence of chance, opportunity and work, my life contains, including the freedom and means by which I'm able to be here.

*A*nd this:

Just as each arriving task possesses its own element of reconnection, my first errands, rather than briskly ticked off a checklist, morph into a visit.

At the post office, Ron hurries over in spite of the bulky ankle brace the Medical Center's rigged him up with, evidence of his latest misstep in the garden. But he's only eager to tell me about the doe and fawn he's seen in the woods near our house, within striking distance, he claims, of my rhododendrons. "That fawn's no bigger than your dog but the mom's already showing it the ropes."

At the plumber's, Lewis tilts back his cap and holds up a small device he's just removed from a customer's toilet tank, and sputters, "Probably some guy got paid a hundred thousand bucks to come up with this bad idea. A restrictor on a filler? Why don't we just go out in the woods and be done with it?"

Crossing the street in the village, I stop to admire Jeff's new pickup, and he's eager to tell me that his dad, still refusing a hearing aid, climbed into the truck cab the first time, immediately cranked up the radio, cranked it up further, then shook his head, saying, "Your last one didn't work neither."

And had I heard about Dave's sweet old dog Charlie and how he got into Dougie's chickens? "Yep, took out six of them." Did I know Art was selling his antiques business? Don't I agree that Margaret's "got too wicked thin?"

But it's at the diminutive Periwinkle Shop where the early summer sun has yet to chase out the winter chill from its pine plank walls but is already chockablock with books, newspapers, cards, magazines, sweatshirts, skeins of yarn, penny candy, calendars and tide charts, all owned, stocked and managed by a one-woman wonder closing in on 90, that I linger longest. Standing behind her big brass register, Neva is, as one friend calls her, the "island oracle." In early June, however, I think of her as the appointed keeper of Who's-Arrived-For-The-Season and Who's-Due-When, as though she were an air traffic controller with up-to-the-minute flight information. Or that, like a customs official with an ink pad behind her counter, she's required to stamp the credentials of all new arrivals and respond to inquiries about which summer folks have returned and when. And for whom, her greeting, "So I was wondering when you people would be arriving," is meant as a true welcome.

Unquestionably, a ferry dock is a necessary link between bridge-less islands and the mainland, a point of disembarkation and transformation, the connector between away and home. Where it's possible to see who's been off-island, who's about to depart, and, maybe, why. On this island, bridged since 1939, the Periwinkle is a sort of ferry dock stand-in for some of us bonded in the rituals of arrival and departure, in a shared short season book-ended by "Hi, when did you get here?" and " 'Bye, see you next summer."

In the Periwinkle, I'm often reminded that if it's anonymity I'm after, I'd best live someplace else. Though not exactly beneath a bell jar, life on a 12 by 6-mile island means everybody knows more about you than you think they do. And, as much a part of the fabric as fog in August, they talk about you. When my husband and I bought our house nine years ago, it was March, the month the island is just beginning to unzip its winter parka. By the time we arrived for the summer in late May, there was hardly a person I had to tell that we'd finally bought our own place. In other less benign versions of "Pass It On," what's said may be touted as bona fide truth, but when it loops back, fact often comes as surprising news. As in other small communities, knowing our neighbors and their business can be both blessing and curse, a recognized pastime and an art form in which, often, the distinctions between oral historian and exquisite gossip blur.

For a long time, favorite subjects of island chatter were a few wealthy newcomers building houses the size of which the island had never known, folks "living at right angles to the land," as writer Lawrence Durrell would've said. And spending big bucks to do it, judging by the numbers being tossed around. But who knows for sure if one such newcomer paid an off-island landscaper hundreds of thousands of dollars just to haul in some trees? It's widely known that one islander on our road, after his wife died years ago, drew the blinds and closed up their house. Allegedly, no one has crossed the threshold since. Of even more dubious certainty is that, with all the devotion of a grieving husband building his Taj Mahal, he refused to change a thing inside. One reportedly good and no doubt self-proclaimed authority recently told me, "Not only are all her clothes still hanging in the closet, the same sugar's in the sugar bowl." A find, apparently, the mice have yet to discover.

But make no mistake. Any time of day or night, word also goes out for essential purposes. Government officials could well learn a few lessons from members of the island's fishing community and their response to possible catastrophe. No political concerns and red tape hinder them. Rather than cooling their heels on shore while waiting for state agency boats to arrive, they hop into pontoons and join the volunteer fire department's bucket brigade attempting to put out a fire on a small nearby island. To radio reports that a lobster boat has gone missing, the first lobsterman likely to circle the waters and the last one to give up the search may well be the same fellow who, as the result of unsettled grievances running back generations or a feud over disputed fishing territory, hasn't so much as tipped his cap in the direction of the missing man. One winter, during a blizzard in the middle of the night, the island's all-volunteer ambulance corps had to transport a woman having a heart attack to the hospital on the mainland. The going was rough but only possible because islanders quick with their trucks and plows preceded them all the way to the bridge.

The world is complete without us. A physical place, independent of us, is more stable and reliable than our bodies or the relationships we share in it with those we love. And yet, though it outlives us, isn't a place richer, stronger, more able to endure when layered with our memories, spackled with our stories? Were it possible to slice off a piece of this island down to bedrock, surely the exposed strata would reveal not just quartz and alpite, but layers of personal history, accumulated experiences and rituals, all deeply veined with a collective narrative shared on a village street, in the post office, buying the newspaper in a small shop.

With as much certainty as resides in the moment when ferry or mail boat bumps against a dock and the landing ramp is lowered, I stop at Periwinkle and know my seasonal journey is at an end.

NAMES

"...and gives airy nothing
A local habitation and a name."
                                    Shakespeare

*T*oday's discovery on my morning walk: our road sign is missing.
Okay, it's been stolen. Again. I've ordered a new one, but for now I have
to figure that people who need to find us can. Like the new UPS driver.
It probably wouldn't help him much knowing we're the driveway just
before the island selectman's.

I sort of understand why this sudden rash of sign-snatching is
attracted to certain road names—Deep Hole, for example, or Sweet
Speed Drive. But Bunchberry Lane? Such designation was one of the
least appealing things about this place when we bought it nine years ago.
A bit too precious for my taste. But at least it possesses some relevance
to a physical feature of our woods' native landscape, unlike the way most
developers in their name choices try to mitigate taking possession of the
landscape and forever changing it. Like a developer naming a shopping
mall Old Orchard, deciding, apparently, that name alone would honor
acres of bulldozed apple trees.

In the switch to Maine's statewide 9-1-1 system, when all previously
identifying fire-road numbers gave way to road names, Bob and I were
still summer renters. We didn't get in on the one-time naming opportunity afforded property owners, efforts that, by the following season, were
manifested in the official blue street signs that for most of us familiar
with lifestyles elsewhere veer way too close to the suburban. Up went
the predictable: family names like Stacy Circle, Caleb's Way, Walker's
Point. Other names highlighted topographical features. Some—Sunny

21

Crest and Deer Haven—seemed to aspire to the poetic. One homeowner expressed disappointment upon hearing his choice had already been taken. On The Rocks, he'd been so certain, would doubly pertain—to his cottage's location on a granite ledge and his appreciation of a perfect gin martini. I have to believe clues to a state of mind when name applications were due or to the issue itself reside in Bottom Line Road or Unnecessary Lane. And Thissa Way must surely, in the sign-snatchers' lair, be good company to our more prosaic Bunchberry Lane.

*N*ames are thresholds through which I've gradually come to know this island.

To better understand the workings of the tides early on, I learned ebb and flood, neap and slack. Of the conifer I most admire here, I discovered that larch, as it's known elsewhere, is, in Maine, a tamarack, but locally, is a hackmatack. A steady wind, I was told, is "fresh" and the absence of wind makes for a "flat-ass" calm sea. In summer, the prevailing winds are out of the southwest but if they blow northeast well into late June, it generally spells bad news for the lobstermen. I've yet to find out whether winds here have names, as they do, for example, in Rome: the westerly sea breeze *ponentino*, the steely northerly wind *tramontana*, and the blistery hot African import, *scirocco*. Given all the mischief they stir up here, I have to wager that our island winds, like their Italian cousins, have specific names, albeit with fewer vowels. I've yet to ask any lobstermen though.

Now, however, I know some to ask. Back when I first came here, neither street name nor fire-road number would have made much difference to anyone other than the volunteer fire department. No one was looking for me. No one here knew who I was. That first summer, I came alone to a rented cottage perched on a tidal cove. The owner's sister lived next door but we never met. I spent much of my time on the cove-facing deck, field guide in hand, and, despite their indifference, made acquaintance with deftly probing Lesser Yellow Legs and high-stepping Black-bellied Plovers. Not so hard to identify was the bald eagle that several times looped overhead although it took some time to identify the osprey circling its eagle-look-alike nest on Little Crow Island. As if with needle and thread, they each began to bind me, stitch me into the fabric of this place.

The following summer, I returned to that house on the cove and Bob got to know it, too. As did our dog, Ben. But first, I again spent two weeks alone, this time in a white clapboard camp on a southern part of the island with a spectacular but potentially brutal exposure to the open

Atlantic. Not much larger than its original single room and built decades before any shorefront setback restrictions, it clung like a limpet to the edge of a massive granite ledge.

My first morning there and for the duration of my stay, no matter what wind and waves delivered, a diminutive black seabird with distinctive white wing patches rode the swells at varying distances off the shore or hunkered nearby in the lee of a huge, storm-lashed boulder. Soon, looking for it became my morning habit. As reliable a fixture as Mark Island Light, that little seabird I identified in the field guide as a Black Guillemot evolved into a kind of companion.

In the same family as the Atlantic puffin, guillemots sport dark sharp bills, bright red feet and short, stubby wings which, when necessary, can propel the little fellows low across the water. Much more proficient at swimming and diving, they cluster in colonies but are not particularly gregarious. My companion appeared to be traveling solo. Most surprising, I learned guillemots are pelagic, meaning the open ocean is their only home. Only briefly do they come ashore to breed and lay eggs, not in any downy roosts but on the bare rocks of shore, islands or cliffs.

While at the camp, I learned other names. Of the nuthatch that built a nest an arm's reach from a small upstairs window. Of the small islands—Andrew and Fort—just off the shore of a small beach down the road. "Happy recognitions," as writer Annie Dillard might've called them, each in its own way changing my morning inventories, my afternoon walks. True, I didn't find the nuthatch one whit less engaging before knowing its name, or the small islands less lovely. Yet naming, that human necessity, was a way of becoming acquainted with my new surroundings. It also comforted.

Like the guillemot, I wasn't particularly gregarious. Not that summer. I'd come to the camp for solitude. Also back then, I didn't know many people on the island. Still, in learning some of the names, I was, in a way, getting to know the neighbors. In a new place, I began to feel connected, part of some broader community, and was reassured thinking that someone preceding me, either by years or by vast swaths of time, had given this tree, this plant, this bird, this road or trail, beach or island, a name.

Those nights when rain and wind lashed the little cottage's windows, when shallow-rooted spruce thrashed the shingles overhead, and, if the tide was up and waves heaved water just steps from the front door, I lit the room's single lamp and hunkered in front of the fire. Knowing the Black Guillemot, my little bow-heavy buddy, was sharing this night, riding out the storm's tempest in his home—that very same immense, pitching sea—not only earned my respect but made the small camp feel less unfamiliar. I had no specific name for a one-room house on a rock above a storm-wracked sea, the wind threatening to rip away the roof and douse the amber light of its single parchment-shaded lamp, but in the familiarity of knowing *black guillemot*, I had come closer to a place I might call home.

*T*hat second summer on the cove, I did meet the sister next door. Our exchange of names opened doors and launched us on a path to getting acquainted. Soon, I was buying some of her cut flowers bunched in empty coffee cans at her driveway's edge. When passing on walks with my dog, she waved and called to me by name. Over coffee, she became the first islander to try to clear up my confusion about "downeast."

Although sometimes disputed, it's commonly put forth that Deer Isle is a part of Maine known as Downeast, an identifier that derives from the nautical. Because prevailing winds blow from the west, it's been customary for more than a century to say you're headed downeast when you're going in the general direction of Canada. And so, but still confusingly, there doesn't seem to be much need for "north" or "south."

She tried to explain things even more simply. "Look, think of it this way: you go *up* to Boston or Portland"—never mind, apparently, that it may seem you're heading south. And when you drive north off the island? "Why then," she said, "you're going *down* to the mainland." Here, it seemed, was another one of those that's-the-way-it-is-and-has-always-been explanations, and it more or less worked until I was forced back into reconsideration with the discovery that America's easternmost frontier with Canada is *West* Quoddy Head.

Maybe I'll always be a person for whom such distinctions are, if not important, at least interesting. Perhaps, too, my early confusion and intrigue identified me in a way I knew nothing about. In her memoir about moving from Manhattan to a small town in upstate New York, Le Anne Schreiber observes that, for a period of time, often years, a newcomer is likely to be known by "an evolving set of identifying labels." The same seems to hold true here. One of my early identifying labels may well have evolved to: Woman Renting the Beck Camp Who Is Confused By Downeast.

Even now, after nine years of owning what a deed tells us is our house, I'm still known to some folks on this road as the Woman Who Bought the Robinson House. More generally, I'm the Woman Who Writes Poetry. Bob has become the Fellow Who Rides A Red Motor

Scooter, a label uniquely his, given that, best I can tell, he's the only person on the island with a red Vespa.

Such identifying labels tell more about a person than just his or her name. About places, too. Eggemoggin is the stretch of water known as a reach over which our island's suspension bridge spans. In Passamaquoddy from which it derives, it is the Place Of The Great Fish Weir and so offers by name alone historical reference and meaning.

I've always appreciated how many Native American names confer meaning on things and places. Apaches, in their native language, use precise place names that are more like guides pointing to specific locations. In them, pictures are suggested, images our imaginations can work with. Like: Trail Extends Across A Long Ridge With Alder Trees. Or, Cluster Of Big Walnut Tree Stands Bushing Out. According to anthropologist Keith Basso, Apaches consider useless any place names that don't provide pictures to the mind, in part because image-conferring names are often used to stand in for stories. They refer to what happens or has happened at a location. Place Where Wind Gathers. Or, Place Of Falling Trees.

On this island, a somewhat similar version of naming exists. Sure, we may know the name Perez Cross Road, but for a few of us living close by, an altogether different name memorializes what happened there, and, Apache-like, summons up pictures—Road Where Running Dog Punctured Artery And Left a Trail of Blood. Given that the dog was our beloved Ben, I can append: Road Where Heart-Thumping Ride To Mainland Vet Began.

Closer to home—literally—I can't help but wonder what my choice might've been for our lane's name. Rather than taking my cue from the bunchberry, I'd have likely focused instead on our massive red oak, although I suspect the state may have balked at: Place Where Tree Of Big Arms Shelters House.

*N*ames are, of course, often labels. And some do a better job of defining what something or someone is not.

Browse any dictionary and I'm certain you won't find *From Away* or *Person From Away*. Definitions for those are privately held, commonly understood. Synonyms, too. Like Summer Complaints. Or Flatlanders. Also—though of decidedly obsolete usage—rusticators. And then there are the subsets. Summer People are distinguished between owners and renters, the former most often eligible for full Summer People status, though renters can cross over if, as Bob and I did, they rent for several seasons. By moving here full-time, Summer People become

Year-Rounders. Or Transplants. Or, possibly, Retirees With Too Much Time On Their Hands. But never do they become From Here.

The *from* in this case is, as I've learned, particularly important. To be From Here is a distinction not readily conferred nor easily obtained. You and a number of your ancestors must have been born on the island, and as writer Phil Crossman of nearby Vinalhaven Island once observed, "If someone named in the Bible is one of your ancestors, it helps."

Over the years, I seem to have sorted out that a person may settle here, live here year-round, have children and die here, and still essentially she *was* here, but she was not *from* here. And, I'm to understand, this remains true of her children and her children's children even if they stay on and marry into a local family. The reverse, however, doesn't hold. A From Here may leave the island, marry a Not From Here, have and raise their children somewhere not here, and yet each time he and his Not-From-Here family visit the island, he's welcomed as a native son, regardless, say, any acquired Virginia twang twining among the Downeast nasals.

While to my mind, *native* smacks of colonialism, it's what most island-born-belonging folks seem to prefer calling themselves. *Local* is, apparently, some subtle subcategory. And maybe such designation makes sense, if you put aside—as it often is—the recognition that on this vast continent few can claim legitimate linkage to the country's true native population.

Native derives from *nasci*, meaning to be born and thus implying indigenous—unlike From Aways who, like gypsy moths or purple loose-strife, are introduced, usually without invitation, into the local habitat, aliens that over time adapt, modify and exist in such increasing numbers, it's hard to recall they were ever from some other place. Until someone notices, for instance, how loosestrife has taken over the marsh.

We People From Away are not without our distant kin—folks who elsewhere are known as Wash Ashores or Non-Belongers. In Rome, the Trastevere neighborhood is home to the annual Festa di Noantri. *Noantri* means us, a derivation of *noialtri* that signifies "people like us" as opposed to *voialtri*, "Romans from elsewhere." This distinction reinforces the Trasteverini notion of being *veraci* or authentic—the "real Romans." Never mind that there's ample evidence to suggest their origin is Corsican. Travel writer R.V. Morton once asked his Roman host how long a pedigree was necessary and he was told rather authoritatively that no less than seven generations might qualify you as a genuine Romano di Roma.

On the island, answers to such a question are vague. It requires four generations, some say. Others scoff. At a recent island event, our electrician told me, "I've been living here for decades, but only my children's children's children will ever be considered Locals." Our neighbor, a long-time island lobsterman, disagreed. "That'll never happen. Take me. My wife was born here but I'll always be a From Away because my family moved here from Connecticut when I was a week old." Also getting in on it, the wife of a native lobsterman admitted, "I don't know that I can even call myself a Local. I was born on the other side of the bridge." In Brooklin, 18 miles away.

Perhaps best summing things up may be the well-circulated story of a young Maine student whose two-sentence biographical "essay" was said to have read: "George Washington was the first President of the United States. He was born off-island."

Such names and distinctions are more confusing than Downeast. And though possibly more germane, are they more important?

Last summer, at the island historical society, I asked a fellow volunteer, a long-time islander, which she thought best: Native or Local?

"Neither, far as I'm concerned. It's all foolishness to me. My husband and his people were born on this island. I've been here fifty-seven years. Folks can call me what they want. We're all in this together." Pausing, she added: "'Course now, some folks do come here and they must not—I don't know—amount to much in whatever puddle they're in back where they come from. Because time's they come here, why, for heaven sakes, they try and *be* the puddle."

While I refuse to think Puddler has the potential to become another subset, her response seems to suggests to someone who still finds herself wondering from time to time, So what does all this make me?—and do I care?—that Neighbor may be the name that matters most. Certainly it would help clear up confusion. And one generally agreed-upon island definition seems to exist already. From what I've gathered in my anything-but-scientific discoveries, a neighbor, after proving by the passage of time that she's here for the long haul and not aiming to change things too much, keeps her nose clean, pays her bills on time, knows when to speak up and when to keep her mouth shut, gives a lot and takes a little. A *good* neighbor, that is. And so it goes. Adjectives themselves making distinctions.

And maybe we can't help ourselves. Naming is an intuitive human necessity. As old as Adam. It's how, starting early, we find our place in the world, become acquainted with and claim our surroundings. For several months in his toddlerhood, my nephew teetered from object to object and, pointing, exclaimed, "Dee, Dee," his one-syllable name for

the dizzying and vast array of things in his new world. In further exploration not many months later, he'd point and ask, "What name this?" and of
whatever was next in range, demand again, "What name this?" He kept
at it until some response sounded to his young, taxonomist-in-the-mak-
ing ears adequately specific.

Even early on, it seems, accuracy matters. A friend recently related
the story of a five-year-old who'd come to the island to visit her grandmother. As the two of them stood at a window overlooking the yard, the
grandmother said, "Oh, look, there's a hummingbird." To which the child
responded, "At our house, Grandma, we have singing birds."

*I*t's a slow process learning names. And being known by our name. As
it should be—no?—since many of us who have chosen to come to this
island have done so partly to escape what too often characterizes what
we've left behind: speed. We leave the terrain of the sprinters to take up
with the distance runners who pick their pace early and stick to it for the
long haul.

Still, from time to time, we may find ourselves wondering if it was
better before we knew the names of things. Joan Didion, in her essay,
"Good-Bye to All That," writes about her early life in New York when she
thought the Triborough Bridge was the Brooklyn Bridge. Claims Didion,
"Those days before I knew the names of all the bridges were happier than
those that came later."

Of course her reasons were personal, many and complex. As they
are for most of us who may journey to a new place and after some span
of time there find we might prefer being, if not unknown, a little less
known. Of "counting for little" as Schreiber puts it. Being so, she points
out, leaves more room for solitude and "elective affinities." Also, tolerance. It's hard to offend, she claims, or "give scandal when no one cares or
expects too much."

Some days, for all my interest in names and naming, a part of me
yearns for my early days on the island, those weeks of discovering its
natural beauty, the as-yet-nameless wonders of its coves and shores,
tides and forests. Those days before I knew about the distinctions
between Native and Local and From Away, or about old deep-seated
competitions between the island's two towns and, though fewer now,
the lingering resentments. Before I recognized the names signed to
the local newspaper's Letters to the Editor that too often become
verbal slugfests between folks holding opposing views. Before I
could guess the identities of who's behind the newspaper's citations

of "Lemons & Laurels." Before I knew whose yards sprouted which political campaign signs, where they were bound to be vandalized or stolen, and by whom. Before I had to choose sides.

Some days I prefer not being known. Like the morning when, out of spontaneous desperation with a new and suddenly ratcheted-up gray squirrel population that had been persistently destroying our bird feeders, I surprised myself by stopping at our local hardware store and, assuming it would only scare and not injure, inquired about a pellet-firing pistol. Not that I even knew if such a thing existed. I wish no one who knew my name had been standing at the nearby register as a well-meaning clerk, in response to my murmured request, said—or, to my ears, shouted—and half a dozen faces turned in our direction, "So it has to be a pistol? We only carry rifles." About to helpfully pull one off a rack, she had no idea she was talking to Woman Generally Horrified By Guns. Who in fact had never held a real one.

I may not be a coffee-klatcher by nature, but in various places on the island, I routinely gather with friends and neighbors who introduce me to folks I don't know. Together we imbibe a hearty stew of island news, rumors, and scuttlebutt, of stories, jokes, and advice, an untangling of family lineage and ancestral histories. A compote of fact, speculation, humor. Inherent in all this, I suppose, along with our wish to know, is our desire to be known, a satisfaction, perhaps, of our adolescent need to be accepted and understood. A throwback to the high school cafeteria which, in a large student body, can be a nightmarish place when there is no table at which you seem welcome, no hands going up to signal you over. A fear that I'm convinced for years kept me out of restaurants when I traveled solo.

*O*nly a small wooden sign marks the turn-off to Hillside Cemetery. A gravel road winds past a couple of houses with vegetable gardens, cars, and kayaks, with animals in the yard, laundry on the line, window boxes that sprout not flowers but some old, brightly painted lobster buoys. It's an unlikely approach, surely a wrong turn. Or if not, then another example of a place whose name is in major disconnect to the topography. But there, finally, on a bit of a rise that more or less qualifies as a hill, is a mown oblong clearing densely bordered by trees.

It's early morning and the sun has yet to push out the chill and clouds from an overnight shower. The grass is wet. An old hydrangea tree's full-flowered wands droop and drip, spackling the ferns beneath it. In the trees, warblers flit but their melodies seem muted, simple, oddly respectful, as if they've agreed to maintain a requisite hush. I seem to be the only person who early on a Friday morning has pulled in, parked her car.

The headstones are, as I remembered, mostly modest here. Shiny and smooth, rough and honed, some splotched with orange and green lichen. A few of the older ones tilt. The simplest are natural granite boulders with metal plates bolted to them. Others, more intricate, are incised with hearts, angels, clasped hands, fishing boats, a detailed forest scene. On each, dates and years. And, of course, names.

A few headstones provide birthdates, the oldest going back to 1808— Hephzibah Small who, given the perils of her day, admirably spanned nearly a century before her death in 1892. One gravestone etched with a schooner amidst tossing waves provides a specific birth date in 1860 but is sketchy with the particular date of death. Henry J. Lufkin, the stone reads, "Died on the coast of Africa at 34 years of age." Some headstones provide the dates that book-end a life. One goes a step further and specifies: "70 years, 11 months, 24 days." Often the math is left up to us, an easy if not heartbreaking computation when the answer is only eight days.

This is no purely historical cemetery absent offspring or friends who visit. Here, what poet Thomas Lynch calls the "ancient agreement," the remembrance of the dead by the living, is upheld. In addition to the many small flags commemorating veterans, numerous other objects adorn the gravesites. Some look weathered, others as though they were placed just yesterday. Affixed to metal posts are twinkling wind chimes and swaying lanterns shaped like small lighthouses. Nestled in the grass or propped against the headstones are all manner of figurines—angels, doves, reclining lambs and fawns. Elsewhere, small ship models, miniature lobster buoys, a stone anchor encrusted with sea glass and the shells of sea urchins, whelks, and razor clams. Striking an even more personal note are stuffed animals, toy cars, baseballs, and, at one gravesite, two basketballs, one old, one new

When I first visited this cemetery eight years ago, the names on these headstones meant little to me. They didn't signify neighbor or friend, young son or local fisherman. I had little of substance to put to the names. I could, as I still can, compute life spans, the heartbreakingly brief, the long-but-never-long-enough. But just as genealogical charts stingy with details cannot reduce a life to the dry facts of dates, a headstone says almost nothing of a life lived even when inscribed with "Mother" or "Husband," or carved with "Together Forever" epitaphs. These tell so little of the story.

Now, I walk among these stones and I recognize some names—Eaton,

Stinson, Snowden—that stretch back, are linked with the island's history. Maybe I wasn't acquainted with the woman in what I'm certain is the newest grave to be dug here, but I know how she died, how important she was to islanders important to me. I also recognize names of people with whom I was familiar, even if obliquely. The gravesite piled with stuffed animal and tiny angel statuettes, with a dog's collar and a child's base-ball cap, is that of a popular fifth-grade boy tragically killed in an ATV accident, the son of a man who once worked at our house. Like other islanders, I, too, was stunned by a local nineteen-year old's drowning, the swirling stories, rumors, and accusations, and how, an accident or not, it probably involved drugs and debt. I know some of his schoolmates who, with old sneakers, caps, a yearbook, and homecoming crown, have made of his headstone a sort of shrine. I know where his body was brought ashore and recognize on the road there the remnants of words his friends spray-painted onto the asphalt instructing us all to remember. Knowing that one gravesite belongs to a hardworking young fisherman pitched into the sea from a scallop dragger better explains the family's choice of the Psalm chiseled into his headstone: "They that go down to the sea in ships, that do business in great waters; these see the works of the Lord, and his wonders in the deep."

Maybe I was first drawn here for the quiet and odd peace that often draws me to cemeteries wherever I travel. Maybe, as a relative newcomer, I came here in pursuit of a bit of history. Now, after nearly seventeen years of coming to the island, after having owned a house here for nine of them and spending several months each year here, I'm still a newcomer. My history and that of my family does not reach back generations. No branches of my family tree intertwine with the histories of those families that do. In the nearby historical society, you'll find no mention of me or my family in the archives. From many of the island-born natives, I still get few points for having chosen to come rather than being born here.

It doesn't matter. First visiting this cemetery years ago, history was evoked by dates stretching back to 1808, by the engraved fact of an island sailor lost a world away. Walking here now, history is still evoked, and has, with my deepening knowledge, expanded. True, I may not be able to claim relationship by blood or close friendship to anyone com-memorated here. My hands, were they not to have come empty, prob-ably wouldn't know what beloved or symbolic objects to place, or where. Perhaps it's easy among a cemetery's *memento mori* to recognize how we all are linked, native-born or those from away who by various routes traveled here, and remained. The same inevitable outcome awaits us all. But so too, regardless our paths, how long or short our chapters, we're also joined by something else—the hope that someone later will get our stories straight and that our mere name alone may one day prompt their telling.

*L*ong before our street sign went missing the first time, I'd learned that bunchberry is the common name for a species of dwarf dogwood. Averaging no more than six inches tall, bunchberry is a diminutive cousin to the hardy upright, brightly-twigged shrub types of dogwood and the gracefully branched, copiously blooming pagoda dogwood tree. Resemblance is by way of leaf shape and white bracted flowers. A native plant, bunchberry predates any of the islander's first settlers to whom some current residents claim bragging rights.

This week, I've been snooping around in local gardening books. I want to know if bunchberry, a creeping perennial that reproduces by way of underground rhizomes, is a good candidate for naturalizing. Can it be transplanted? Will it spread? My aim is not merely to bolster the population of what's suggested by our lane's name. I want to better integrate the adjoining woods with our yard and perennial garden. I like the idea of having a bordering, untended woodland garden that might better marry the natural with the maintained and cultivated—and named—specimens I've imposed on the landscape.

I've learned that a preferred spot for bunchberry is beneath conifers, a location predominantly shaded yet receiving some dappled light, with soil both acidic and consistently moist. Says one local gardening book, transplanted bunchberry will thrive "if it finds itself in the right situation."

Bunchberry has much going for it. About the time in spring when you think that a hard winter with little snow cover has decimated even its thickest colony, bunchberry, almost without fail, stirs to life with vibrant green and is followed weeks later by small, star-shaped, creamy-white flowers. By late summer, it's generous with bright-red berries, and, come fall, with a last leaf color that can approach vermillion. More important to me, bunchberry has become another essential marker of the seasons. As is the resident osprey that returns to nearby Heart Island. Hard to believe I once could've confused an osprey's wing-flapping flight with an eagle's pinion-spread soar. Now it's as easy to distinguish between them as it is to identify, by distant silhouette alone, low-slung loon from high-riding cormorant.

Each was a part of a process that's taken time, a slow accretion of names and knowledge that is never over. Just this week, I learned that the connecting sandbar formation at the causeway linking us to the mainland is called a tombolo. On a new island friend's boat, I at last had the opportunity to connect *sculpin* to the actual spiny, armor-headed bottom-dweller he hauled up in a lobster trap. Yesterday, I was able to translate mere information—a new woman who walks our road every morning—into Dorothy, who this summer moved to nearby Deer Run.

I'm not sure what I'll do with such knowledge. Doubtless there will be countless times I cross the causeway without giving its geographical makeup and moniker a single thought. I may never again encounter a sculpin. Any relationship with Dorothy may not extend much past a wave on the road. Still, names matter. To know a name, to be known by a name. How else does the abstract ever tilt toward the intimate?

"The difference in naming is a difference in seeing," Schreiber notes. For her, seeing only a "chunky dark bird" on a particular date in March would never be the equivalent of seeing the first cowbird return on its migration north. A name was the door that first opened into knowledge about a particular species, its habits and migratory patterns. Now it informs her that it's spring. Cowbird brings the promise of another cycle repeating itself. As does bunchberry for me. And osprey. Or, at the far end of the same season, a hackmatack that by its conifer-like appearance alone doesn't suggest its needles will bronze, grow as golden as if dipped into flame, then drop, ushering in the next phase of an annual cycle that in one way or another touches us all.

Like Schreiber's, my calendar's been remade. The names of the months may remain the same, but they've evolved, derived new meaning. After my having been here through many cycles, dates now mark rituals and anniversaries, all of which, and by way of learning names first, are closely observed, celebrated, praised.

To a delivery truck driver in June, I am and may likely remain a mere name on a dispatcher's roster. Perhaps, until my road sign's been replaced, I'm Woman Who Lives On Lane With No Name. Certainly, I can't expect him, a Just Passing Through, to know much more.

OF TWO WORLDS

*L*ike many people in a northern climate of four distinct seasons, I await the harbingers that herald a new season's turning, particularly those signaling winter giving way to spring. In my Illinois yard, there's no more reliable messenger than the male cardinal who perches atop our small hawthorn tree, a carmine point around which a dreary end-of-winter gray collapses. The cardinal's a bright chap who seems at first a bit overdressed, but after several mornings of unrelenting, heart-bursting melody in which he repledges his ardor to his mate and warns off any would-be suitors, appears instead to have been yoked to all of spring's renewing color and hauls it into view, even as the sparrows, those opportunistic nineteenth-century imports, go about their brisk business in dull unchanging brown, as though trying to blend in unnoticed. On the island, spring—or at least mud season—is announced when ice eases out of the coves and Frost Heave warnings are posted on the roads. When warblers begin again to mob the feeder and peepers burst forth with song in ponds and flooded hollows.

And then there are the nearby Heart Island ospreys. Usually, I'm not on the island until my seasonal return in late May, so ospreys are less a sign of spring for me. They're a measure of arrival. Mine.

In the first days back on the island, I go about my usual rituals of reconnecting and renewal, of inscribing new chapters in what I hope will be a long history here. I'm drawn into the garden like a salamander to a vernal pool, and, inevitably, begin another season's long To-Do list. But it's not until I hear the high-pitched *kew, kew, kew* of the Heart Island ospreys that I recognize what I've been waiting for. The confirmation I need—the ospreys have indeed returned to their nest. At last, I can truly settle in.

Once, I knew little about ospreys—that, for example, they are one of only six species to appear on each of our planet's continents except Antarctica. Or how, in March, just as I'm beginning to get serious about my late-May trip back to the island—perhaps showing some of the same kinds of restlessness birds exhibit prior to embarking on their migratory journey—ospreys, possibly Heart Island's among them, begin leaving their wintering territories in South America. Compelled by an urgency to nest and mate, they travel north, covering 100 to 200 miles a day along a 4,000-mile migratory flyway, much of the route over open water and with hurdles along the way—and all making, relatively speaking, my first day's island-bound and otherwise impressive 700-mile Interstate drive in a car rigged with cooler, music and audio books a somewhat puny accomplishment.

Over the years, as the nearby Heart Island ospreys have helped make our house and property home, I've become more convinced that I can now better translate their high-pitched cheeps as begging, peevish warning, or vigilant alert. More important, I've heeded their demands to pay closer attention to the skies. Early on, they instructed me to buy better binoculars, and, with my ringside seat to their aerial displays, I've been rewarded ever since. Were these resident birds not to return, as I feared for a time last year, it would be a loss I'd have a hard time accepting.

Once, the entire country was impoverished by a loss of ospreys. Following its widespread use for decades, the pesticide DDT seeped into the food chain. A fat-soluble compound, DDT doesn't break down and can pass from one organism to another, accumulating in fatty tissues and magnifying in concentration as it works its way up the chain to top predators, including raptors such as ospreys. Between 1950 and 1975, DDT wiped out nearly 90% of our country's osprey population. One insidious result of DDT ingestion is the thinning of eggshells. Thanks in large part to Rachel Carson's landmark *Silent Spring*, of "a spring without voices," folks began to understand why the weight of incubating osprey parents was turning the potential offspring beneath them into what more closely resembled the makings of our omelets on a Sunday morning.

Often called fish hawks, ospreys can reach 24 inches tall with an impressive wingspan of six feet. Predominately black above and white below, they sport prominent black cheek patches and handsome checked markings on the undersides of wings and tail. Sure, they may lack the regal bearing of a black-and-white immaculately clad bald eagle with just the right accessorizing touches of yellow, but a tufted crown and white pantaloons give ospreys a decidedly cosmopolitan air. And they're tough. Hitting the scale at about four pounds, an osprey is capable of pulling from ocean, pond, or lake a fish more than half its size. A prize catch often carefully noted by a nearby "king of skies" eagle that, abandoning any noblesse oblige and engaging in persistent midflight harassment more common to the masses, will attempt to steal.

Ospreys are also quite adept at nest-building. Returning in spring, they frequently spend days or even weeks repairing winter damage, or, as though in the spirit of *This Old House*, revamping and adding on. The nest built atop one of Heart Island's tallest spruces is visible to the unglassed eye from our deck, but it is not a whopper. Nowhere close to nest sizes known to reach four feet tall and weigh nearly a quarter ton, it is, however, emblematic of the large, often messy arrangement of sticks, warp, and cleverly recycled scavenged finds. In *Return of the Osprey*, David Gessner writes of one nest he observed throughout an entire season on Cape Cod. Among its building components was the clever reuse of a partially clad Barbie doll, surely not a purpose the Mattel folks had in mind.

To watch an osprey dive is to watch an athlete at the top of his game. As much as 100 feet above the water, it hovers with rapid kingfisher-like wing beats. Then, having made any necessary adjustments, the osprey tucks its folded wings, and, at speeds up to 40 mph, plunges headlong toward the water. Just before hitting, it flips, wings thrust back, talons forward, and strikes the water, disappearing in total immersion. Moments later, it resurfaces with thrashing wings, and, if the dive was successful, rises with a fish clasped headfirst, torpedo-like, in expert aerodynamic fashion. Seldom have I witnessed such an accomplishment. More numerous are the times I've watched repeated, admirable attempts that come up short, usually in aborted dives when whatever calculations osprey make apparently require recalibration. All very exhilarating to be sure, but in each is a sober reminder of the incredible maneuvers required to fill a belly—no mere stroll to the refrigerator as Gessner adroitly points out.

Nearly as impressive to me is how at least half the ospreys born to an area return to the same spot. Osprey pairs are considered monogamous, a trait that, be it in osprey, swan, or wolf, we humans seem eager to recognize, as though certain birds and mammals are in the business of trying to emulate us. But such faithfulness, osprey expert Alan Poole claims, is more a commitment to a nesting site than to one another. More to a place than a partner. Were a supposedly beloved mate to prove suddenly incapable of bearing offspring, she'd be sent packing. Any unattached replacement candidates sense this and begin hanging out nearby. Who knows? Maybe that's what the commotion was about two summers ago when, inexplicably, very early in the season, three ospreys, often in full cry, circled Heart Island for days. I assumed an unhitched offspring was hanging out, but maybe an impending new bride was already visualizing how she'd reposition the furniture.

Next to producing offspring and filling bellies, the deepest instinct ospreys possess is a biological imperative that's tangibly lived in their allegiance to a particular place. Returning to it, they're pulled by an instinctual and unyielding urge, following inner compasses beyond even a scientist's explanation.

Their journeys are, of course, different from mine. And yet I feel we're kindred spirits. Somehow, perhaps, we experience similar stirrings in the blood, irresistible seasonal urges. Scientists tell us that on their migratory journeys, ospreys recognize landmarks along the way. So what, I wonder, are the landmarks for the Heart Island ospreys as they home in on their final leg? The bridge crossing the Piscataqua? Or, in this neighborhood, our bridge spanning the Reach? What do they hold in the sweep of their aerial view—far greater, obviously, than mine atop Caterpillar Hill? Closing in, do they open into full high-pitched cry the way my heart pings turning onto Route 15? Is it possible that, for the pair nesting on Heart Island, our shoreline and maybe even our house are among their recognized landmarks? And tell them that they, too, have arrived? Birds of two places, two worlds. Of, like me, here and away.

EBB AND FLOW

*S*ummer days begin early. Even when fog blankets the coast and coves, obscures the spruce tops and thumping lobster boats putting out from the harbor, I rise just before dawn. I make coffee, feed the dog, linger a bit in the garden to deadhead and prune or to water the herb pots on the deck. Before embarking on the rest of my morning, the best of which includes a few hours of writing, I put away last night's dishes, make the bed. I straighten.

I descend from a long line of straighteners, women who daily aligned, put things right, performed what I presumed back in the 1950s was a necessary housewifely art, like pressed handkerchiefs and Sunday pot roasts. Often, my mother's straightening took on a near Calvinistic zeal. It produced tangible results—a polished tabletop, a dusted *Encyclopaedia Brittannica* bookshelf, a counter cleared of all but the percolator, cookie jar, and rotary phone. But other days, dust rag in hand, she moved through our red brick ranch on Oakdale Avenue in an almost aimless wander, as though with her attempts to straighten, something inside her was expanding, allowing for an *un*-straightening.

By the time I took any notice of her ritual, I had begun to climb alone into my primitive backyard tree house and lose myself to daydreams and adolescent yearnings. I was still years away from understanding how in such housewifely gestures my mother found it possible to withdraw into herself, free there to contemplate whatever she wished, travel wherever consciousness might take her. To my mind, mothers and daydreamers were still worlds apart.

I wasn't taught to straighten. Unlike other tasks—ironing blouses, for example, with her directive to always start with the collars—the command "Go straighten your room" came with only vague instruction. In it, however, dwelled specific expectation and the understanding that the unlikely had occurred—a tornado had dropped down on our house and blown with singular mayhem through my room. Unenthused, I picked up, stashed, stacked and stowed. I took none of the pleasure I now do in laying my hands on favorite objects—polished rocks from Boom Beach, a local potter's small vases glazed in that dusky sunset violet the sky takes on just before all light over the Camden Hills is extinguished. Now in my own actions, I recognize my mother's ritual, how she lingered before the open shelves of the dining room hutch, arranging her flow blue transferware and Blue Willow–patterned plates. Some mornings, a bit like her, I drift. In a doorway, I pause to admire how the light, fixed in a particular moment—Octavio Paz's "time thinking about itself"—gilds the petals of a white rose in a glass on the sill.

Straightening has, of course, its practical sides. Behind a framed photograph, I find the lost earring. I discover while restacking magazines the mark a wet vase has made on a table. I renew my love of a forgotten object. I honor the beauty of a made thing. Striving for effects, I clear a space around a blue bowl of oranges and make them, to my eye, more appealing. I suppose I could worry that I'm succumbing to the tyranny of inanimate objects, but I prefer to believe straightening helps make the spaces I inhabit more beautiful, a not-so-unworthy result of what is largely seen as a mostly gender-specific pursuit. Or, as colorfully observed by writer John Fowles—with men, it's the "challenging of getting," with women "the elaboration of the got."

No apologies. I'm neat. I need straightened surroundings. I require a tranquil place from which to leave and return, launch and retreat. I'm certainly mindful of the writing that doesn't get done when I spend time and energy attending to tasks lacking any real urgency. I don't thumb my nose at such a concern. But as I clear and open physical spaces in a drawer or on a shelf or desktop, it's as if physical and psychological spaces open up in me, places where lines or phrases begin to trickle in, like the ebb's merest seepage when the tide first turns. And though it's been said that only amidst disorder do muses stroll, might they not from time to time in a surprise visit appreciate a cleared path?

Most important, I straighten in an attempt to create order. Bob may stack his shirts on our closet shelf regardless of type, season, or color, but I encourage them into straight stacks. His desk is awash with files, envelopes, clipped articles and letters, but he commandeers them like regimented soldiers into tidy rows, all so perfectly aligned, the right angles could've been the work of a T-square. To my way of looking, that almost works.

In my straightened house, I may be tempted to think that I alone am the controlling principle. Perhaps over mere objects I am. But even that notion seems refuted by the evidence of our junk drawer, that burgeoning, almost life-of-its-own growth of receipts, ticket stubs, odd screws, coupons, rubber bands and obsolete appliance manuals.

*F*or all its often overwhelming beauty, the northeastern Atlantic can be wild and unpredictable, a dangerous place. Wherever I am on this island, some aspect of its waters is in walking distance. From almost every room in this house I see it, the reminder of a powerful and potentially disordering force.

Deep water has always scared me. Otherwise fairly athletic, I'm a poor and clumsy swimmer. I possess no skills at pool or beach as I do on diamond, court or track. Since childhood, I watch with envy as family and friends dive and move through water with the confidence of a dolphin or seal. On the rare occasions I find myself in deep water, I feel just an arm-stroke away from being sucked under. To reside in all my puniness at the edge of the sea's indifferent immensity and to know here joy and peace sometimes still comes as a surprise to me.

Clearly, I didn't anticipate the pull of the sea, its complexities and contradictions that attracted—attracts still—a flailing swimmer from the Midwest. Nor did I expect the northeast Atlantic's many gifts, chief among them its unrelenting tides.

With a reliability that puts to shame any clock in my house, tides, at specific times, heave and collapse. They empty then fill coves and harbors, reveal bars and small offshore islands accessible on foot but only for the narrow window of time a tidal cycle allows. They strand boats on their moorings or maroon boaters who turn too late for passage out of a narrow tidal cove. Many times, I've watched amateur paddlers go ashore at nearby tiny Heart Island and fail to pull their kayaks above the high tide line so that later my neighbor or I often hear them halooing for help.

Day and night, in all seasons and weather, tides alter this coastline, expose tidal pools and vast mudflats depended upon by the creatures who hunt there—gulls and wild mink and men who carry hods and rakes. The difference between a tidal cove and a lake, the old saying goes, is when you return, the lake is exactly where you left it.

Like a boater in foreign waters studying nautical charts, who must memorize the locations of channel markers and bell buoys, I had to acquire new language when learning about the island's tides. The outgoing ebb. The incoming flood. The sluggish neap. Slack tide—that brief period of in-between, the equivalent, in tide-parlance, of time standing still. Although, even then, movement, a drift and sway.

Behind all this orchestration of movement is, of course, the moon, which, simply put, pulls toward it the closest of Earth's water and pushes away the water on her far side. In what appears to us as shape-shifting phases more than 200,000 miles away, the moon adheres to a rigid schedule, and of the tides, demands a similar, to-the-minute chartable precision.

Once, I thought spring tides with their greatest extremes of high and low levels referred to a season. But the causes behind them relate to astronomy, to how and when and to what degree the moon either tugs or shoves. Occurring around a full or new moon phase, a spring tide's waters brim as though with newly acquired energy. They "spring" forward. Perhaps a more colorful if inaccurate measurement of a spring tide's swing is the promise a recent houseguest made when departing for a low-tide walk on the shore: "I'll be back when my butt gets wet."

Averaging 11 feet, our island tides are impressive. But consider those farther Downeast. In some places there, tides rise and fall more than 20 feet. The "main tide" running from the shore and islands can move at speeds up to eight or ten knots, making it all but impossible for lobstermen to haul traps in anything other than slack tide.

Unlike them, I don't live by the tides. I'm not a fisherman wrestling tidal currents or a clammer working mudflats. Still, I rely on tides. They're often a gauge of my day. They help create its rhythms, determine when I'm likely to take a break and visit the shore or walk the narrow finger of an exposed bar. There, in the small pocket of time I've been given before the incoming tide returns and reclaims, they demand awareness, a concentrated attention. So, too, tidal constancy connects me to the world. Daily, I'm aware of ebb or flow, how each incrementally shifts our shorelines, alters my view. I look up from my desk and the amount of change tells me the time. I awake and listen on a windless summer night, know in slap or murmuring slide whether the tide is in advance or retreat. In each is the assurance the cosmos is still intact.

And such supreme straighteners the tides can be. Daily at work on the shore, a high tide sweeps in and routinely attempts to tidy up all the messy evidence of a seemingly endless banquet another retreating tide leaves behind. Each cycle arranges, rearranges. Presents something new. But it takes away, too, like the treasure of a nearly complete heron skeleton I discovered one morning on our shoreline and was gone the next. Tides straighten. They take and give. Leave and return. And in them, always, flux.

*F*or all they might signify or deliver, there's no ceremony when a tide first turns. When the day is still and a cove is quiet, there's no big drama in the incoming tide, even with the push of the sea behind it, although potential tumult dwells there, ready to be assisted by the slightest shift in wind or weather. Nor might it seem like much drama resides within the little tidal pools revealed by the ebb. But it does.

A guide to tidal zones finer than the late Rachel Carson has probably yet to be found. Her words still masterfully instruct us to consider even the smallest of tidal pools as miniature seas, the adjoining exposed flats and neighboring tidal shorelines little communities of activity. In them, parts of the ancient continuum are enacted daily. Mostly they're old stories—something being eaten by something in danger of being eaten, though whatever the narrative thread, it's the absence or presence of water that unravels it, not light or dark, dawn or dusk.

Not surprisingly, most intertidal creatures are, of necessity, linked. But the rules governing them are neither kind nor just. A sea star gropes its slow way up to the high tide line to feast, but only at its peril once the ebb begins. A herring gull patiently waits out the tide to catch then hoist above some shell-shattering rocks a hapless mollusk, only to have it snatched by a lazier but quicker gull.

To survive the alternate land and water worlds that tides create twice daily, true tidal creatures must adapt. The green crab scuttles into the rockweed's messy closet and ducks behind heavy, dripping folds to wait out the ebb. Perhaps at some point in its evolution, the pale sand shrimp shelved in a neat stack its once more colorful shirt and now sports conservative garb in colors native to its habitat. The less particular hermit crab, on the other hand, merely rummages in the shoreline's junk drawer of flotsam—amidst sea glass bits, bitter ends of washed-ashore rope, a few iron-caked bolts, and the remnants of a shorebird's recent lunch for whatever empty armoring shell he can scramble into and claim as his own.

On the uppermost reaches of the high tide zones, even in spots where only the surf's occasional spray is enough to keep them wet, barnacles offer few signs of active life. Once situated, they don't budge from the porch. To all but the most discerning eye, they appear to snooze beneath their coolie-shaped sun hats until, like a pizza delivery guy, the sea hands over the next meal. Nearby, periwinkles in astonishing numbers thrive, claiming as home every imaginable rock, seam, and crevice. Few creatures are less dramatic than a grazing periwinkle, but a large population of them scraping about for food can, over time—albeit imperceptibly—erode rocks, deepen tidal pools.

Further into the mid-tidal zone, the simple architectural lines of a limpet's cone-shaped shell belie the genius of its precise engineering. As the tides push and pull, a limpet only has to fasten itself to a rock face, shut tight its operculum, and hold on as water washes over its sloped roof. The more forceful the waves, the more firmly limpet is pressed into place. Aristotle was among the first to point out that a limpet, even if looking every bit as much the lounge lizard as the barnacle, actually goes afield to feed. As the tide rises, it wanders nearby rocks. Prior to the ebb, however, the limpet returns, often by the same path, and always to the same precise place, its home made as recognizable by a particular depression or scar as does a welcome mat or the color of shutters to the owner of a clapboard Cape.

For every creature that survives the shoreline's daily drama, who can say how many don't? The number may be unknown but not for lack of evidence. With each ebb tide, the shore is strewn with the debris of the once-living—bleached shells of whelks and moon snails, split carapaces of green crabs, shattered remnants of sea urchins, the unhinged halves of surf clams and mussels, skeletal bits of seabirds and fish. Tangled in the heaps of black wrack are pulverized bits of whatever once swam, crawled, crept, siphoned, and spit, and have, in death, been shattered, pummeled, and dragged. A stadium of mortality. A junk drawer's jumble of chance and contingency. Of universality and certainty.

There are so many casualties in the tidal zones. So many deaths. The numbers, were they known, would be staggering. Sadly, with almost every walk I take on the tide-exposed shoreline below our house, I add to it. As though intended as a carpet, periwinkle-encrusted rocks stretch out in all directions. When the tide is out, it's almost impossible for me to step anywhere and not hear a telltale crunch. Heavy-footed and clumsy at times, I scramble over rockweed beneath which crabs or sea stars might be waiting out the ebb, or where a large moon snail, en route to its lunch, has protracted its fleshy, plowing foot, none of which can compete against the press of a size eight thick-soled Teva. Out on the flats, who can say how many unintended casualties clammers working a tide produce?

We go down to the shore or emptied tidal cove and most times we're indifferent to death's untidy aftermath. We stumble and crunch, overcome instead with the larger picture of sculpted cumulus, like continents on a map, ballooning across the distant horizon, or the panoramic swaths of saturated color seeping into the sea at sunrise. Or perhaps we're mesmerized by the masterful orchestration overhead of an osprey's hover and dive. Even when we attentively rummage in what's underfoot, we're apt to forget these are the remains of so many small and unexceptional deaths. We strive instead to find in that breakage beauty, objects we slip into a pocket and carry home to arrange on table or shelf, make of them something different, as if it were in our power to transform.

For Cape Cod writer Robert Finch, so much tide-revealed wreckage enlivens. In emptied vessels and shattered remains delivered up for our inspection by the obliging tides is evidence of the richness of life. Neither sentimental nor neat, this strewn, disorderly spectacle is a testimony to existence's harshness and the endurance of living in spite of it. And without such mangled and battered remains of extinguished life, wouldn't the shore, Finch asks, be a "barren, morbid and ultimately terrifying place?" What if the comings and goings of the tides revealed to us none of the discarded signs of life's continuity? We'd be left with trying to decipher the empty wrack line like mysterious hieroglyphics on a cave's wall. Without crunch or squish, we'd walk the shore in search of links broken, crucial cycles stopped. In death's messy evidence, the tides deliver to us certainty. Life, they tell us, persists.

"What are you looking for?" A human voice startles me. It's John, a neighbor who lives down the road.

I'm standing still and mute, head bent, ankle-deep—my blue heron imitation—in a small sandy-bottomed tidal pool. The tide has only just turned, begun to seep back toward shore. It's a glorious morning, without the merest hint of breeze. The intertidal water is flat, clear. Shortly after sunrise, I came down to the shore to take advantage of one of maybe only a dozen times this year that a big spring tide will occur during daylight hours.

I can't say how long I've been standing in this same spot, but my sandaled feet are almost too numb from the cold water to feel what look to be sand shrimp skittering over them as if they were rocks. Just as John posed his question, one had come to rest on my big toe. Moments before that, a small flat fish—a juvenile flounder? a good sign for our local fish population as surely as the stands of swaying eel grass further out—shuddered itself out of the sand, then skimmed toward some draping rockweed and disappeared.

Undetected, John has paddled up in his kayak, making it easier for me to understand how a kayaker might steal up on a seal snoozing on a sun-warmed ledge.

"Oh, well," I fumble in answer to his question. "I'm just—" I raise my hands to shade my eyes. The sun is higher but it doesn't tell me how much time I've spent on the shore. Enough to have made it out to a cluster of boulders splotched with rose-colored coralline algae revealed only at the spring tides' extremes. Not far from where John floats, I earlier came upon a trove of sea stars in varying shades of purple, blue, and pink. One bigger than my hand was in the middle of breakfast. With strong arms and supple suction-cup feet, the sea star had pried open and through its mouth emptied its stomach into a meaty mussel. No doubt digestive enzymes, with a blender's puree-cycle efficiency, were already turning the bivalve into slurpable slop.

I don't divulge to John the nearby cache of overharvested sand dollars or the spot where in a tide as big as this you can dig a mess of hen clams. Nor do I tell him that despite their decline in the years since divers descended on the island each November to satisfy appetites in far-off Japan, there are large colonies of sea urchins among the coralline-crusted rocks just off our shore. I'm tempted to report that while wading out past the spring tide's low-water mark, I discovered a brittle star, a nocturnally active dweller typically found in deeper water. But I don't know John well. And I can't really fault him for what's feeling more and more to me like an intrusion. I comment instead on the beauty of the day, and comfortably we retreat into weather's neutral territory, the recent stretch of fine days, those still being promised in the forecast. As he paddles away, I turn for shore, still, I realize, mulling over his question.

I do not come down to the shore as a scientist or expert of any kind. I don't search for an epiphany, though it's possible in such a messy realm to sweep out a few cobwebs. Maybe not actively searching for one, I sometimes stumble on a phrase or line that, like a well-placed squirt of oil, helps ignite the sputtering engine of some stalled essay or poem. Or perhaps I see again how the shoreline routinely makes good on its promise to delight, even amaze.

But John didn't ask, "What do you see?" Not even "What are you looking *at?*"

His question suggested I'd not come down to the shore for an aimless walk, but was driven here by a purpose, by a need yet to be met. Or was the purpose his? His readiness to be helpful if needed—if, say, I was after something I'd lost, something I had to find.

What, he asked, are you looking *for?*

*I*t's supposed to be a walk to observe birds. Several of us have joined two birders associated with an island conservation group. Our destination: the Mill Pond's tidal flats in Sunset, a place I know well. One August several years ago, Bob and I rented a house on a nearby tidal cove, the terrain of numerous visiting shorebird species, and it's here the walk starts, just as the tide is approaching its lowest ebb and the last of the morning's fog is burning off.

A developed eye is needed to appreciate the beauty of exposed mud-flats. In what might appear as a barren stretch of pungent smell and muck over which the wind routinely sweeps but elicits no deep-water waves' shimmer and shine is a terrain of small holes and mounds, scrapes and troughs, the traces of what crawls or trails away, what, to survive, must burrow and hide. A place where grazing shorebirds probe and poke, etching the mud with calligraphic scribblings.

Once, in another cottage we rented, a houseguest waking his first morning to a similarly emptied tidal cove, proclaimed, "You'd better get your money back. Someone has stolen all the water." Other guests, holding their noses, greeted the exposed flats with less humor. Even our dog Ben, always keen in his younger days for a walk at any time, hesitated when the afternoon's adventure included a low-tide hike across muddy flats.

For the clammer who makes his living by digging a tide, the exposed flats are where he punches in, the equivalent elsewhere of office, assembly line, or construction site. It's no place for a slouch. The work here demands physical effort and produces by day's end oodles of discomfort. With upper body bent low over a short-handled rake, the clammer works the lengthening flats in a repetitive chop and scrape. Ankle deep in muck, each rubber-booted step requires a sucking pop of release. For the birds that inhabit them, the tide-exposed flats are essential, the equivalent of a well-stocked supermarket or brimming salad bar. They, too, go to work here. But hands down, and even though clammer and shorebird alike recognize the telltale signs in the flats of where to bend and poke or rake, it's the feathered forager that makes the enterprise look easy.

No sooner do we walkers park our cars than a *"Whew, whew, whew"* prompts Matt to announce, "Greater yellow legs," this bird's three syllables alone distinguishing it from a lesser yellow leg's two. On the rocky shoreline, Carl sets up his spotting scope, and the smallest of the distant birds is noted first—least sandpipers, or peeps, each of which weighs no more than a few ounces but in migration to and from the Hudson Bay fly thousands of miles. Atop a rocky outcropping perch several Bonaparte gulls. Farther out are a few stout-billed semi-palmated plovers that, with their quick steps and abrupt pause before each probe, remind me of my childhood game of "Freeze."

I love lists. Always have. Making them, keeping them. Using lists, I prioritize, create structure, invite and maintain order. A To-Do list in itself displays industriousness, the promise of tangible accomplishment. Satisfaction resides in checking off each item and moving on to the next. A life list is a list of a different sort. As the tally of all bird species seen in a lifetime, its value resides in what is added, not taken away. There's no burden in how such a list expands. Indeed each new entry is eagerly sought, none more so than a type of bird seen for the first time. What in bird-speak is known as a "lifer."

Clearly, my novice rank and infant life list assure me numerous lifers still await. On walks such as this, with notebook and field guide in hand, I've yet to confirm great numbers of the newly observed or what with some practice I'll be able to identify with more than a mere name. Like the stout, mottled bird Matt waves me over to sight in his scope. Looking like a dapper chap sporting a tweed jacket over a rust-colored sweater, this bird, with its straight prominent bill twice the size of its head, is one I'm certain I've seen but until now I'd not, albeit with Matt's help, identified—a short-billed dowitcher. Actually, there are three of them on the far side of the cove, each intent and singularly focused, though their movements are the same, and now to my eye unmistakable. Methodically, they step across a shallow pool, their heads in perpetual up and down motion, their long bills repeatedly probing. The "sewing-machine bird" stitching patterns in the mud.

Itself like a small flock of birds, our gathered group has made its way out to a small point. With much less grace and lightness of foot, we step over the slick tide-exposed rocks near shore, trying to stay safely out of muck's reach. Soon the tide will turn, and this cove, I remember, quickly fills once the flood tide reaches the cove's narrowing neck, pressed by the deep waters of Sylvester Cove and Penobscot Bay beyond. Already, seepage into the cove has begun. Soon, the shorebirds' salad bar will be shut down.

Time on the flats is measured in what the tides grant. And we've got enough of it, Carl assures us, to make it around the point and to a small marshy area. I already know that near there, above a tide-exposed track leading to Sheephead Island, is an osprey nest with three unfledged juveniles who by their Baby Huey proportions alone threaten to topple the nest and whose big appetites and loud demands seem to be exhausting beyond reason their attentive, bedraggled parents. Often in this marsh are birds I'm less familiar with, including, as recently reported sightings suggest, some red knots I'm eager now to confirm.

But this is before the whale.

"Oh, look. There it is." A woman late to our group points toward land, to the wrack line and a long dark hump almost obscured by large boulders close to the wooded shore.

"Don't go near it. It stinks," she warns, continuing on to the marsh as four of us peel off and approach the dead whale's body. Despite her warning, I've yet to be overpowered by any putrefying stench. Nor is the congress of flies as thick and riotous as I expect. Surprisingly, there's little significant evidence that the busiest and most opportunistic shoreline scavengers, the gulls and crows, have been at work peppering the dead creature with open shotgun-like wounds. The eye sockets have yet to be fully emptied, ravaged clean. Clearly though, the elements have had a hand in whatever natural process of disintegration began when the whale's dark skin and fatty layer meant to retain heat in cold water baked the whale once it stranded. Up close, it's possible to see that the skin, once smooth and rubbery, has split, and, like fruit, is peeling away in thick ragged sheets. The body is swollen, blown up, but with an odd density more than gaseous bloat. It looks sodden and lumpish, heavy, as though by sheer weight alone it's becoming part of the earth. Still, the animal it once was is distinguishable. Tall, curved dorsal fin, broad flukes, long and thin flippers, a slender tail that once could thrust. A conspicuous watery-world presence, even if what once gave this creature of the sea its speed and grace has vanished.

So this is it. What I was so sorry to miss. Just five days ago, in one of those startling juxtapositions offered up by this little island, when many of us were joining the New Orleans musicians invited here for the annual JazzFest in a Mardi-Gras-type line dance winding down Stonington's Main Street, other islanders were ringing Sylvester Cove to observe the rare occurrence of a whale who'd come close to shore and was by all accounts cavorting among moored boats and putting on its own show. News of the sighting soon percolated its way around the island, but few of us knew until the following morning that later the whale followed the tide into the Mill Pond, this cove that, as one worried resident declared, "empties right out." Whatever attempts were made to direct it back into the Bay failed. The whale, stranded, died. And only later still did news circulate that the whale thought first to be a minke and later a pilot is in fact a Risso's dolphin.

As we circle, stoop, squat for a closer look, it's easy to see how the mistake was made. The dolphin's eleven-foot length and the square blunt shape of its head would telegraph "whale" to those on shore. But the perceived scratches and scars reported to marine biologists by the Mill Pond residents who first feared a stranding are actually the white markings of a Risso's dolphin. Even now, though much of the splitting skin has peeled and frayed, it's possible to see them—irregular lines and scratches, smudged splotches, some almost circular, like the remnants of chalk marks on a blackboard carelessly erased. Such dolphins, I've since read, travel in pods, typically offshore, and are known to prefer warmer temperatures and tropical waters. Some may, though rarely, migrate north to cooler waters during summer calving season. Were this dolphin a bird, it might be tempting to identify it as an accidental, a species that has wandered far from its normal range.

A stranded cetacean of any type is a rare occurrence and an even rarer sighting. Truly, for me, a lifer. But by way of unfortunate circumstance. What drove this creature to a quiet tidal cove that became treacherous, the outgoing tide less a merciful shot to the head than a slow, tortuous suffocation? Had the dolphin's sonar misguided it? Was this, as some suggest, an intentional beaching because of illness or internal injury? Had parasites made a mushy mess of the brain, or did a twisting spaghetti-mass of nematode worms infect the inner ear, disrupt navigation? Only an autopsy will reveal answers to the marine researchers at nearby College of the Atlantic who most of us thought had already hauled the dolphin's body away. Instead, here it is.

All around us on the cove are the small deaths customary to our shorelines. The broken detritus, the extinguished remains, the crunch beneath our pitiless feet. But just as the images of oil-soaked birds and otters call to us from our television screens, big and visible deaths such as this, particularly of what is stranded, netted, assaulted by accident or environmental tragedy, capture our attention. Deaths more extraordinary, more exceptional. Deaths, perhaps, which bear more resemblance to our own.

Among us humans, the act of dying is often kept hidden, and more so certainly its aftermath, what happens to the body after life is extinguished. None in this small group here are medical people, homicide detectives, or soldiers who've been in battle. Most likely we've never witnessed beloved bodies transforming into untidy, rotting husks. It's hard for me to imagine what any of us squatting here would look like after several days cooked on a granite ledge.

With textbook knowledge, I know that the dolphin and I are linked by similar mammalian characteristics. Yet I bear no physical similarity to it. The underwater world can never be home to me. Even temporarily, I'm unable to swim with even a smidgeon of the dolphin's liquid grace. Yet for a time, we breathed the same air.

"I had no idea skin could do this," Nancy, squatting beside me, says in not much more than a whisper. A fiber artist I knew only by her work in local galleries until we met as fellow walkers this morning, she's obviously sensitive to surface and texture. About this body before us, she is understandably, appropriately, amazed. And a bit horrified. As am I. Yet neither of us seems ready to resume the walk around the point.

Maybe behind her observation and our mutual unwillingness to move on or look away is the recognition: we, too, are this.

Finally I stand. The sea, unrelenting, is inching up. Eventually, after we're forced to leave, it will reach the dolphin's body, this creature now so very much of the earth. Even without being tethered, as I would've thought the researchers would instruct, while they await necessary marine mammal removal permits, the dolphin's body shows no signs of being budged loose by the tides. While it's certain the tidal cycle played a key role in the dolphin's death and at some point nudged the body to the wrack line, the tide will, in this quiet cove, need some big assists to fully reclaim it, like wind whipping up waves or the moon surging a spring tide to highest water levels. Eventually, were the dolphin's body not destined for the COA labs, the sea, in cahoots with whatever scavengers find the carcass, with whatever mysterious internal process of decay the plethora of munching bacteria have long been hastening, the mush-and-muck, gas-and-rot evidence of which, were we able to flip the dolphin over would on its underside display, will break the body down, scatter whatever bones and bits remain—flotsam helpless against a current, all reclaimed by an outgoing tide, and, perhaps, in fragments small enough to be pocketed, be tossed ashore again.

*T*his morning, I sat at my desk, attempted a new poem. I don't usually write in form, but I'd challenged myself to compose and strictly adhere to the identifying characteristics of a fourteen-line sonnet. What I wound up with wasn't a sonnet. Among other reasons, its apparent subject didn't trigger me to a *volta* at the end of the eighth line, nor, as it turns out, to anything else worth keeping. Instead, I shifted my attention to other drafts, to prose bearing no form similar to that which eluded me in the sonnet. And certainly not to any found in a sestina's regimented number of lines, its precise order of key end-line words repeated in as precise a sequence as the tide's charted rise and fall.

No stranger to form, Robert Frost famously likened free verse to playing tennis without a net. He also proclaimed that poetry is a "momentary stay against confusion." Of course, the same can be said about other types of writing, not just poetry. How we order and lay out words on a page, attempt to straighten the jumbled bits of our untidy minds. How we strive to make something out of, and are thereby able to live with, disorder, all the world's chaos. Like an ebb tide against a stiff onshore breeze, words incrementally, stubbornly, fill the page. And there, among truths waiting to be revealed, forms and patterns emerge.

As they do elsewhere. In symmetrical architectural designs. In the clipped geometrical hedges that in formal gardens and cultivated countrysides attempt to banish chance, declare victory over untamed wildness. Or in the ebb and flow of our daily lives when the fear of life's unpredictable hazards throws a long shadow. There, shaken, we turn our faces to regularity's bright light. Reliable patterns emerge, rituals and habits. Perhaps we routinely choose to set our dinner table with cloth mats and napkins and flowers from the garden rather than squeeze out a haphazard space between teetering piles of books, magazines, and unopened mail. With deep satisfaction, we stack clean, neatly folded towels on a shelf. Or, with an aesthetic that through practice and intention has become routine as much as it may be physically inherent, we pluck from a cabinet a cobalt plate because its color alone is perfect for the lemons.

"Fragments I have shored against my ruins," writer Joan Didion declared in her memoir, recounting the time following her husband's death and her daughter's critical and eventually fatal illness. Didion was referring to the fragments of her domestic life's repeated rituals in which, as wife and mother, she once believed she could find meaning. In deep mourning, she believed in them still, even if, at a well-laid table in their routine dinner-at-home ritual, her husband had slumped, head to plate, in an almost immediately fatal cardiac arrest.

Order and disorder reside, not parallel, but intertwined. They mingle, as do, briefly, currents at their tidal turn. We live with both. Sometimes, like a boat, even if carefully tethered, we're pulled by a flood tide from our mooring. Or, in spite of all our armoring against, we collapse at the loss of someone we love, and like an eroding chunk of coastline in a spring tide's surge backed by a strong northeasterly wind, a vital piece of ourselves is swept into a sea of grief. Daily we're open to revision, vulnerable to change.

And isn't that how it should be? Uncertainty helps make life possible, doesn't it? If my brother, who couldn't survive without a liver transplant, had been told it was certain he'd never get one, how could he have gone on the last year of his life?

Embedded in human experience are contradictions and polarities between which we must reside. What we attach ourselves to, what we're forced to relinquish. The tides' reliable reassurance, their reckless indifference. Our attempts to stay the current, our recognition that we're bits of flotsam powerless against it. The certainty of uncertainty.

Of course I know all this. I know the ritual of sipping tea from a favorite mug at the same hour each day offers little more than comfort. I know no amount of straightening or rearranging will prevent loss. No order I can impose arrests the inevitable. Relentlessly, in a world where so much of what comes next is unknown, tides predictably, in spite of us, rise and fall. Tides leave, always return. The blessing and the curse.

The tidal sculptures of Andy Goldsworthy remind me of this. Erected between tides at the sea's edge and constructed of sticks and stones, even bracken, leaves and ice, they're beautiful, often intricate, but never bulwark-sturdy. Goldsworthy's intention isn't permanence. His sculptural constructions attract in part because they're ephemeral, temporary. Part of their making is the unmaking, what occurs when the rising tide slowly, incrementally, but inevitably and irretrievably undermines, claims. In a documentary of Goldsworthy's water-edge sculptures, we watch as he constructs, in an estuary's upper tidal zone, a large dome of washed-up, bleached-gray branches collected from a nearby embankment. Laboriously, as the tide advances, he stacks the sticks around him, the last of which he places around the dome's top hole at a height taller than he is, before scooting out of a small opening at its base. Soon, the rising water touches the branches, begins to lift the dome. As it slowly rises, a few bottom branches float off. And then a few more. An aerial view shows them radiating out and away. The water continues to rise and the dome, as though untethered, begins to move, revolve in the current, until, with more branches floating off, what remains of the dome is carried upstream. Watching, Goldsworthy is visibly excited about his success. He's achieved his aim: "to make works that anticipate but do not attempt to predict or control the future." Change is integral to his work, to the dome that Goldsworthy observes is being taken into another plane, another world. The dome, he's convinced, "becomes stronger and more complete as it falls apart, and disappears."

Tides impose a kind of order on what, by its very nature, is water's formlessness. They mandate at what time, as directed by the moon, water will measurably rise and fall. But the tides cannot direct or control a heap of other factors—wind and weather and season—the confluences of which, along with the assists of chance and contingency, can't be predicted. Tides impose an order but do not alone control the sea. As with a Goldsworthy sculpture, the precise when of its impending destruction may be known, but not the how of a dome's or cairn's demise. The Mill Pond onlookers on a Sunday night knew the precise time a dolphin's final trouble would begin but not the *if* of the other factors that might yet assist in steering it out to the bay. The uncertainty of certainty.

Yet the tides with their charted accuracy do provide a unifying principle amidst disorder, what we writers may be trying to achieve as we push words across a page, or, pushing away from our desks, go down to the shore to find. There, amidst evidence of deaths large and small, we discover again the reminder that permanence, like the order in my junk drawer that will probably forever elude me, can't be ours. Nothing is permanent in spite of our efforts to endure, no matter the predictable regularity sustained with ritual and routine. If, with a sonnet-making intention, I make surprising turns, none can reroute me from where, inevitably, I'll wind up.

This morning, before I sat down to write, I returned form to the unmade, rumpled bed, structured order out of last night's kitchen clutter. I straightened. I put my hands into the current that carries me back to my knowable past, my hands linked to my mother's as they still are each time I iron, her hands guiding mine across first-primer handkerchiefs, lessons my young granddaughters in their hyperscheduled worlds of fleece, denim, and spandex may never know to miss. Through ritual and routine, I gathered to me pieces scattered by time and distance, and in spaces newly cleared, infused them with possible new meaning.

Soon, I'll go down to the shore. Out in the bay, the distant eelgrass streaming with the current will tell me if the tide is in advance or retreat. Either way, I'm in it, too, heading in the same direction as every living thing. I'll wade out into the sloshing, formless sea, among the remains of what's already extinguished. Again, in the tides' certainty, I'll find life persists. Again, I'll plunge my hands in.

PROTECTING THE DREAMER

$\mathcal{B}$arely 7 a.m. but a light-squelching fog on a muffled June morning almost makes the hour irrelevant. I'm still in pajama bottoms and a sweatshirt when Lewis our plumber arrives, his van rattling up the drive and spattering gravel into the stillness like gunshot.

"I reckon it is an ungodly hour when the weather doesn't give much reason to get up and on with something," he says, making it clear in the next breath that I'm his second call. By his standards, this day is well underway.

Unfortunately, I long ago discovered that no summer season is complete without a plumbing problem. This time it's the water filter on the fritz, a tall cylindrical device the previous owners installed beside the water pump and the likely culprit behind the alarmingly gray-tinged water that's begun to spew from our faucets.

"If you're going to be the captain of the ship," Lewis instructs, "you'd better know how to run it." This morning, we both descend into the cellar.

I'm always learning something new from Lewis, a tall, lean 80-something island native still living on the piece of land he was born to and who each year fails to make good on his threat to retire. "So let's see what's up with this creature," he suggests, pushing back the bill of his cap which, in the years he's come to our house or on the road when I've waved to him in his truck, I've never seen him without. Were he not to wear it, I'm not sure I'd recognize him.

"Lookit here, you need to know what this is," he says, and points at a sprocketed gear. "This here's her timing device." Today, I find out our water filter system has a gender. Naturally, it's female, as are, it seems, going back to Adam, most things likely to stir up trouble. Only in recent years do hurricanes hurtling up the coast bear names like Andrew or Ivan. Best I know, a neighbor on our road is one of the few to christen a lobster boat, those objects of endless devotion and aggravation, with a name such as *Sir Shawn*.

After just a few minutes of wordless investigation—Lewis is nothing if not laconic—he determines the problem resides with the filter's timing device. "Seems she's gone a little off. Probably from all those power outages back in early spring." Though easily fixed, he'll need to flush the backwash lines into the floor drain. "Have you got a cold chisel?" he asks. "Mine's back at the shop."

"Not only do we not have a cold chisel, I never knew such a thing existed. And though Lewis manages to pry the drain open with hammer and screwdriver, I know that sometime soon, I'll head over to AJ's and buy one for tasks as yet unknown. Clearly no workbench should be without its cold chisel.

"So let's let her rest a bit," Lewis suggests. "We got her pretty riled up. She should settle back down some by afternoon."

As if all *she* needs is a good cry.

I've always thought that to become intimate with a house is to know in which corners at which times of day the sun shines it warmest light, to know the sound of rain unique to a particular place on the roof, to be certain when the wind howls where the house creaks its loudest or moans at its highest pitch, and in a storm, beneath which doors and windows water will seep. To know its bones. Its basement and attic.

Numerous apartments notwithstanding, I've never lived in a house without a basement. Houses raised on stilts or tacked smack onto a concrete slab seem to me houses without roots, without a foundation to carry a house's weight, the heft of joy or the burden of sorrows within. To a basement we retreat when winds threaten. There we head when mechanical problems compromise our comfort. And there, a child in a crowded house seeks privacy and quiet.

Chalk it up to regional parlance perhaps, but what in my native Midwest is a basement, I decline to call here anything but a cellar. It's also a matter, I suppose, of use, purpose, and structure. Cool and dark, lit only by a couple of pull-chain lightbulbs and three small windows, our cellar is a little creepy. In its corners, the desiccated remains of mice are discovered each spring. Once, a salamander that must've squeezed in through a screen seemed happily adjusted to life on a sweating pipe. Often damp and predisposed to mildew in late-spring thaw and rain, our cellar is a place of pure function, a netherworld of pipes and drains, the home to machines that filter and pump and heat our water, to electrical boxes and switches that provide power to wash clothes or warm a bowl of chowder. At one end, the concrete floor slopes upward to follow the contour of the underlying granite ledge, a place where not even I of modest height can stand upright. On this, my house of light and energy and dreams stands.

Though it's a distant cousin to our basement in Illinois, that well-lit place of bookshelves and washing machine, of cedar closet and brimming storage bins, or to my childhood home's knotty-pine-paneled basement rec room with TV and wet bar, our cellar here bears no resemblance to either. Nor, I predict, will it ever.

Still, despite its more direct lineage to the New England root cellar, and if, as philosopher Gaston Bachelard claims, our past houses are physically inscribed in us, then each time I empty-handedly climb the narrow cellar stairs of this house, I'm carrying up a load of warm laundry, a garment bag of winter woolens, a box of Christmas decorations. Or I'm the adolescent newly unchained from another subterranean summer afternoon's chore of ironing primer pillowcases and handkerchiefs, or I'm fresh from one more reinvention of my teenage self who in lip-sync belted out Petula Clark's "Downtown" to one of my 45s while upstairs my family went about their obviously more mundane lives. Each experience has been physically impressed on tissue and bone even if, as the cellar door thunks shut behind me, I enter a bright, light-filled house that by its architectural style—and surely by its location on the edge of an edge of an island—resembles no house I've ever called home.

A house is a child's first universe, one of the first things she draws. Out of sofa cushions, appliance cartons, a pink flannel blanket draped over iron porch railings, it's one of her first creations. "A dreamer of houses sees them everywhere," Bachelard tells us. She also coaxes.

Each summer, in a shallow hollow, beneath spruce trees not far from this house, I invite our grandchildren and nephew to build miniature "gnome homes" out of forest and beach finds. Together we drop crosslegged onto the forest floor with gathered birch bark, mussel shells, sticks, and balsam cones. We tramp shore and woods, landscapes rife not just with potential building materials but houses themselves. In the wrack above the high-tide line, taking a page from Bachelard's playbook, I hold up a whorled, spiral-ridged dogwinkle shell and say, "Imagine living in here"—within bleached, corrugated outer walls, in a single room deeply lustered like an old silk lamp shade in subtle variegations of lavender, orange and pink, a spiral staircase climbing to a small turreted tower. At nearby Ames Pond, I try to convince them the turtle roused from a log has retreated into its shingled, one-room watery palace of dark glossy halls dimly lit by a single lamp.

A house protects the dreamer, Bachelard claims. A house shelters the imagination, invites reverie and many essential musings. It's a world within worlds, a personal cosmos. But first, and throughout history, whatever its type, however primitive its form, a house helps insure survival.

Little did I know that much of what has always attracted me to particular houses, including this one, is due in part to what geographer Jay Appleton calls the inherent need we hunter-gatherers possess for outlook and shelter, prospect and refuge. A place from which to spot peril or tonight's dinner. A "womb with a view." Small wonder then that our species seems to have evolved by having long ago bunked down in savannah landscapes, home to open vistas and sheltering trees.

I credit Bob with first heeding that ancestral pull when we considered buying this house. Prospect tugged first and hardest on him. Somewhat predictably, studies show men are drawn to the familiar domain of hunter while we women put effort into refuge, into those spaces too often disparagingly labeled "domestic." A big bright space with broad view is one definition of *prospect,* and that we've got in spades here, as became apparent the first time we saw this place. But the snug-and-protective-haven aspect of things? It mattered little to Bob that the kitchen of our possible new house was in need of major renovation. Or that the living area with its narrow width would limit furniture placement and pose challenges for looking out from a comfortable chair to the enviable prospect which, following one brief circuit of the interior, he'd retreated to the outside deck to more properly ponder. He didn't question as I did the sudden disappearance of our long-held dream of a snug New England Cape or a classic cedar-shingle camp or a rambling and worn saltwater farmhouse. In this contemporary-styled refuge, I sought some likely alcoves and nooks in open, high-ceilinged spaces. On multiple-windowed walls, I searched for places to put bookshelves, hang art. Was he not horrified by the color palette (a more-at-home-in-the-tropics yellow, pink and green combo—but on a small Maine island for Pete's sake—and signifying perhaps other less obvious flaws?) or by the shag carpeting, including in (what were they thinking?) the bathrooms?

That afternoon, we'd quite unknowingly fallen into lockstep with men and women who for millennia preceded us—even, more recently, my parents. One summer afternoon of my adolescence, as my mother and I drove off to look at paint and fabrics for her latest café curtain re-do of the bedroom my sister and I shared, we waved to my father busily hauling out pruner and shears. By the time we returned, the mere buzz cut he'd promised to give the evergreen border had morphed into the near elimination of those sheltering shrubs, my mother's attempt at a privacy screen, and he'd already retreated back into the garage, offspring of the basement with its engines, gadgets, and sharpened tools of the hunt.

Bob, of course, was right. Not that a contemporary-styled, shed-roofed house with shortcomings not easily fixed was my first choice. But that over time we'd work to coax out of it the havens we needed to sleep, eat, laugh, welcome family and friends, heal illness, lick our wounds. We'd change colors, rip up carpet. And the prospect of the unbounded sea and sky our house looked upon? Or as one male friend proclaimed, our "million dollar view?" That needed little assist from either of us.

*T*rue, my interest in my house's design and décor could be dismissed as trifling. A concern too slight. The pursuit of a useless beauty. Even architecture, we're reminded by Alain de Botton in *The Architecture of Happiness,* is not free from a degree of suspicion. Doubts, he claims, have long been raised about its seriousness, its moral worth and cost. Many of the world's most intelligent people disdain such interest and equate contentment with "discarnate and invisible matters instead." A contradictory notion, however, acknowledges how much our identities are indelibly connected to our locations, are influenced by our surroundings. How a house can more than just hold us but shape us like a shell its resident snail.

To critics who would sniff at my pursuits, to how I spend time, not just over what piece of furniture goes where or from what perspective I wish to look out window or at computer screen but on the chair itself, its fabric upon which I plunk my bum, I offer up in a defensive crouch: "Yes, but I also work here." Here is where, as a writer, I attempt loftier subjects, higher planes of thought. I'm defined by those thoughts my words make manifest, but also by the language of materials and colors and objects within my house. Through them, I declare to others: this, too, is who I am.

I welcome my linkage back to ancestral gatherers squatting beside a streambed, harvesting greens, and who in their cave homes couldn't resist picking up a stick or whatever was the equivalent of paintbrush or chisel. I've long been fascinated by prehistoric cave paintings, their simple but sophisticated animals and abstract-patterned finger flutings, though I'm most taken by images of red ochre hands, splayed palms not so much traced as pressed against cool rock. It's been theorized that in some caves this is the work of shamans. But I've got my chips down that at least some of them were done by women, perhaps while pausing in the midst of performing other necessary tasks. Are they, I wonder, a claim of ownership or a form of identity? An early human insistence that our houses, no matter how primitive, are our biographies? Or might they be evidence of our ancient and persistent-through-the-ages urge to create, to make what is ours beautiful, even in times of peril, out of whatever is at hand?

Of course, a fully inhabited house needn't be beautiful. Nor is beauty without a somber reality—envy and aggression can as easily as peace and kindness call a beautiful house home. Sadists, dictators and racists can emerge from its rooms. Stendahl declared, "Beauty is the promise of happiness." No doubt countless arguments have been made and countless more remain as to whether there is such a link. Defining happiness or beauty, or, for that matter, taste, a major component of beauty, is fodder for realms both lofty and not. Definitions aside, de Botton suggests that Stendahl seems to have succeeded in plucking out of an aesthetics-fueled argument the integration of our love of beauty with our more or less universally-held wish for happiness, one of the qualities we need to prosper as human beings.

Indeed, I'm happy when I find the right chair for my house—like, say, the one left behind by the previous owners which, when stripped of its floral print, I slipcovered in plain parchment canvas. Positioning it just so makes of it a refuge with prospect so that while I write or read, I can also look up to watch monarchs hovering over the coneflowers in my garden or, come evening, the final hurrah of some ruddy-bellied nimbus hunkering on the horizon. And yet I'll admit I'm often no more or less happy there than on other days sitting in other chairs in this house. On days, for example, when I move with the sun as it travels from room to room, and in those other places where it shines its brightest, I take up other tasks, engage other selves. Those other Me's.

*F*or years, while renting various summer cottages on the island, Bob and I made numerous trips to our Illinois basement, hauling down pieces of furniture, old mirrors, quilts, lamps, boxes of objects labeled "Save For Maine." No house of our own had yet come within our reach but the shape of one, blurry in outline, fuzzy in detail, persisted. When at last we bought this place, we pulled into its driveway with a rented truck. The following summer we downsized to a rented van. Ever since, my car on its annual cross-country trips is densely packed.

I arrive with updated photo albums, kitchen gadgets, bottles and jars of foodstuffs not readily available to me here. And, of course, books. Boxes of them. I unload the car and carry in cartons and files, framed prints, various finds and purchases of emotional and utilitarian import that in the intervening months I became convinced belong here—like a crudely carved bird striving to resemble a loon if only by way of its red-painted eyes and despite their rather maniacal un-loon-like gaze. Or one more platter, another tray, as if my intention is to serve the entire island population in a single sitting.

Home is a "place where every day is multiplied by all the days before it," claimed the late explorer Freya Stark. It's also a place layered with our possessions—the objects, fragments, pieces of our lives, the beautiful and the ordinary, the potential for, were this ancient Rome, an archeological dig. In many ways, we are what we have. What's mine is me.

Obviously, not all our stuff possesses value or meaning. And let's be clear: I'm not talking about coffee makers and blenders, the mere mundane and way-more-than-we-need commodities too soon outdated and unwanted, as evidenced by brimming curbside bins and landfills (albeit by way of the more rigorous cabinet-and-closet cullers among us). I mean objects that can, for example, exert powerful and potentially positive influence. Like how, on the eve of brain surgery, our twelve-year-old grandson, defying the stigma linking adolescent boys to stuffed toys, brought to the hospital his ragged, resurrected-from-the-back-of-the-closet "Lambie."

Our desire to possess and collect seems instinctive, doesn't it? Watch how a child herds his Cheerios into the corner of his highchair's tray, a small collection that in just a few years may balloon into hoards of Hot Wheels or, thanks to the marketing departments of Disney and Pixar, myriad must-have action figures. Maybe then rocks, shells, stamps. And later, possibly, in a glass vitrine, autographed baseballs.

Naturally, this can lead to excess in need of correction. The *horror vacui* that compelled Victorians to stuff their rooms and embellish their furnishings eventually paved the way to an antithetical midcentury modern minimalism. Since, in more recent postmodern decades, such spareness has morphed again, fueled by what social commentator George Will once observed is the "endless inculcation of envy."

But hey, it might be argued, consumerism and consumption is the stuff on which American economic engines run, no? And so why then, I often wonder, while leafing through those euphemistically called "shelter magazines," do houses appear clutter-free, even as they're glossily depicted in pages brimming with ads urging readers to buy more and more? Maybe such tidy houses don't so much speak to our buying less than to spending more in clever ways to store all our stuff out of sight. I'm reminded of the summer an island friend hosted a party for visiting author and social activist Studs Terkel. A young man by way of introduction said he was an organizer. Not surprisingly, Terkel immediately launched into a lively conversation with what he'd taken as a labor organizer, only to discover the objects of the young man's organizing skills were closets.

The bond between me and my possessions—okay, *some* possessions—can be important. Culture scholar Russell Belk claims that the accumulation of possessions can help tell us who we were, where we have come from, and perhaps where we are going. They also offer, perhaps, a record of what matters to us most.

Fleeing a forest fire or hurricane suddenly bearing down with a new, unpredicted force, we instinctively grab family photographs, important documents, perhaps a prized painting, an heirloom brooch, and then, if we have time, objects diverse, ordinary, and important. Later, maybe, we surprise even ourselves with our odd choices. In the comfort of my home, spared such disaster, I watch the stunned faces of the less fortunate on TV. I see the fear and despair of debt and injury, dollars and insurance, and the immediate question: Where tonight and tomorrow will my family rest their heads? But I see, too, a sense of betrayal. Of how a house, that familiar place invested with time and love and honored with memories, failed to protect and hold. All that a person may own. Things sanctified by love. Objects honored by a family's history. I look at those faces on cots in a gym, how loss is burrowing in. I watch as a middle-aged woman who, though grateful her family is safe, picks through charred remains, plucks from them a twisted metal picture frame, a shard of china, the spoked wheel of what had been her daughter's tricycle. She brushes back the hair from her brow and, turning to the camera, motions toward the blackened heap, her face saying, This, too, is me.

On this island more obviously and generously endowed than Robinson Crusoe's, I'm nevertheless reminded of his reference to "the strange multitudes of little things necessary." Much of what I carry into this house isn't, admittedly, necessary. But I've come to believe that more of it than I'd originally thought is, even here where I'm closer to the natural world with its multitudes of freely offered gifts, of little—and big—necessities.

Matter matters. The squat pitcher holding flowers plucked from my yard may not have belonged to my deceased mother, but in it her spirit emerges, her love of gardening is present. So, too, in the painted tramp-art table, an odd chip-carved yellow thing as stacked and layered as an ornate wedding cake that an electrician working here stared at as though it were a caged animal in a zoo before asking, "Is that supposed to be a table?" Though not a handed-down relic, it possesses my mother's love of the old, the found, and the scrounged that's been passed on to me. Her cracked but cherished Blue Willow–patterned platter doesn't make my house hers. But as an object that carries the vibrancy of her attention and care, it's transported some of her presence here. And it instructs, "Remember."

Recently I came across the term *wabi sabi,* what in Japanese is the "perfect imperfection"—what in certain objects bears the evidence of their making, or, reflecting time's passage, are made more beautiful with use. That never-the-same quality certain old things possess. Our dining table is more beautiful to me because its wide-planked top bears the darkened phantom remains of three long-gone hinges and a latch, evidence that in its former life as a nineteenth-century door, it was banged shut who knows where or by how many hands.

In his essay, "Toward an Impure Poetry," Pablo Neruda exhorted fellow poets to seek what is rich with the "impurity of the human condition," like the objects that are "worn with the hand's obligations…steeped in sweat and in smoke," but his opening instruction to "look closely at the world of objects at rest" is a general invitation to pause over dusty wheels and sacks, barrels and baskets, the handles and hafts from the carpenter's tool chest. We're encouraged to examine the used surface of things, the wear that busy hands give them. In each is the "abiding presence of the human engulfing all artifacts."

Again and again, I run my hand over the deep depression worn into the top of the cobbler's bench now used as our coffee table. It refers back to a life's ownership, tells me where it withstood the most weight, the brunt of tool and boot. I raise the yellow-and-green painted lid of a funky, scavenged sewing stand, and my fingers rest in the same spot worn smooth by women I will never know, whose stories I can't construct. An island friend who splits cords of firewood with an expert precision I'll never possess uses an axe that belonged to his grandfather, a man I never met though the axe's gouged and weathered handle tells me where for three generations it was held, where it held up. Surely when Neruda exhorted fellow poets to look closely at the world of objects, to note in them "the abiding presence of the human," he meant, for example, my mother's filigreed sewing scissors with their scarred and dented blades.

After he was rescued from his island and returned to England where he drank his "real tea, surrounded by uninteresting lumber," Robinson Crusoe, in a poem by Elizabeth Bishop, speaks of his now shelved knife which once "reeked of meaning, like a crucifix. It lived." Later, he asks, "How many years did I beg it, implore it, not to break?" Crusoe knew "each nick and scratch by heart, the bluish blade, the broken tip...." Now, at a remove from its purpose and place, the knife's "living soul has dribbled away." Crusoe will give it to the museum that wants it, yet wonders, "How can anyone want such things?"

But many of us do. We're among those likely to argue that a house and much of what it houses aren't merely inanimate. Do we need again to dissect the role of Laura's glass menagerie in Tennessee Williams' play? Or recall once more the "Time Passes" section in Woolf's *To the Lighthouse*, when, following a spate of sudden family deaths, the abandoned Ramsay house and its objects become containers of spirit?

Yes, some accumulations are pure rubbish, the result in part of greed, neglect, and waste. Others are the intended collections of objects which may suggest, say folks who study such things, our attempts to protect against loss, as though there is, in fact, a charmed safety in numbers. But objects in their unique singularity also memorialize our past, reveal fragile and lost bits of our selves. They speak to our fear of forgetting, our desire to remember. There's no denying the stillness in a room to which the person once living there will never return. Or in objects that, after, honor or commemorate the dead—unearthed like relics from an Etruscan tomb. Or are simply lifted from a closet shelf in a house on an island in Maine.

Yesterday, for the first time in months, I held in my hands my brother's black zip-neck shirt, the one he wore the last time I saw him during my Arizona visit shortly before his sudden death, and which he wears in the framed photograph on my desk I see daily. Lifting the shirt from the shelf, in the brutal brightness of a late summer afternoon seeming to thrum with more sunlight than it could possibly contain, I felt a deep ache, a nearly overwhelming tenderness. This time, though, and I'm not sure what this says, I didn't cry. My brother is gone but his shirt is in this house, animating it with his presence. I am living with his shirt, *learning* to live with all it represents. The necessity of it—like a compass in the new terrain of this journey with sorrow, in my new acquaintanceship with grief. Neatly folded, long sleeves tucked securely inside, that shirt held me in a way that at that moment no human could, spoke to me when words could not. My brother's unheroic shirt.

*O*riginally, I came to this house dedicated to the belief that this would be a time to cull, pare back, streamline. Even as we emptied a part of our Illinois basement into the rented truck we drove east, and for months before that when myriad house-improvement schemes flooded my mind, I maintained, if not a truly Thoreauvian commitment to "simplify, simplify, simplify," at least the good intention that each object transported here was or would be transformed into the necessary. I was certain that here, with a Robinson Crusoe–type independence, I'd have less stuff. I'd enjoy a freedom almost guaranteed by a smaller house with fewer closets and a damp cellar rather than a basement, a house of seasonal use, of warm months inviting outdoor living, encouraging play. Even as I unloaded the rented truck, dreams of Henry Beston in his rustic Outer Beach dune shack played in my head. As if each packed box I carried in was somehow linked to a deeper involvement with the natural world. As if each equated to longer hours of contemplation on an empty beach. Here, I reminded myself in multiple trips between truck and house, I'd be somehow different, unencumbered. Each June, I'd return to a freer, cleansed version of myself, as though I were making a yearly pilgrimage to one of those rigorous health spas that demand fasting and a detoxifying purge.

In the years since, so much has found its way here—the meaningful and necessary, but so, too, the redundant, the not needed, what elsewhere didn't fit, what I couldn't bear to part with. The attractive and quirky. The valuable or what one day might be. With much of it, there are relationships I'm not ready to sever yet. Like tattered journals and notebooks, Bob's old 78s, and, memorialized in some early family photographs, his pilled yellow sweater I'm convinced one of the grandsons will one day want.

I've never lived in a house with a real attic, and yet for many years an attic has been vividly fixed in my head. There it resides with its exposed bones-of-the-house rafters and prickly sheets of insulation. An old lamp sits atop a chest shoved beneath steeply canted eaves among boxes, garment bags, trunks. Through a small unwashed window, sunlight, even on the brightest afternoons, only dimly peeks. It's a dusty and cobwebbed place, the air hot and stifling, an oppression that in summer an attic fan does little to disperse. All of this is so clear to me, it's as if mounting narrow, steep stairs into a dimly lit attic, loose floorboards protesting beneath my feet, has been physically inscribed deep within. Or should have been.

With such long-held attic envy and an increasing year-by-year accumulation of possessions, I now look around and wonder, Did anything change here? Did I truly—naively?—think I'd claim some distant linkage to Thoreau or Beston? Or that, with empty closets and less furniture, I'd achieve some nostalgic reach back to the past when life was—wasn't it?—simpler?

Maybe it's easier to live a rustic life from afar. The way that on vacation we think we'll get away from it all, only to find that our busy minds packed their bags and came along, too. Was my original simplifying intention a real desire, a sincere wish or need, or some perceived obligatory justification? That here, blessed with much, I'd do with less. That here I'd have my finest thoughts, write my best. Unburdened, greater would be my deeds, my acts of kindness. Happier, I'd be more generous with family and friends. But if, as I've claimed, it's in this place where I feel most at home, then it's natural, isn't it, that I'd transfer here not just things, but my propensity to collect and honor, to retain not just objects but my way of looking at them? Using them with willful intention to help make beautiful what around me has shaped and shapes me still?

Often I return to my yearning to be unweighted by possessions, unencumbered by the time and concern a house such as I've made demands. And yet, no compelling desire has risen up, grabbed me by the hand, demanded that I cull and parse. Years after making my pledge to do with less, I've discovered there are interests and connections I'm not willing to shed, not even, it seems, in a summer house on an island. Here, I continue to love beautiful objects, what the simplest of them can mean. I embrace the double bind of bounty and burden. Unwilling to renounce the possibility of unearthing some valuable piece of the past from my house's stratified layers, I choose to live in a space increasingly weighted with trigger points for memories and recollected histories.

Perhaps such conflicting urges to be both bound and free are kin to the impulses Michael Pollan describes in *A Place of My Own*. Our centripetal wish, he writes, pulls us into enclosure, toward protection in what in my case is my object-weighted house. A centrifugal impulse pushes us outward, like fledglings nudged from their nest. It urges us to fling wide our windows and doors and go forth into the surrounding landscape. Such twin urges aren't necessarily in conflict, Pollan claims. In fact, they're reflected in certain particularly American architecture styles going all the way back to Thoreau and *Walden*, to his enclosure "so slightly clad," Thoreau boasted, he "did not need to go outdoors to take the air."

And what are such bound-and-free urges but a sign of the world itself? In all its complexity, the world draws us up and out of ourselves, demands our attention and wonder and then delivers us, enriched, back to ourselves. It sends us indoors, deep within, and later leads us out again. Casting attention outward as well as inward is the work of a person deeply engaged, a question—isn't it?—either in house or world, of fully inhabiting. Indeed, a house amply stocked but not deeply occupied can cease being a safe and protective place. In *To the Lighthouse* (that word *to*, centrifugal or centripetal, or both?), Woolf shows us how the unoccupied Ramsay home, in spite of all the emblematic objects it houses, threatens to expire, collapse. An image for me as lonely and parched as an empty, swept-clean attic.

Sometimes, with a painting, a still life, say, you have to step back and away to fully see it. So, too, this house. From a distance of 1,300 miles, all through a long Midwestern winter, I've come to see that in the way a Cape looks most at ease rubbing shoulders on a village street, this house responds to its physical location atop a small bluff, above a tidal shoreline that shifts daily between land and water. Such location demands of my house an openness. It also requires, with such an exposure to whatever sea and sky hurl at it, a hefty helping of ballast. For all my early dreams of the house we'd one day own here presenting itself as a center-entry Cape with sloped ceilings and narrow-paned windows, and with, yes, an attic, it's this attic-less house with its expansive view, securely bound by cellar to granite ledge, a house weighted by possessions, beloved objects and relics of the past, that eloquently expresses my twin urges to go forth and retreat. In comfortable, personalized niches I created here, I drift inward. Or, as easily, I fling wide the sliding glass doors and numerous windows to the world beyond.

I'm well aware of the choices I could still make about how and where to live. But each year I'm more certain that even if this house's design was not originally of my choosing, this life in it in this place is. And actually, maybe from the very first, this house asserted itself, in the way Ben as an eight-week old puppy barreled his way over his littermates to leap at Bob's bootlaces, choosing us. This house, like the island, grabbed me by the collar and demanded, "Look." It's also helped me understand how a loved and deeply occupied house doesn't impede a journey of discovery. A way of living that is not simplified can nevertheless be clear.

*A*fter a dinner out with friends, I park my car at the top of the slope near the garage. It's a still night, and because of dense cloud cover, very dark. No moon or stars over the water. No filtering porch light—I forgot to leave it on. But the lamp in the living room is lit. Into the damp night with a threat of fog by sunrise, it gives off a soft, amber glow. I crunch my way down the gravel drive, a route I know by feel, inscribed within by the many times I've walked from my car, pushed the wheelbarrow from the garage, carried in loads of wood.

How inviting my house looks with its single amber light—a lamp in the window the house's eye, Bachelard claimed. The eye of a vigilant house. That circle of light pulling me in and toward it, propelling me even further, into the primitive wall-painted huts of my ancient ancestors gathered around the fire.

One summer, a microburst barreled through here, and with minimal damage, my house stood steadfast against the storm's destructive threats. Triumphant, it answered the question: "Will you survive?" In a thunderstorm three nights ago, it kept me dry. Winds blow and rain hurls its full weight and my house struggles not to betray me. But a house is a fragile thing. Tonight, I approach the threshold across which I will soon lie in safety, even as I know my house, like anyone's, can't always turn away grief, illness or disease, can no more guarantee not to collapse beneath death or a poverty of spirit than a tornado or hurricane can promise to respect a locked door.

In just a couple of months, before autumn trees are tattered and leaves splatter this gravel drive and choke the gutters, it'll be time again to empty the refrigerator, store linens, cover the furniture, pack the car, and drive off. Nights in long succession will descend upon my house. As will wind, storms, a winter gale. As will the sun that more than the wind or an occasional storm knows its way around. Many are the times I've watched it confidently move over the dining room table or light the mantel and hearth, embrace a dresser's square-edged bulk, finger with feather-light touch ceramic pots on the sill. Surely in the months to come, it will nose around corners and illuminate the empty wastebaskets, flowerless vases, unopened books snug on their shelves. During moments I know nothing about, the sun will lavish light on a particular object as though it has been specially chosen and, with burnishing gleam, is cherished.

And perhaps for a time, in ways similar to those suggested by de Botton, my house enjoys its emptiness. In privacy, it freely creaks or moans, expanding its joints after a long cold night. Blanket to chin, it snoozes after a summer of houseguests and banging screen doors, of dents, abrasions, scuffs, and scrapes. For a few months, it's freed from wasps busily probing the eaves. It doesn't have to endure the crows' noisy early morning assembly on the roof as they await their daily ration of peanuts. It's not called on to witness a woman crying over her dead brother's black zip-neck shirt. It's not required to make room for one more child's haphazard collection of shattered mussel shells or the surprise of forty people showing up for a rained-out picnic on an otherwise quiet Sunday afternoon.

My house, my refuge, the guardian of my many selves—with or without me, it exists. But maybe it only fully constructs with the crunch of my footsteps in early summer, when I insert the key, push open the door, and my eyes, refreshed after a long winter away, look. Only then does my house open, room to room, each object flinging itself into form. Because I look. Because I carry in more boxes, fill again the cabinet shelves, open windows that in autumn I lock, and, as night comes, switch on the lamp that now is lit. In a house that waits.

OLD DOG

"We live in the same country,
the same household, and our burning
comes from the same lamp."

Mary Oliver

At nearly fifteen, Ben's obviously not the dog he used to be. Just last year he willingly walked to the road. And the year before that, in the heartbreaking compression of dog-time, he keenly explored the roadside's wooded paths. There, years past his puppyhood and exuberant adolescence, he gifted me with glimpses of desire and nose-to-the ground focus, the power and athleticism of his running that seemed to extend beyond purpose, beyond the drive of what in the blood makes a pointer most fully himself. I've known few dogs that could run as fast for as long, or with as much eloquence.

Now, seriously arthritic in hips and spine, Ben at his quickest briefly gallops, an odd gait assisted by a kind of back-leg bunny hop. He can't do stairs, haul himself onto the sofa, make it through the night without assists from me getting him out the door and back to his bed, two or even three round-trips before dawn. On winter's ice or the kitchen's tiled floor, his nails scrabble for purchase. Some evidence of his massive chest remains, but the once powerful haunches are now thin, meager things, and his hip joints, when I massage him there, feel like bone on bone.

No longer is he the freely wandering, purposeful inspector of our property or the adjoining woods we share on either side with neighbors. His range has shrunk to the garden, the lawn and clearing, the peripheries where each borders woods. He still expects his accompanied daily walks, however circumscribed they've become to a single lap of our

71

gravel drive out to the lane, the part that extends around a small copse of trees and, in presumable safety, directs us back to the house. Sometimes, though, even on so short a journey, he seems uncertain, a bit anxious. With short, tentative steps he walks ahead of me, stops, looks back, as though to seek confirmation that this is far enough. And when I agree and turn for home, his whole body registers relief in a brief burst of speed, each step carrying him away from the uncertainty of road, the possibility that this walk might've been his last.

And so tonight, in waning light with rain coming on, it's a surprise when Ben doesn't take our lane's fork homeward but turns instead toward the neighbor's. Like Bob, they're away on a trip and I've yet to see their garden. I let Ben lead.

Leaning over the back gate, I find much to admire in Jane's tended, luxurious beds but am also selfishly gratified to see that her lavender, like mine, barely survived an especially hard winter's wallop. Meanwhile, Ben creakily totters across the lawn toward the other side of the house, reading the world with his nose, whatever gets communicated in the pages of damp dirt and tall wet grass. When I turn, ready to go, he's nowhere in sight.

By breed—a Vizsla—Ben's naturally alert, predisposed to being tuned in to whatever goes on around him, a capacity that for most of his life he engaged in overdrive. Likely that enabled him to slip past us for who knows how long the fact that he'd become deaf. Now, as I walk around to the shore side of our neighbor's house, I check to see if the gate to the front enclosure that routinely corrals their schnauzer Mary might be open. Finding it secure, I scan the woods that separate our houses. It's becoming painfully clear that this time Ben has somehow physically slipped past me.

Walking back to our house, I'm certain I'll see his telltale russet color and unmistakable long-legged but now somewhat humped silhouette nose-sniffing along the gravel drive or waiting patiently at the back door. But I don't. Nor can I hear the rattle of his metal collar tags. The wind is kicking up. The rain's begun. Stupidly, I call out his name. Panic is beginning to set in. A deaf dog in his dotage in the dark is not a picture I want to paint.

And suppose he's injured? That somehow in such a short period of time, he's gotten into another fix? That's he's not exhausted his supply of what I'd come to assume were merely youthful scrapes? Like his falling through a pond's ice or nearly plummeting off a headland on Wass Island. Or slicing open a paw pad to the bone when chasing after deer or puncturing an artery in his leg miles from home. All the trouble to which a keen nose can lead.

I take a deep breath and let past experience suggest a narrative. The obvious begins to take shape. Something at the edge of my neighbor's yard where it abuts a small bluff must've proved irresistible and lured him to squeeze around the schnauzer's wire fence. There, he'd have to descend the bluff a bit, most likely in the spot where a mix of small trees, rugosas, large rocks and tall grasses makes the descent not as steep. But once on the way down and without strength in hips or withered haunches to muscle him back up, he'd have no choice but to continue, even tumble, all the way to the shore.

Quickly I take our beach stairs down. The tide, I discover, is nearly up, the shoreline already a narrow strip. My heart sinks. He's not there. But my neighbor's house sits on a small point and the shoreline wrapping around the other side isn't visible from here. I wade into the cold flooding tide, scramble over a few old fallen trees and several large wet boulders. The rain's really hammering now. And I've forgotten that this part of shoreline I seldom walk suddenly shifts to a stretch of jagged, narrow slabs of shale with sharp-edged crevices tough to maneuver. In shoes not made for such terrain, I grope my way around the point.

And there, on a shale-sharded strip, the tide lapping close, I find Ben. He's down on his side. Blood splatters his front leg. He looks exhausted but his head is up, his grizzled old face turned toward me as though he never doubted I'd be coming and from this precise direction. But he doesn't struggle to his feet. Nor do ears lift or tail thump in customary greeting. His whole body registers defeat, a resignation to whatever might come next.

And what comes next seems, in the moment anyway, not to surprise me in the least. Somehow in the rain, I manage to straddle two large shale slabs. Precariously balanced, I stoop and lift my seventy-pound dog. I heave him up against my chest, then clumsily clamber over jagged shards toward my neighbor's stairs. Already huffing, my heart banging, one ankle rock-scraped where I almost went down, I pause, briefly assess. There are forty-two steps to the top of the bluff. And I'm holding Ben in a dead-weight long-legged sprawl. He's all I can manage. I won't be able to free either hand and grab hold of a railing to steady myself. I have to hope he'll hang limp in my arms and not begin to thrash. Otherwise, we won't make it.

Finally, up top, staggering and soaked with rain and sweat, my legs trembling with fatigue, I set Ben down. His back end immediately collapses and he nearly topples over. But I catch and hold him until he's hauled himself upright. Wobbling, he lurches forward, takes a step, then another. His cut, I'm relieved to see, probably won't need stitches, and nothing seems broken. His wounds, the physical ones anyway, aren't serious. In the rain, we shamble home.

*T*he first messenger arrives in late May.

Near dusk, while reading the newspaper in a favorite chair near the living room's glass sliders, with Ben curled sleep-deep in his fleecy dog bed nearby, I hear an unfamiliar pattering of feet against wood. Of something larger than one of the red squirrels who busily traffic our deck's length as though it were a transporting interstate. I turn my head and look out. A tawny fox kit, its nose nearly pressed against glass, is looking in.

As though equally surprised in its discovery as I am in mine, the kit slowly backs away until, suddenly, in an abrupt turn, it trots down the stairs and onto the lawn. Expecting the kit to flee, I begin to stand so I can watch it dash for the nearby woods. Instead, in obvious familiarity with the route, the kit deftly hurtles back up the steps and trots back to the same spot. Now, in our close mutual inspection, it cocks its head to one side. Black-tipped ears prick forward, back. White patches mark either side of its narrow muzzle, as though they've been recently dipped in a bowl of milk.

In no obvious hurry to scuttle off, a thought bubble over the kit's head might read, "Who are you? And just what are *you* doing here?" More than just curious, this little visitor seems to be declaring proprietary claims established prior to my seasonal arrival, a sort of defiant "I was here first" assertion in spite of its physical, not-much-larger-than-a-cat and cute-as-all-get-out demeanor.

For several days after, I do not see the kit again. My presence alone has no doubt convinced it the deck is now off limits. But, as I've discovered more recently, little else on our property is. The message, increasingly clear: a family of foxes resides someplace nearby. Also equally certain: an old dog no longer poses a threat serious enough to keep them away, doesn't demand they recognize perimeters or respect borders, as protracted as they might've become.

I know the sighting of foxes is not all that unusual. In some places, they're often spotted on suburban streets, even urban alleys. Here, from time to time, I've seen them trotting down our road, streaking across a clearing, darting into the woods. Some folks I've told about the resident fox family show little interest, are even blasé. One friend immediately warned, "Don't go near them." Another, about the kit, "Don't touch it." As though I might get that close.

By my count, there are four kits, and their world, it's clear, is expanding. Each time I see them, they appear more curious, confident. Routinely now they venture out on their own. Mom, obviously enjoying the break, often saunters solo on her daily patrol of bluff's edge. She's filled out some since the morning just a couple of weeks ago when she sprawled in the sun near our garage with her bumbling kits, a post they only reluctantly abandoned after a few sentinel crows summoned the whole raucous crew and blasted mayhem into the trees, not settling again until the foxes took off into the woods as if scattered by gunshot. I've learned since that I can as effectively scatter foxes if I no more than nudge open the door. Stepping outside or down from the deck, I quickly transform into what terrifies, threatens.

The kits, redder now, their black stockings and white-tipped tails more pronounced, are a lively bunch—a *skulk*, as the field guide instructs. This morning, from the back door, I'm watching all four of them transform our oak tree and a patch of lawn into a vulpine playground. I know they're practicing for tougher tasks ahead, but it's hard not to call this a game as they chase each other around the oak, abruptly change direction, tackle, tussle, tag, dart off, and, after fanning out into the woods adjoining the drive, poke their heads from behind trees or above tall ferns in some foxy version of hide-and-seek.

Behind me, Ben hauls himself out of his bed and minces his way toward the kitchen. As he nail-scrabbles across the tile, I push open the screen door. Once outside, he studiously presses nose to grass, circles the oak, raises his head and, nostrils flaring, snuffles the air. Though the kits disappeared at the door's opening scrape, Ben stares down the lane as if some dim memory is taking shape. Not unlike the way, when he's lying on the deck watching the squirrels tauntingly patter near, his look says, "Buddy, a few years ago, you would've been toast." Though in a squirrel's direction he may still occasionally feint, he seems no more tempted to go after it than to follow fox scent into the woods.

His business done, Ben turns toward the house, one last squirt midway. Heaving himself up a single granite step, he makes a wobbly beeline for his food dish, kibble alone still fueling desire, stoking life's engine. I stand ready with the sling I've rigged up from an old beach towel. With it I keep his back end hoisted. No point in being mere bystander as one of his last remaining pleasures is marred by creaking joints and weak, painfully quivering hind legs.

*D*ogs. They've been with us a long time. Hunters at our sides, vigilant guardians before our fires. According to Maine science writer Hannah Holmes, every canid who walks this region of North America is a descendant of some weasel-like critters that climbed trees more than 60 million years ago. After the dinos died off and left behind an indisputably big niche, these early canid ancestors climbed down from the trees looking to add something meatier to their diets. Their evolving brains and teeth obliged, and about 10 million years later, bigger-brained carnivores divided into two groups, the "cattish" and the "doggish." Later, the doggish branch of the family split further and, says Holmes, "umpteen more pre-dog species evolved toward dogness." Some research suggests that during another long episode of glacial mischief-making and reshaping of the planet's continents, what finally succeeded in the equivalent of our current North American Southwest was a fox species. From it, it's believed, our current wolves, foxes, jackals, coyotes, and wild and domesticated dogs may have descended. But whatever the long lineage or however extended the time line, it's certain, claims Holmes, that "Man and Dog walked into North America near the end of the last ice age, and things would never be the same."

Ever since, the survival of dogs has been ensured by domestication. As cave paintings depict, canines achieved a favored status early on. They demonstrated that they could be tamed, their behavior trained. Our messages to them were clear: Old hunter, stay alert, protect me from danger. Pack animal, bend to my alpha dog will. Later, when we humans stayed put and moved indoors, we needed ample proof our dogs-as-household-pets would submit to us. Eagerly and wisely, if longevity's the goal, they obliged. Soon we human tinkerers selected dogs' best traits, and with desire standing in for blind nature, ensured what got passed on to future generations. Dogs evolved into a willing powerlessness, into an outright eagerness to get along with us if defined by slobber and slather and coffee-table-clearing tail wagging. Indeed, they've come to rely on us, accepting, most of the time, the rules we impose.

And so we invite dogs into our houses. They bound across the welcome mat and swap carcass for kibble. It's assumed they leave their wildness at the door. And yet there have been many times over the years when I've discovered Ben gulping down the last bits of a baby rabbit, rolling in fresh possum roadkill, or running toward me, mouth open, its pink ridges and white teeth clumped with some wild animal's shit. At night, I've watched him stop and stare into the black woods, his fur lifting along his spine, his entire body twitching with the nerve-ending quiver of the chase, and I've known that he still lives in two worlds. Even if such episodes are brief, and for a long time now have come only by way of a leg-twitching, mouth-chuffing dream in which he runs with his ancestral pack, Ben goes back to his other life. He returns to wildness. For a time, it is the only world he knows.

On the shore, rescuing Ben, heaving him up those many stairs, I took control. I assumed the traditional role of master. Is such mastery a reason we love our dogs? Or our belief that we know them, and that they, in gratitude or through long habit or dependence, reflect back on us the emotion we're so often told dogs do not possess? When they take off after a fox in unfamiliar terrain or a deer on a pond's thin spring ice, we fear what can happen to them. But aren't we frightened, too, a little, by their pursuit of what we cannot know?

Our dogs bolt and we stand helpless in the face of an instinctive and ancestral urge pulling them away from us, our beloved pets who sleep in our beds or nap on our furniture. We trust they'll heed our call and return to hearth and kibble, to tidbits fed from the table. We rely on their relinquishing the chase or carcass, to their giving themselves over to a hose's cold spray and a brisk scrubbing down with soapy brush. They've been bred to obey, trained to return. And for this we're rewarded. Not only by our desired and, at times, necessary bond, but by our mastery, our control, as deluded as we may be.

I've been to the meadow to pick the last of the nearly spent lupines, and now, walking the lane home, one of the fox kits plunges from the woods and streaks across the lane just a few feet in front of me. It's carrying something limp, presumably dead, and nearly a third the young fox's size.

From my desk just a few days ago, I watched a kit in the clearing practice its developing hunter skills. With characteristic foxy style, it leapt with all fours off the ground and pounced on a hapless vole. After several such acrobatic maneuvers, the kit picked up the vole by the tail, whirled it overhead, flung it to the ground, then decisively and repeatedly pounce-leaped again, as though the purpose wasn't so much to rustle up some lunch as to entertain—an unlikely defiant embodiment of my mother's long-ago reprimand: "Don't play with your food." As spectator I had no choice but to pity vole, applaud vulpine.

Now, on the lane, just weeks past the plush-toy-look-alike stage, this kit offers me a fresher glimpse of the stealthy, crafty creature it's becoming. In the wild where rules are neither nice nor neat, the kit's an animal with sharp teeth cunningly employed. Soon, the young rabbit or squirrel that just as freely traveled these woods a short while ago will be transformed into bits of fur and bone. Mama will be proud.

Though still resembling at times a passel of tussling puppies, the kits are developing skill sets. At the apex of their survival is food, but it's not presented in a bowl or by mother's hand. Nor is it available in easy trips to refrigerator or restaurant. To survive, a fox can possess neither pity nor mercy. It's a lesson early learned.

For several minutes, I scan the woods, but to my eyes the kit has vanished. Keen pupil in learning what to hunt, in what or whom to avoid, it already knows its way in these woods. Like the quiet rabbit or clean-stepping deer, the kit is already more intimate with this land's physicality than folks long ago born here. It possesses an unconscious competence we humans will never know—the innate ability to go smoothly, silently into the woods and, without a rustle, disappear, something most of us upright blunderers can only, even at our best, merely imitate.

On what interior parts, I wonder, is such knowing mapped? Is it so very different from Ben's? Though surely, the hands-down winner for the most intimate in-the-body knowing of the land's topography, its actual physical contours, has to be the snake, no? Imagine how we humans would know the land differently if we had to get down on our bellies to travel over rock or through duff. Or, on hands and knees, lower face to food rather than, with the miracles of hands and thumbs, lift bowl or fork to mouth.

Suddenly, further up the lane, my neighbor's schnauzer, Mary, erupts into frenzied barking. She's obviously spotted the kit as it hauls homeward its prize, and for such accomplishment collects at den's threshold the fox equivalent of a high five.

As for Mary's owners, they've recently returned from their trip and confirmed the presence of a den located somewhere just over the bluff's edge at one side of their front yard, the obvious source of intrigue that drew Ben nose-first into mishap on a rainy night. According to Jane, before I arrived on the island for the season, the vixen had already begun to parade out her offspring—tawny balls of big-eared, pointy-muzzled fluff. Sprawled on the lawn, they nursed just steps from the porch while Jane took photographs through the window and tried to contain Mary in the house. After being away for a few weeks, Jane's surprised at the change.

"They've gotten so brazen," she exclaims. Now, in addition to the part of the yard just beyond the fence where the kits still stake claim, they also dart under her porch and garden shed. "And, you know, they taunt Mary." The kits, Jane makes clear, are no longer cute.

*T*oday, I'm tackling my sprawling garden. I need to shear the cranesbill to encourage a second bloom, snip old rugosa blooms before they set into fat orange hips, tie up the shrub roses so they don't shade the asters yet to approach their peak.

Gardening demands knowledge and faith. It requires decisiveness, a frequent unflinching brutality. To shear, deadhead, prune. To cut back, cut down, cut out. Deriving from an old German word meaning enclosure, the garden is a place that is at once with nature and, as Michael Pollan notes, "unapologetically set against it." Indeed, with its expanding perennial beds claiming more of what was once lawn, and on one side of the house pushing up against woods' edge, my garden increasingly bears the shape of what my hands dig into it, and, sometimes mercilessly, yank out. It also reflects my desire and imagination. And my willful insistence.

Gardens have always revealed human nature's wish to possess and control, in spite of the season-after-season evidence that this is an ability we'll never achieve, old news even if delivered in some new packaging of thrip or gold canker, or delivered, perhaps, by Asiatic long-horn beetles and other messengers new to the terrain.

Not that all uninvited visitors are unwelcome in my garden. Last week, Lew, another neighbor, told me, "Keep those foxes in your yard. I've got bunnies in mine." But rabbits are welcome here, too, now that I get my lettuce from Yellow Birch Farm and what we've come to let pass as lawn is really a crazy quilt patched with rye, sorrel, dandelion, hawkweed, wild yarrow and, a bunny's favorite, red clover. I'm even willing to share my land with a family of deer, including two newborn spindle-legged fawns. But can't they please merely cruise by my lilies and phlox?

In fact, as much as to shear and prune, I've come to the garden to investigate where, early this morning, one of the fox kits high-stepped into the monkshood, nosed behind the veronica, muzzled past the hydrangea, and ducked under the deck. From my vantage point inside, I could only estimate where the kit went in and where a few minutes later it scuttled out, head held high, nose pointing skyward, and balanced between its picket teeth something still quite alive—a spotted salamander it looked like.

Now, leaning in, it's hard to find any traces. Had I not seen the kit, I might never have known it was here. Just the faintest depression of dirt around the coreopsis, a bent coneflower stem, a bit of the bee balm pushed aside. Nothing chewed, sheared or mown down. Hungry deer or Ben lumbering in wouldn't have been so kind. Nor am I as I squat to peer beneath the deck and try not to squash the coral bells.

My garden hosts an abundance of plant species. Most aren't native. The ancestry of its showiest specimens are foreign-born, brought to our shores intentionally. Others, to get here, freeloaded, often in their seed stage infancy, and, like the Asiatic long-horned beetle, stowed away amidst ballast and packing crates. Arriving on our melting pot shores, some fussy outsiders took years to adapt, were slow to spread. Not so, though, with great numbers of invasives, the hardy types that possess few manners, that don't so much search out a niche as barge in and seize, happily grabbing a territory and claiming it as their own. And they're not shy about it. Of Asiatic bittersweet, Holmes says, "Give it a millimeter and it'll take a mile." Sadly, unchecked, it does. In the woods and far from any battles with virus or fungi, it'll twine, choke, throttle, tree after tree.

And we humans? How do we fit in? Observes science writer David Quammen, we're "a weedy species." Easily we multiply, sprawl, adapt to myriad conditions. But as the pluckor, not the pluckee, we're definitely more potent than weeds. And we're not confined to the garden.

We hominids are everywhere, a special case, claims Holmes, of the Superinvasive Species. Indeed, with few limits, with multiple means of travel at our disposal, we require few assists. We need merely pack our dogs and go. From place to place, we're also likely to haul along with us the bullying stranglehold of purple loosestrife, bittersweet, and honeysuckle. After all, it's our ancestors who, even if with admirable intentions, boarded boats with starlings and English sparrows—obviously the idea of having on our shores every bird mentioned in Shakespeare's plays must've seemed at the time like a good one.

Native or outsider? This is a question often vigorously debated here, a popular pastime sport among the island's human residents, specifically between the island-born and the people "from away." But it's a broader question Holmes takes on by delving further back into our ancestral heritage. Despite some of our aggressive, elbowing-aside characteristics, she champions *Homo sapiens* as belonging in the native category. In one hominid installment or another, we've been part of North America's ecosystems for maybe as long as 30,000 years. (Such numbers certainly trump our fourth-generation islanders who claim unequivocal native status.) But as heated exchanges here testify, wrangling with who and what is native or is not is generally a dicey issue.

Certainly disparate views between islanders aren't easily resolved. Nor, in my garden, are the choices of what stays or goes, what is pulled and yanked, always clear or necessary. For too long I was blinded to purple loosestrife's smothering sprawl, seduced by its craftily evolved flamboyance and ease. So stunning is its show that to a novice's eye loose-strife can resemble lupines, another, albeit more conservatively mannered, non-native that many Mainers accept as the state flower.

Native, outsider, invader, intruder. Such labels appear not to apply to dogs. More keenly observed are the names of breeds registered by the American Kennel Club and the strict adherence to standards and specific traits demanded of each breed, most of which, as with flowers, favor beauty over utility. Dogs share significant DNA with wolves, indisputable evidence that from them dogs descend. But dogs, we humans have made clear, unlike their distant forefathers, belong here. So universal is our acceptance of our hearthside pals, so solid our interspecies bonds, it's estimated that 400 million dogs inhabit the planet, 75 million of which live in this country alone—leaving a lot less room for its 400,000 or so wolves. Clearly, our human tinkering's been successful. Dogs, it seems, and under any circumstances, are here to stay.

"We've got to get rid of them." Jane says, transitioning our phone conversation from an upcoming potluck dinner to resident fox.

At first I think the kits' novelty has merely worn off. Certainly at this point they're not the diminutive babies with Disney-esque facial features intended to protect them—usually a sure-fire ploy unless, for example, you're a baby harp seal whose round face and black, baleful eyes do little to blunt the pelt collector's cudgel. Puppies clearly have a better chance. As do adult dogs with bred-in infantile characteristics, like the immensely popular pugs, bulldogs, and Boston terriers. Through human intervention and controlled trait selection, they've been increasingly bred to accentuate their round heads and big eyes that now protrude from sockets as though ready to explode from their skulls. And never mind that most of those big-headed and nearly bug-eyed puppies eliciting their dedicated owners' and breeders' "oohs" and "ahs" can only be delivered through Caesarean section. Cuteness obviously has its price.

Our resident fox kits, adolescents now and in deepening colors ranging from scarlet-orange to russet-red, are bigger, taller. It's easier to see how their brush tails will eventually equal their body's length and add to the illusion that they're much larger than they are.

"We've got to do something," Jane repeats. The collective *we* raises some questions. Nor am I sure what's behind *something*.

"What do you mean?" I ask, guarded but certain she's not talking about poison-laced baiting. Jane is, after all, a gentle and sweet woman who voiced not a single expletive when deer jumped the fence into her garden and in a feeding frenzy sheared away all her prized phlox. And surely she's not referring to guns. Numerous times, we've talked about whether or not to post our properties as we close up in October and drive off just as hunting season is about to roll around, when we and our dogs, were we to remain, would need to don blaze orange merely to walk our road. I'm much less afraid of a fox than a loaded gun. I have to believe she is, too.

Jane asks, "Aren't there people around here who trap wild animals? Maybe they can move them someplace else."

"All of them?" It's hard to imagine how such an enterprise would work. One curious kit maybe, but wily as they are, how would you get the others to fall for the same trick? And where would they be taken?

"I'm not sure," I say, "if that would work."

But Jane seems convinced it's worth a try. She relates the latest evidence working against the fox's favor—the uh-oh grisly remains of a new fawn's leg. Having been dragged near her garden shed, it's become for the kits both a source of food and entertainment. I'm about to suggest that maybe fox is getting a bum rap for the handiwork of cousin coyote.

Though I've not seen any, other islanders have recently spotted coyote near Pressey Village Road, the cause, perhaps, behind the loud gunshots that recently interrupted dinner at a friend's home near there. Gunfire, several pops, a hair-raising sound erupting in the dark that brought up stories among us non-hunter types about the illegal but widely known practice of jacking. And the prevalent belief that nothing that happens on private property is off limits. As once observed by essayist and birder Jonathan Rosen, "There's no such thing as an endangered species on private property."

Let's be clear. Hunters aren't generally irresponsible. I know many and I respect them. And I can appreciate the sad necessity of culling. Still, when relating stories about our resident fox family, I've seen some of the knee-jerk reactions of folks who, if they were in on this conversation about Jane's quest for a trap, would translate Have-A-Heart to Get-Your-Gun.

And then the real reason is out. Jane says, "I'm worried about Mary."

To rescue Ben from his fix on the shore was the responsible—and only—thing to do. Just as when a young Ben chased deer off our property and went missing for two days, it was necessary that I stuff mailboxes with flyers and tack up lost dog signs, and, long before that, collar him with the ID tags crucial in his eventual retrieval. We invite dogs into our homes, attempt to train whatever bits of wildness still courses in their blood, and we must be responsible.

But what is responsible or appropriate when it comes to the vixen and her kits? Trap and transport them to some distant habitat as my neighbor now suggests? But what cog of the intricate machinery of our coexistence does this remove? To how much, with our will and intellect, with our orderly notions and by whatever means possible, our hands with their opposable thumbs guiding the till, are we entitled? What exactly must I give up—if anything—to catch a glimpse of a fox? What exactly do I lose—if anything—when, just steps from my door, the fox deposits a disemboweled vole or a gull's tattered wing? Maybe Mary is confined to a fenced yard and Ben no longer sprints after squirrels, rabbits or deer, but other pets do. Any number of my friends here have cats who daily bolt from the house and run free, who routinely carry home a trophy not unlike the ones left by the fox kits. But they are seldom chastened, nor are they refused entry for such doorstep-deposited gifts, as though this were a kind of reciprocity for filling a plastic bowl with another heaping helping of Tidy Bits.

But I do understand responsibility. I understand how crucial our dogs can become, how in ways both heroic and uncanny they're able to haul us away from danger, literally save our lives, or seem to, in hard-to-explain ways. How they come to us in times of illness or sorrow and with paw or muzzle, or with simple shared breathing, they comfort without comment, even if some nights our sadness is for them, their decline, the emptier days ahead. I understand.

I try to explain to Jane that I don't think she has to worry about Mary. From all I've read since first seeing a fluff ball of fox kit trot onto my deck, foxes aren't known to go after dogs unless a den is directly under siege. Usually just the presence of a resident dog is enough to make the nearby neighborhood off limits. Unless, obviously, those specimens are small, inconsequential yammerers or old gimpy-legged geezers.

Clearly the vixen did not build her den for the benefit of our snapping pictures from the window or for providing us with multiple moments of entertainment. Nor did she choose her spot to aggravate or scare. She needed a safe and protected place to birth her kits A wide-mouthed hole among a thick tangle of exposed tree and rugosa roots in the side of a bluff, out of sight but within striking distance of shore and woods, must've seemed to her ideal. That it's also steps from someone's porch is purely incidental and was without consequence until late May's migration brought to the neighborhood its upright, two-legged seasonal residents.

Surely foxes don't need us. Do we need them?

"I don't know," Jane says, after my attempts to reassure her about

Mary and in response to my asking her what she thinks she might do.

"*B*oy, Grandma, you must be strong."

In the eyes of Jimmy, my seven-year-old sports-loving grandson, I seem to have been elevated to the level of hero worship typically reserved for major league baseball players and NBA stars. On the telephone, he's still asking for more details about Ben's rescue, how I carried him up those forty-two stairs.

Jimmy knows the distance well. Last summer, during a visit here, we spent many hours on the shore. Each trip back up top, he usually toted a bucket of "treasure," specimens of shell and claw, bits of driftwood and bone. Wading tidal pools, he soon excelled at capturing hermit crabs and spotting sea stars among the rocks. From the deck, he also learned what to look for when trying to spot the occasional passing porpoise or seal.

"Have you seen any porpoises?" he asks.

In fact, I had, earlier that morning, not far beyond where the tide ebbs its lowest. Conditions were perfect—few clouds, no wind, the water still. Cruising the coastline, the harbor porpoise submerged and then, a short distance away, the water ruffling, rose with a wet *"Phff,"* dorsal fin and sleek back arching out of the water.

"I heard it, too," I tell him.

"Really?" he almost whispers, as though privy to a secret. Or to one of earth's wonders—as surely seemed the case last summer in a young child's first-time witness of a porpoise swimming free, not confined to a theme park's saltwater tank and trained to jump through hoops for a few tossed fish.

Only seven, but how far he's already traveled since the afternoon we celebrated his first birthday when, in his high chair, he not so much ate a chunk of cake as explored it with uninhibited gusto. Grabbing it by the fistful, he squeezed white, yellow and blue frosting through his fingers. He smeared pulverized cake onto chin and cheek. As though applying face paint in a tribal initiation, he plastered gooey palm against forehead, spiked blond hair blue. He drew mysterious hieroglyphics and abstract shapes onto his high chair's tray. A one-year-old, he'd recently begun to teeter into upright locomotion but had yet to arrive at the threshold of language. He still knew the world best through his body, primarily his hands with their wondrous, make-so-much-possible thumbs. *Cake* not a word but an in-the-body sensual feast.

As I talk with Jimmy, Ben sleeps at my side. I stroke the space between his ears, the little dip between bone, the ridged rise at the top of his skull—the "knowledge bump" we've always called it—and the little familiar toggle of skin that seems to hook right ear to head.

For a time, prior to the thrill of a child attempting his first tottering steps, our offspring, down on all fours, views the world from a perspective not unlike a puppy's. And not unlike, I have to assume, a fox kit's. Without language, a child still emitting gibberish may even sound like a mewling puppy or chattering kit. For a time this is the closest our species gets to being of the animal world. Maybe that's why our young offspring seem so fearless and ready to press face and body to any puppy or kitten they encounter. And when they do, the warnings some of us worried adults shout convey meaning not through words but in decibel and tone, and all less effective for a time than our hands that yank or arms that scoop up.

Beside me, Ben groans, twitches. He's breathing hard. Growling from someplace deep, he emits a few muffled yelps.

"What's that?" Jimmy asks.

"Dreams. Old dreams," I say, patting Ben's flanks hillocked with fatty old-age bumps and small knobby cysts until his eyes open.

To Ben, who cannot hear me, I have become a being of purely physical gesture and movement, like a raised index finger or open palm, each of which, thanks to some early training, still has meaning and, when consistently delivered, elicits a predictable sit-or-stay response. It is now the way my dog and I "talk." Even if Ben could hear me, my words, no matter their sequence or inflection, tone or cadence, would mean little. Not in the sense of true comprehension. Oh, a few words or phrases may be recognizable—I once read that some dogs possess the cognitive abilities of a two-year-old. But isn't it mostly a matter of repetition, of signal and gesture? An exchange that translates to "I say this, you do that." I've lived with this beloved dog for fifteen years, but no matter my urge to verbally communicate to him meaning, if only a thank you, I cannot.

The fox, however, wordlessly communicates with Ben. Nearly daily now there are more deposits of scat and fur and tattered wing near the door or along the gravel drive, just steps from the garden. Ben lingers long in these places. He sniffs, snorts, squirts. To me, such calling cards are challenges. A fox family's staking its claim. Once I'd have feared the outcome, but now it's as if, neither rival nor combatant, Ben noses through the pages of an old photo album and comes upon some unknown but dimly recognized distant cousin.

"Grandma," Jimmy says, "tell me more about the foxes."

Patting Ben, I describe the fox kit that this morning crouched near the butterfly bush in wait for the next red admiral to flutter within reach, and how the kit leaped and slapped at it, fell back, leaped again, an acrobatic yet balletic dance in which the kit chased the butterfly across the lawn. A dance and a game and a sort of joyous celebration. Leap, slap, fall back, leap again.

"But did he get it?" Jimmy wants to know. Clearly, batting averages, even among foxes, count for something, too.

I've been reading some old *Down East* essays by Caskie Stinnet. In one, he claims that, given her skill sets, if his boxer Margaret were human, she'd be put in charge of Customer Service.

And Ben?

No doubt he'd have an adjoining office. Inspector General is a title that seems appropriate. Once, nothing much got past him. Few folks managed to enter our house without his physical inspection—a full frontal assault a more apt description. Even in later years, when flak-jacket protection was no longer necessary, Ben's approach was so democratic and equally inflected to whoever crossed our threshold, a friend once declared him the canine equivalent of the Walmart greeter.

Today, I've hauled one of his fleecy beds outside so that he can get some sun and fresh air in all the comfort a retiree from a long and illustrious career so richly deserves. He's fallen into the deep sleep of the old and deaf when provided abundant security and ease.

It's a beautiful afternoon. The sun has moved above the spruce and there's ample breeze. Clouds billow and scud. Far offshore, a pair of ospreys rides the thermals. Nearby, even though the oak has yet to bonk the roof with its acorns, the red squirrels are indefatigably busy. They remind me I haven't seen much of the rabbits. Are they still seeking sanctuary at Lew's? Even the carrot greens I spread out for them on the lawn went untouched. Not that I know if rabbits even like carrot tops. Maybe such a lure has a taint to it and is destined to fail.

Not far from where Ben snoozes, I'm attempting again to stake the toppling aster and cranesbill. The garden's definitely moved a further notch toward end-of-summer. Just about everything here seems to be preparing already for the final act. As I shear off the spent heads of bee balm, it's almost easy to forget their earlier flamboyance. Tinkered with to exploit their beauty, the bee balms' long-lasting blooms, especially when stuck in a vase, are sure strategies for survival. Certainly, were I a flower, I'd want to look as attractive to the gardener flipping pages in a plant catalogue in January as to bees hauling around my pollen in July.

As I lean back to survey my handiwork, a movement over my left shoulder, not far from Ben and me, catches my eye. It's the vixen. Without the merest trace of alarm or hurry, she's emerged from the woods. She looks briefly at us, then sets off on a slow trot across the lawn at bluff's edge. About to pass a small clump of hay-scented fern, she stops, sniffs the ground, and sits. She raises her left hind leg and scratches an ear. Looking around, she's both casual and attentive, like a passenger awaiting the next train. She raises her narrow muzzle, sniffs the air, looks toward the house, the woods on the other side. Abruptly she rises and bolts across the lawn, disappearing into the trees beyond the clearing.

Ben, once vigilant, misses it all. I don't know whether to be grateful or to find in this another reason for heartbreak. One thing's clear: the fox makes it harder to tell where cultivated yard and garden and all its altered and tinkered-with species ends and the world of the naturally evolved begins.

Dogs and wolves may well share ancestral heritage, but Ben and vixen are linked, too, and in ways more numerous than the shared dichromatic vision that limits how much of the green in my garden either is able to see. Not that this necessarily makes things any less perilous for fox than brethren wolf. Too often, survival means how well other species adapt to living among us, or, like gulls at the dump, how and to what extent they depend on us in ways that may be annoying or unappealing but harm us not. The verdict often rests with what we upright *Homo sapiens* wish to protect, eradicate, ignore or plunder. While loosestrife may gum up the works in a marsh and the starlings push out their neighbors who were here first, it's our species that, in unconfined invasive sprawl, bulldozes and spills, clearcuts and paves. As though our only aim is to extricate the wildness out of the wild.

This afternoon I crossed the threshold of my house and entered the outside world without roof or door or address. Ben, too, left behind sawn timber and hammered shingle to join me in the garden that is forever changing, evolving, thanks to and in spite of my tinkering. A vixen crossed the lawn. She did nothing exceptional. Still, for a few moments, she brought a little disorder to the garden, an unexpected flash of color, a russet-orange hue not so different from Ben's. Like a flame not long before it dies out.

The decision my neighbors have reached about not trapping and moving the fox seems to me an easy one. With impinged upon ranges making foxes more prevalent visitors to our tamed landscapes, they seem to be demonstrating an ability to live among us. And yet they bring to us, too, the proof that pockets of wildness exist. Small islands within islands. We may well be the "wheel that drives our world," as poet Mary Oliver claims, but it is a shared world. I dwell here not just in the company of family, friends and neighbors, but also creatures that trot and yip, dig and soar. Each of us linked by the drive to survive.

Maybe Jane became convinced Mary is safe. Or she reached the same conclusion as mine. I need both. Dog and fox.

Nearby, Ben at last stirs, opens his eyes. In the bright sun, it's hard to see the scrim that in recent months has dropped over them. I might almost believe they've retrieved their old polished luster. He lifts his head, his nose working the air. In it, too late, he's learning about the vixen's fleeting presence. Slowly, he hauls himself up, teeters, wobbles a few steps, then makes his way to the place where the vixen emerged from the woods. Highly-evolved nose to the ground, he crosses time lines, travels distances, retrieves through smell alone what I can barely imagine.

Not so many years ago, a younger Ben might not have gotten himself into such a fix at the neighbor's bluff. He'd have worked the scent of the fox with unflagging ardor. He'd have charged up and down the bluff's face, crashed in and out of the trees, parsed the grasses with his lowered nose, whatever it took, what his species had been bred to do but seemed so uniquely his. Eventually, maybe long after it had grown dark, he'd have bounded back to me, alive in all his otherness, a quivering embodiment of joy at having visited the world of his distant kin. To have run again with the pack. In spite of my vexation and fear, I'd have understood. He had returned to the wildness that is his ancestral home. And is, a bit, mine, too, this daughter of distant forebears who to survive required fur pelts on their bodies, meat over their fires.

At the woods' edge, Ben pauses, stares into the trees, to where in another time his nose would have led. His whole body trembles, with arthritic discomfort or in instinctive anticipation, I can't say. When at last he turns back in my direction, I'm struck again by how grizzled and white his face has become, how hunched his spine. Old dog, my companion of no words.

As though along a path of certainties, he slowly walks toward me. He seems in no particular hurry, but of course he's racing. He's never stopped.

WHAT THE BODY KNOWS

*M*y friend Marianne's chosen well. The shoreline we're heading for is known for its smooth granite ledges and large tumbled boulders. At low tide, crevices and niches abound. It's a great place for children, as she and her young granddaughter Elsa discovered during her summer visit last year. While Marianne and I walk and talk, occasionally pausing to glass a bobbing loon or hovering osprey, Elsa pokes about in the wrack line with a stick, occasionally pocketing a stone or broken bit of shell. A few steps behind us, she's quietly humming.

But as soon as we round the point, she flings aside her stick and cries, "There they are!" and begins running toward a mass of granite outcroppings as though, despite her life's brief time line, they were old acquaintances.

Soon, with a little hoisting assist from us, she's climbing onto a broad ledge. From there it's an easy scramble to some immense, heaped up boulders, old sentinel reminders of glacial force and heave. Dropping onto her bum, she scoots toward the largest of them, and then, flipping onto her belly and ducking her head, she begins to slither forward and down into what, until then, I'd not seen as a narrow passage. Though Elsa is slender, the opening's a snug fit. We watch as she wriggles and thrusts herself forward with her sneakered feet and more of her slender body disappears beneath the ledge's overhang.

"Be careful," Marianne warns, her grin betraying the same wish as mine. And, perhaps, the same yearning. From somewhere deep within the rocky crevice, Elsa giggles.

Picking our way over the sprawling boulders to the other side, Marianne and I arrive just as Elsa's head and narrow shoulders emerge. With open arms, palms splayed against smooth rock, she begins to pull herself forward. Looking up at us, she breaks into a huge smile.

"Oh see, Grandma," she proclaims. "The rocks remember me!"

*W*hen I was a student not much older than Elsa, I often muddled *geology* and *geography*. Eventually I learned that, although related and both deriving from *geo,* Latin for *earth,* they are, of course, different. Geologists study the materials of the earth, not just its rocks, as we armchair scientists might assume, but also its liquid matters—how all are structured and how processes, most often natural (earthquakes, volcanic eruptions, tsunamis) but also man-made (deep-sea drilling and a belching oil spill, the oil-and-water-never-mix outcome you don't need to be a scientist to understand) act upon them.

By contrast, the stuff of geography, the study of land, its features, its living inhabitants and its phenomena may seem not less important but more the handiwork of statisticians and cartographers and all made so much simpler, no?, by satellite cameras and GPS systems. But geographers define what they do as essential to understanding Earth and all its human and natural complexities—in other words, not merely where things are but how they came to be there, how they have changed, and what with future change they may become. A combination, some claim, of "science and art."

As a recent survey suggests, geography is something about which we Americans are woefully ignorant. About world geography, yes, but also about what is where within our own borders. Certainly we admire the Rockies' towering, jagged peaks, those majestic subjects of patriotic praise imprinted on our collective memory, but where are they exactly? Where are those unencroached-upon coasts and stretches of forest ubiquitously featured in calendar photos? All those seemingly unpeopled landscapes? And what about those oft-depicted towns with litter-free village greens or those sprawling cities with only clean, burnished skylines? Though memorialized to a point verging on romantic myth, some of these places actually exist. And if I want to know where, I don't have to hop a plane. Nor, thanks to the Internet, do I have to haul out a heavy atlas.

Of course, many of us do board planes and travel to places new to us. And there we may say, "I want to get the lay of the land," unfolding a map, acquainting ourselves with roads and distances. Maps have long attempted to tell us much, even of places never visited or only vividly imagined. Early map-making often had to rely on dispatches, reports, even the mind's creative imaginings. Recently, I read that Renaissance cartographers drew maps of Hell based on distances and proportions described in Dante's *Inferno*. Informed by this work of fiction and using elements of geometry, Galileo lectured on the mapping of Hell, its calculated depths, dimensions, and entry points. The kind of place that would challenge even the best GPS.

When traveling, I, too, consult maps. I may also say I've come to a place for its landscape, for the geography of a place that is uniquely its own. Say, the Badlands. Or the Okefenokee Swamp. But what I call landscape may well be only *scenery* if I don't at least leave my car and climb down from an overlook to get my hiking boots dusty walking a trail, if I don't pick up a paddle and get my feet wet boarding a canoe to meander among the cypress, if what's captured in a moment of time is merely a digitized vista corralled within the perimeter of a photograph, either as pretty subject in itself or as interesting backdrop to my grinning friends.

Derived from the Greek word for stage, scenery has long been linked to theater as the decorative, static backdrop against which the stories of lives are played out. Not that scenery in and of itself can't step to center stage. Certainly the unfamiliar can be more than backdrop. The viewed-from-afar sweep of it—of mountains or sea, of forests or plains—can beckon, inspire more attentive looking, embolden the senses. Without any previous intention of doing so, my just being in the snowy Colorado Rockies for the first time convinced me to strap on a pair of rental skis. But does a beginner's snaking her tortuous way down a few runs and afterwards sipping wine in the mountain-base restaurants with stupendous views make them more landscape than scenery? And what should I call that which, more recently, quelled disquiet, salved, if only for a short time, the wounds carved by fresh grief? How, not long after my brother's death, just looking out over the vast Sonoran desert, a landscape known and beloved by him, became for me a welcome solace—even if it was then, and remains for me still, something closer to scenery.

It probably matters not a whit if a young girl's joyful scrambling, her duck-your-head-and-slither-your-body kind of exploration of glacially upheaved rocks on a familiar, increasingly known-to-her stretch of shoreline is more akin to geography than geology. Surely most important to her is the experience itself, and what, in the memory of it, becomes story. But neither can occur without the shoreline setting, without a tangible, physical context. Just as without a particular kind of knowing, scenery can't become landscape. Become place.

I no longer need a map to find my way around the island or when crossing its bridge to the mainland. A map for what, unfortunately, too often with brief glimpses, I drive by or hurry through. When what is familiar and known to me becomes mere backdrop for whatever action in my life is taking place, if only it's my lip-syncing lyrics to a song playing on the radio. Or when, fully conscious of it or not, I feel beneath the tires the familiar dip and sway of Route 175 as it rises and falls over hills, curves around a cove. Or when I feel in my steering wheel's pull the island's serpentine causeway S-ing its way over the bar flanked on either side by exposed, oddly beautiful tide-tugged mudflats with foraging seabirds—a route that seems not to have been bulldozed through the land but exists to honor it, work in tandem with its contours, be attendant to the spared trees and marsh, and telegraph each into my body.

At times, I may be seemingly unmindful of such places as I go about my daily busy-nesses, but when they're familiar and known to me, haven't they already been transformed from scenery into landscape? Into what by definition are the physical features of an area of land, including, along with landforms, its flora and fauna, light and weather, human activity and man-made structures? In other words, some of the very things I might admire in a landscape painter's composed, detailed, and carefully chosen point of view—whether she's a painter of *en plein air* tradition setting up an easel at the causeway's edge and feeling the *whoosh* of passing cars, hearing nearby gulls squawk over their low tide's plunder, maybe waving to a clammer carrying hod and rake onto the flats, or is a painter who journeys back to her studio and transports to canvas what's retrieved with the mind's eye by way of hand and brush.

Geographer D.W. Meinig has claimed, "Landscape is composed not only of what lies before our eyes but what lies within our heads." And isn't landscape, too, what's within our bodies? Within our "small, bonebound island," as Dylan Thomas in his notebooks referred to his body. What, with our eyes and ears, appendages and tongue, we physically experience?

Like a migrating bird that retraces routes laid down eons ago and recalled through markers stored in the body, I return to the island each May. In my first approach of a new season, and, depending on the tides, either in briny, iodine-laden or mudflat-bordering-on-stink air, I catch sight of the glittering wide ribbon of the Reach. Beyond it is the expansive bay studded with outlying islands. Closer in is a clutch of houses clinging to a rocky spruce-clad shore and a few blunt-nosed lobster boats moored in a cove. All of it is a familiar and known—and now beloved—landscape. And yet, I only fully recognize it when, behind the wheel and as though I were taxiing down a runway, I approach the ramped, narrowing road to the island's arching suspension bridge, and, with a small lurch in my stomach, ascend, my hood pointing skyward, tires humming against the reinforced deck. Until, in the descent on the other side of an 1,100-foot span, and as if I've come by way of the sky, I feel I've landed as efficiently and with as much grace as a loon that, in spite of its laboriously clumsy and noisy wing-whapping take-off, returns to the water with hardly a ripple. As though it had never left.

After, on the causeway—again the familiar curve and sway. Again, what, if I had to shut my eyes, would be recognizable by body alone. Feeling once more the place that has imprinted and shaped, I might even be tempted to exclaim, "See, the causeway remembers me!"

*O*kay, so it's silly to think the road can feel my swaying body. Or that rock can feel a squirming child much less *remember* her.

But was it always thus?

"Ooh, the wind is so mad," my four-year old granddaughter solemnly declared one afternoon as she paused while coloring, looked outside and pointed her crayon toward the storm-thrashed trees.

"The sky woke up," my young nephew announced, stumbling into the kitchen very early one morning during his summer island visit. The night before, there'd been no pathetic fallacy at work in his storybook's drooping flowers. Yes, the protagonist might've been sad, but so too were the flowers. For him, no analysis or literary device was necessary—the rain that ultimately revived the fading blooms were the teardrops of a sky that in a simple plot turn brightened and became, again, happy.

For both children, sensibility is not a uniquely human property. It's one shared by trees or flowers—or rocks. Such mutual embrace seems innate, like an at-birth characteristic as certain as the color of hair. Nor should this surprise. Coming into this world, we humans learn through the physical interaction of our young animal bodies. An infant presses against, kneads and grabs. A baby down on all fours crawls, and not so dissimilar to how a dog reads the world with its nose, becomes acquainted with her surroundings via grasping fingers and open mouth. Hers is a wordless conversation in a commonly shared geography, in a community of other material beings all intertwined, be they trees, birds, the sunlight prisming through branches where birds perch or warmly pooling on the floor where she parks her bum. Pouring down over her like rain are words. But they remain sounds. Later, as she begins to acquire language, to totter down a path that increasingly leads her away from what was only physically experienced to words that signify bird or oak, the purely sensate body becomes the speaking self.

For a time though, long before she's likely to accept the age-old assumption that the mind is a uniquely human property, that mankind alone is the carrier of consciousness, she dwells in a world that is home to a wind that gets mad, a sun that blinks its eyes awake, a sky that cries. Where the rocks she touches touch her. Hers is a spontaneous affinity with inanimate and nonhuman beings and they the counterpart to her own sensations. She is an extension of the breathing, pulsing world where the experiences of everything in it are, in the words of philosopher David Abram, "reverberations echoing the pulse and pleasures of our body." A world where, emerging from her snug, body-hugging crevice, a young girl is quick to acknowledge a rocky outcropping's embracing awareness, its ability to welcome her back, as would an old friend.

Too bad more of us don't hold onto some of that early felt-experience belief. If, for example, at least a little, we carried into our adult, mind-clicking years the notion that the nonhuman beings with which we share the planet have some measure of sentience. Of sense perception and feeling. A pinch of awareness. (Okay, I can hear the outrage from fellow gardeners if this extends to slugs or blackflies.) But if more of us were to experience the nonhuman as sensate, might we not take more care? Our actions become more respectful? If convinced the animals with which we inhabit the earth are without feelings, it's undoubtedly easier to raise cudgel or scoped rifle, to set out leg-mangling traps or slow-working, gut-twisting poisons, to test in labs, to pack into cages and pens. And if the planet's critters, particularly fellow mammals, don't stay our hand, what chance for the seemingly mute trees, passive prairie grass, inert rock?

In "Mind in the Forest," essayist Scott Russell Sanders asks, "How can I know a tree's inwardness?" He can't, of course. None of us can. Even if we acknowledge that a certain kind of intelligence is the capacity for exchanging information and responding appropriately to circumstances, as, in a forest, trees do, "the only intelligence I can examine is my own," Sanders observes. For all our meaning-making capacities and comfort in hanging out with abstractions, our access is limited. We may observe and listen, note and draw conclusions, but we cannot get into another's inwardness, not even, really, into the heads of our fellow humans. Suggestions that animals can think—crows using tools, apes solving puzzles—or that they feel or have emotions—a fur seal bleating as her bludgeoned pup is hauled across the ice, elephants circling and milling for days over their dead—have not been (have yet to be?) scientifically proven.

Yet easily and often, and guilty of the anthropomorphism scientists warn us against, so many of us look for the sisters and hunters among the stars. Or say creeks speak rather than burble. That doves in their callings mourn. Even so, a contradictory lot, we may also act as though a particular geography doesn't count for much.

Cleverly equipped, we humans are quick to respond to our bodies' discomforts, its hungry cries for "More!" But for all our brain power smarts, we blessed-with-consciousness beings are too often slow to recognize that we inhabit a world of finite resources. Our words may be gifted, may be articulately, even artistically, reflective of the miraculous workings within our skull's wad of cells. But words aren't equipped with pollen. They don't fertilize blueberry barrens. Nor with any success can they decree a sudden detour in centuries-old migratory routes in sea or sky.

Too seldom, we consider what a future map might look like. We fail to consider the damage done to a place until we recognize in our bodies a geography's polluted rivers, its toxic-leached soils and poisonous waste sites. Too often too late, after harm to our bodies or our children's bodies, we discover neglect can damage. Disregard destroys.

Sure, reading that lobsters are without the capacity to experience pain makes things less complicated when I toss them into a boiling pot. And the resulting taste, one of our local Maine lobstermen will eagerly tell you, is unlike that of any other lobsters from any other place. Likewise, farmers working the "black gold" soil of Iowa will swear that no other sweet corn is finer than theirs. Loggers will defend the premium prices for red cedar specific to their northwest forests. Those who farm, fish, and log, who put mind over matter battling storms, over droughts or the weight of regulations, and routinely put their backs into it, too, need to pay attention to a place's geography. And they often do. Yet with our demands that distances be surmounted and productivity manipulated, geography too often translates into what's meant to be overcome by a freight plane or refrigerated truck, an Internet site or GPS system. Threats of potential exploitation rise. Knowledge of a particular place is severely diminished when only measured by miles or the clicks of a mouse.

We certainly don't have to hold onto a child's view that rocks recognize us and angry winds throttle trees in order to grasp how a particular-to-a-place geography needs more of our awareness, our attention, and our respect. We ought to be able to agree that local geographies give to light and air, soil and water various characteristics specific, and possibly unique, to them. A particular shape, weight or quality. A necessary weather pattern. An essential temperature and current. Literally and figuratively, geographies feed us.

Some days, wandering through the kitchen in late afternoon, it's not that I'm hungry. I crave—but for what I'm not always sure. Yesterday, I tossed a few cashews into my mouth, reached into the freezer and scooped straight from the carton a tablespoon of mocha fudge ice cream. But only when I switched to a peeled clementine did I discover the particular sweetness I'd been after.

Today, rereading Sanders' *Staying Put*, I was reminded how his father, when coming to a new place, "would take a pinch of dirt, sprinkle it into his palm, sniff it, stir it with a blunt finger, squeeze it, then rake it on his tongue." Why eat dirt? the young Sanders asked him. "Just trying to figure out where I am," his father explained.

I've not tasted the dirt here. But I have touched my tongue to a favorite glacial erratic just off our shoreline, a large boulder whose active being is its existence, a reliable and reassuring presence. In a landscape grown familiar to me, it organizes the space around it. Daily, and not just to tell me the time by the whereabouts of the tides sloshing against its flanks, it invites my attention, and often, hopefully, I respond with a reciprocity anchored in recognition but with a freshness of looking, as if with new eyes. I have also pressed my cheek to the staved trunk of our big broad-armed, house-anchoring oak after it bore the brunt of another howling storm that sucked at my house's windows, tore at its roof. A gesture that could be translated into "Thanks" or "I'm glad you made it, too."

I once had the privilege to walk with a maple sugar harvester at work. Collecting buckets of sap from his acreage of trees, he uses a sled and a pair of draft horses. Choices driven, he says, by personal preference and what is better for the environment—the newer, all-encompassing word for landscape. For me, there's also respect in this choice, in how, for example, the noise of machines might be a disturbance not just to him or his dappled team but, possibly, to the trees themselves. Against a backdrop of quietude, of a woodland's feathered browsing and intimate nonhuman conversations, the harvester, on foot and in mind, works his land with a familiarity that extends beyond limbing or tapping, beyond when the ground is likely to thaw or the rain to come. As though he were still dwelling in his child's animal body, before there were words for such knowledge, he and his team move through the bending, watching trees with a few clicks, a toss of the reins. "Language, but not words," poet Tomas Transomer once wrote of his encounter with deer tracks in the snow-covered woods.

Recently, a batch of boulders and an expanse of smooth granite ledge called to a young girl. With their textures and patches of color riven with glacial striations and glinting veins of quartz, those rocks call to my senses, too. As though extending an open palm, they beckon, invite, and from an aging but still willing body coax a remembered agility. By their very existence, they draw to them child and adult, even visitors who, carrying cameras, come only once.

Appealing to the body is one way a place becomes special. At nearby Lily Pond, the island's favorite freshwater swimming hole, a narrow path worn into the duff and dirt by many preceding feet leads to a small granite bluff. There, a thick rope hanging from a tree invites a body-cooling plunge on a hot afternoon. Having been there so long, the rope's become part of the landscape. But first, that spot was a solid bluff beneath bare feet, a big maple's sturdy, leafy limb arching overhead, and the splash of bright sun on dark water that collectively called out to someone who answered with a dive, and, later, a rope.

Maybe there's always an interchange between the body and the landscape. A "sort of silent conversation," as Abram calls it. A continuous dialogue that unfolds below articulated awareness, unspooling without conscious thought. Like not recognizing a craving for clementine until my tongue first telegraphs it. Or not recognizing for so many years my hunger to know a place's geography with the geography of my body. To belong to a place with a stitched-into-sinew-and-bone knowing.

Like that of a young girl whose body has begun to know a stretch of rocky coastline in ways mine once knew its bared-to-summer-legs way of shinnying up a splintery-barked crabapple tree to sit among tossing branches above a suburban alley. To know a place by feel, or by feel be returned to it, the way, perhaps, walking a path along a pond's edge, the ground pressing up against my feet, I'm returned to the Little Calumet River of my youth, its winding trails my feet helped make among the rattling reeds lining its muddy banks. Landscapes that, writes Sanders, "are borne in the mind, lived in the body." The remembering body.

It may have only required a couple of summer trips east to tell me what a map can't convey. To feel how the drive here telescopes down. How my behind-the-wheel journey compresses from the flat open Midwest and its distant horizon sightlines to the hillier terrain of upstate New York and the green heights of the Berkshires, distances between me and the coast diminishing as miles on my odometer accrete. Until, past

Augusta and Belfast and at last traveling down the Blue Hill Peninsula to the Reach, on roads my body knows by their curves and turns, their crowned dips and sways, the distance narrowing further, I feel more and more as if I'm physically in a funnel, the neck of which is the slender cabled bridge that delivers me from the mainland to this island. But to truly know this place where that physical journey ends, to obtain such knowledge through personal intimacy, will take a long time. And given how late I've come to such hunger, maybe all of whatever time I have left.

"*H*er head is in the stars," Mr. M declares.

Cool, I think, suppressing a smile. So much better maybe to have your head thrust up among the fixed, pulsing stars that since ancient times is where we've looked for direction than in the lofting and tumbling, unfixed clouds.

Mr. M's come to help me tackle the transplant of some sprawling dogwoods, a task at which he's as proficient as he is at rigging deer fencing around my rhododendron in autumn or expertly removing the threat to our power lines by winter blow-downs. We've chosen a good day. Some cloud cover is keeping temperatures down. There's breeze enough to hold off most of the bugs. We're each armed with tools appropriate to the job, but again it soon becomes clear that my assist will be less with shovel than with willing ear as he sputters forth his latest frustrations over a teenager niece prone to repeated mishap and mischief.

Mr. M, as I secretly and with much affection call him, is private shorthand for my equally benign-intended and secretly held Mr. Malaprop. Over the past few years, and on multiple occasions, Mr M has gifted me with his unintentional misuses. About his neighbors engaged in dispute last summer: "There was a lot of bittery between them." About his decision in spring: "I won't mow too close or I'll sculp your lawn." Recently, one of his customers was so eager to get a load of "loom," he was "chafing at the hips." Mr. M is still fuming over the mice that invaded his house and got into his pantry by "borrowing" through snowdrifts.

What Mr. M also doesn't know is that he's one of my local guides.

If scenery's to become landscape, we can't just drop into a place and point our cameras. We can, of course, acquire some general geographical understanding from books, or, as Sanders puts it, make an "amateur's raid into the domains of experts." We can also consult maps. But if we genuinely want to know a place, we've got to unpack our bags, park our butts, settle in. We'd also do well, advises essayist Barry Lopez, to seek a local guide. Someone whose knowledge is "intimate not encyclopedic…

human not scholarly." Whose experience comes through exposure. Whose body has stooped over the land and crumbled its soil in her fingers, or whose feet have known where to find the least slippery stones when crossing a cold, swollen river. Who knows in which trees the sap runs best, or where the wintering-over crows are likely to roost. And where, measured by a glacial erratic, the high-water mark of a spring tide is able to reach. Someone for whom a geography has evolved into a known landscape. Into a place that without its stories remains only landscape.

That Mr. M is one of my local guides is a notion he'd likely scoff at. With customary colorful language, he'd likely point to his common-to-us-all memory lapses and ignorance of the precisely named. But as a native-born son, Mr. M has lived his life here except for a few years after which, using his inner map, journeying on foot and along memory's grooves, he carried back from Vietnam his bodily and relived-in-the-mind injuries, wounds that a known place and the many seasons of becoming more intimate with its dirt and roots in deeply remembered soil have helped to heal.

Mr. M and me. We're both cartographers of sorts, just as we all are, carrying within us inward maps on which are inscribed the geographies that, perhaps with the assistance of a good guide, we've come to know. Maps crowded with detail in some spots. In others, less so. Maybe within our map or at its margins are dark blanks or the vaguely if colorfully drawn abstractions we've only imagined. Spanning them are lines that cross, converge, lead. The bulleted straightaways of turnpikes and freight routes. Roads so small and seemingly unimportant as to not need numbers or names. Trails meandering through woods.

Whether inexplicably drawn to this island like iron shavings to a magnet or driven to it with a wind of unknown origin at my back, I arrived in a place for which I had no map. But in cove's exhale and spruce's breath, in ebb tide's gurgle and flood tide's pulsing edge, as though each had been waiting and wanting to be known by me, I recognized my craving. I unpacked that first summer and, in the many since, have settled in. Each year, I continue to walk, explore, photograph, collect, record. Of Mr. M, of my other local guides and fellow islanders, I ask often and often enough the right questions. Details are filling in.

It's unlikely I'll ever tell Mr. M my secret name for him. I'll probably never confess either that I've come to know a boulder by tongue's touch and taste—by salt and scrape and mineral grit. Or that in places in our woods not only do my feet know where a thick moss's spongy spring gives way to granite ledge, but also where, having stretched out there, my head and cheek know its soft, pelted cushion. I'll likely not share with Mr. M how I often return to a familiar stretch of shoreline rocks, their footholds my clambering body knows in a way different from that of a young girl, and am quick to recognize their unique way of being, their retained, day-after-day shape and stable presence. Honoring them, responding to their invitation, I recline there, still my mind's natter. With sun-baked ledge warm against my back, I'm neither purely intelligent body nor impoverished mind. Nor is there any "bittery" between them.

As I push the wheelbarrow from the garage to where Mr. M has just about freed the dogwood's roots, he straightens up from his shovel. Tipping back his cap's visor, he turns and looks toward the bay.

"Yep" he says. "I was right. Storm's coming. Been feeling it in my bones all morning."

Setting down the wheelbarrow beside him, I too look toward the bay and watch the towering clouds darken over the distant islands. Even before doing so, I believed Mr. M. As I do the weather change predictions made by an old-salt lobsterman down the road whose bum shoulder from years of hand-hauling is, I'm convinced, a better indicator than a barometer's dial.

The air swells with new humidity. A quickening breeze agitates the oak leaves overhead. "Yes, you were right," I tell Mr. M.

Beneath my feet, rising up from the moist pile dug around the dogwood's root ball is the fecund, sweet smell of dirt, the kind you might almost want to eat if trying to figure out where you are.

A NECESSARY BALLAST

"Go inside a stone
That would be my way."
Charles Simic

*M*ost days, I walk the shore at low tide to survey what water and wind have tossed up. I'm after the *objets du jour*, serendipity's daily specials. But yesterday, I went with a specific purpose: to find a few smooth, tumbled rocks for the corner of our shower with its new floor of grouted river stones.

Now, from a shower head, warm water rains down on three speckled rocks the size of large cantaloupes. They're inelegantly spattered with shampoo foam and sage-scented bath gel. Other than aesthetic appeal, they serve no purpose. I've warned Bob of their new presence, the perils of stubbed toes. "Flesh and stone: considerable rivals," poet Pablo Neruda once declared.

Not surprisingly, Bob's neither impressed nor especially enthusiastic. Peering in at my new finds and clearly computing the ratio of rock to remaining shower floor, he says, "Hmm, another collection."

"That's stretching it a bit, isn't it?" I leap to my own defense. "Three rocks is hardly a collection."

"Yet."

Okay, so evidence abounds. Irrefutable are the three burgeoning piles of stones on the deck, each color-sorted in shades of tan, gray and rose, and assembled beneath the butterfly bush several large heart-shaped specimens, a modest collection by almost anyone's measure, but one that seems to have birthed offspring stacked in a nearby terra-cotta saucer. On my desktop rise small cairns of flat speckled stones. In the kitchen, a bowl is home to a mound of flat ones I use as knife rests. A shelf holds several celadon-hued beauties hauled from Jasper Beach that serve, I've insisted, a real if only occasionally necessary purpose in holding down napkins at a breezy afternoon picnic.

The larger point is, and this has always seemed obvious to me, you can't love this Maine island if you don't like rock. It's the star of our bold shorelines and ledges, our snug harbors, coves, and fingering inlets. Atop indigenous granite foundations, old Capes hunker. As do their barns and connecting ells. Once, after farmers cleared much of this island's land and until underlying granite in cahoots with poor soil forced them into other trades, rock walls bordered fields, corralled livestock, delineated property lines. Many still exist. In spruce forests that grew up where open fields once sprawled, meandering rock walls speak to a long-gone way of life.

Just about everywhere here, local granite bulwarks wharf pilings, sea walls and breakwaters. It's the stuff of walls, steps, benches and fence posts, of vases, candle holders, trivets and birdbaths. Rocks are still often used to weight down lobster traps. At home, they hold open doors, prop up books. Dig in the garden, and shovel or spade tings against rock. Expanding my perennial bed last spring, the rototiller's blades unearthed several large specimens, the makings of the new bed's edging. As if the earth knew just what I needed.

Most important, rocks have stories to tell.

Just as a botanist can translate a lichen's hieroglyphic script splattering a boulder, a geomorphologist studying Maine's rocky islands and coast is able to interpret much about the earth's surface, its restless movements. According to Island Institute president Philip Conkling, after only a half hour of pick-plinking, a geologist paraphrased one of the stories relinquished by a particular rocky shore: "This is a third-order fold of an ancient mountain chain and is good evidence of a continental collision." Undoubtedly, had the rocks themselves been able to speak, they'd have offered a livelier version.

Indeed, so many other stories rocks would tell if they could. The large boulders now armoring a portion of our shorefront against further erosion might speak of their transport here by dump truck and barge from a blast site just over the bridge. I'd love to hear from the moss-matted remnants of a stone wall bordering our property on its northern edge. I'm hungry for the testimony simple headstones might provide, like those my friend Charles found in his woods, how more than 100 years ago they bore witness to a sea captain's grief when he carried home the illness that killed his two young children. And what else might I learn of the fire on the Holmes property if the rocks of a chimney, all that remain, could find voice?

Mid-island, at the road's edge on Route 15, there's a compact-car-size boulder hard to miss. It's been identified by geologists as part of an end moraine transported here by meltwater from the last ice sheet, the edge of which was many miles away. But at least one island elder rejects such a notion. Offering up not a crumb of scientific evidence, nor feeling that she must, she's exclaimed, "Why that rock couldn't have come any further than Little Deer Isle." Meaning, of course, such a familiar and important landmark couldn't have come from off-island. From away.

Maybe only the boulder itself could set the story straight—just as, after centuries, Stonehenge is still trying to. But most folks here don't seem interested. It's the human story that matters, a boulder mere backdrop. Known as Carman's Rock for as long as most old-timers can remember and according to historical records and photographs dating to the 1890s, its sort-of-billboard purpose was to advertise a particular brand of soap. Now, come each June, it's where the graduating high school seniors make their mark. They freshly paint it with colors unique to their class and emblazon the surface with their names. Not so much graffiti as announcement. An island tradition. Here we are, these paint layers proclaim. Here we go. Into the bright future with our stories and dreams.

Of course Bob knows most of this, too. Still, after inspecting my new additions, he shrugs, goes back to shaving, relieved perhaps by my promise of "just these three." Or maybe he's resigned himself to what in his mind seems inevitable. Though neither drawn toward picking up rocks nor objecting when I do, he asks, "So what do you think it's about with you, all this rock and stone stuff?"

*T*o be moved. That's some part of it, no?

To be able to pick up, pocket a stone, hoist a rock, haul it to kitchen or shower because, and thanks in no small part to my miraculous thumbs, I can. And, of course, that I'm moved to. But by what exactly? The feel of a stone's heft and shape in my palm? A rock's solidity I can with fingers grasp? With rock in hand, I hold an indisputable certainty, my senses telegraphing to brain: this is rock. Maybe I also satisfy the need for closer inspection, fueled by curiosity but also a shifting aesthetic, from the seemingly arbitrary to the collector's specificity calling for a particular color or shape, all of which compel me to keep a stone one day that on the next I might toss back—a process that when he joins me on a walk must surely puzzle or assure Bob.

Or maybe it's about where I look. As a child, I was told "watch where you step." I did and do. Good advice then and still, particularly when hiking the island's cobbled shores or its wooded trails thickly webbed with shallow spruce roots. Unless my bum is safely plunked somewhere or my feet have come to rest where footing is secure, I'm likely to be looking down. No doubt there have been times when I'd have benefitted from the big picture, with looking up, ahead, to taking in a more expansive range of distant possibilities, in whatever span of time I might still have coming to me—that unknown journey which, in part, is also what *move* implies.

But what is equally attractive and dependably reassuring about rocks is that they don't move, except perhaps in our nightmares when certain objects might animate in ways that terrify us—like, say, my chef's knife suddenly leaping up from the counter and pursuing me around the kitchen. Presumably, only in my dreams can the rocks in my shower assemble in the corner and plan an anarchic uprising.

But rocks are moved. By earthquakes, of course, nightmares from which its victims cannot merely awaken. Indeed, the history of our planet's rock is a long one of movement. And what a turbulent ride. Rock's been extruded, thrust, heated, cooled. Pulverized by glacial weight, compressed by ice, drowned by ice melt, driven by seething storm surge, gnawed by lichen, pelted by rain. Perhaps covered, sucked under, hatched anew by who knows how many sequences of cyclical heave and collapse. Ground, scraped, polished. Excavated, blasted, hammered and hauled. And that's just in this neck of the woods after the last glacial dunking 14,000 years ago, one of the more recent and brief chapters when considering the earliest known rocks of the unfathomable-to-our-human-minds span of the Archaean period, a geological pre-Cambrian eon some 4.5 to 2.5 billion years ago.

Mostly, I suspect, we want rocks not to move. To be what they appear. Still and silent objects without history or other life except what we give them. Although it's not so hard—is it?—to imagine how, in another discovery of what seem like endless excavations in Rome, a newly exposed rock might, while blinking in the light, sigh "At last," eager to throw back an espresso and then reveal what it knows.

The inanimate objects we keep around us—rocks and stones not excepted—tell much about who we are. Prominently heaped in an old wooden trencher on my dining room sideboard are my favorite stones. Smooth and black, they each possess, in varying widths, a white band of quartz circling their circumference. I think of them as my Belted Galloways, that breed of black cows naturally encircled at their midsection with broad white "belts," cows that to my eye always look well-dressed, their shirts neatly tucked in.

Collecting these stones, I was first drawn by aesthetics. I liked the way they look herded together, their myriad differences in meeting my demand of an unbroken band both obvious and subtle. Since, I've learned these banded stones are locally known as "wishing stones." And while I may be alone in my most recent desire to indulge a seemingly decorative-driven whim while subjecting large, shore-fetched rocks to shower gel and naked moving-well-past-middle-age body parts, I'm not alone in my attraction to wishing stones. Many folks, I've discovered, collect them.

Indeed, on this island, there's a lot of wishing. Often outspoken about their wishes, a number of native islanders want things "the way they used to be." They echo the late Maine author Ruth Moore who, in a recent edition of her letters, reveals that she missed Maine even when she was at home.

Such a malady is not unique to this island or state. It's widespread. An *in situ* homesickness. Or what some would call nostalgia. Deriving from the Greek *nostos* for homeward journey and *algos* for grief or pain, nostalgia is what a seventeenth-century Swiss doctor identified as the body-sickening longing most of us know as homesickness. According to the late writer Deborah Tall, European medical books described nostalgia as fatal until the nineteenth century, after which it shifted from a physical disease to a psychological one, an issue of time not place. Most commonly today, nostalgia is recognized as a longing in the present for what belongs to a different time, for things, persons or situations of the past. Often, for what is no longer possible.

The advertising folks who try to sell us stuff are especially adept at pulling nostalgia from their trick bag. As do consultants crafting political ads in presidential election years. And so, too, the state tourist boards. Long touted as "Vacationland" (even for those who have to hold down three jobs?), Maine also sports the state-sponsored tag line, "The Way Life Should Be," which, when translated in certain quarters here, reads: "The Way Life Was."

Americans, Tall claims, are "habitually nostalgic." Even as we're taking videos of our children, she observes, we're already looking forward to watching them in future years. The present moment becomes anticipated memory. She, too, finds the statement of my native Chicago's late mayor Richard Daley revealing. Never the wordsmith, he once declared, "I am looking to the future with nostalgia."

Often it seems nostalgia goes hand in hand with the number of years we've clocked in. We reach a certain age, and, in our longing, lament a vanished and always better time. We may recall the 1950s offering tidy brick bungalows, the GI bill, kids saluting the flag, Norman Rockwellian scenes of families around dinner tables, but forget that those years also served up whites-only lunch counters, polio scares, McCarthyism, and women relegated to ruffled aprons, pressed handkerchiefs, and Sunday pot roasts.

Often what we may be wishing for in such nostalgia is not a simple life, but a simpler one. In which, for example, technology doesn't predominate in our staying connected, or stand in for connectedness. Although, when it comes to this, we islanders may say we're luckier than most. Miss those service stations where friendly attendants pumped your gas, actually knew how to fix your car and, while they were at it, asked after your ailing mother? A postmistress who calls your house to remind you of an express delivery package you've yet to pick up? We still have them. Would you like to know whose chickens laid your eggs, whose hands made your bread and fired the plate that holds it, whose maple trees are the source of your pancake syrup? I can sit down to breakfast and give you answers.

But lest I veer too close to boosterism or indulge in nostalgia's sidekick, sentimentality, I need to be clear: we, too, on this island have our complexities, our messy problems. What goes on elsewhere goes on here, and in one way or another always has. On this road alone this year: a divorce of the nastiest sort, a DUI, an inheritance dispute, a threatened lawsuit over property line encroachment, a nine-year-old left behind by his mother when she walked out on his father, a dying woman whose adult offspring never visit. A bit further afield: the burglarized pharmacy, another drug arrest, a stabbing during a Saturday night post-party brawl.

Nostalgic, we may reject change, resist moving on. But it's as foolish to think wishing alone will bring more jobs to the island, return cod to the bay, boost the boat price of lobster, or banish drugs in our schools and obesity in our youth, as it is to imagine change not happening. It will and must. Do all the islanders out on inlets and back roads and still without choice truly prefer dial-up Internet service? Or, as my teenage nephew calls it, "living in the Stone Age?" Would we truly feel better off if the Island Medical Center had never been built?

And yet I understand the urge to imbibe at the well of myth. When I return in mind's eye to my childhood past, I often paint much of it with broad idyllic brushstrokes or peer back through a smeared lens blurring coarse edges with gauzy light. Filtering through are tidy yards, shady sun-dappled streets, endless games of Kick the Can, mothers at each screened doorway calling their kids home. Filtered out are abuse, divorce, the joblessness and booze from which most neighborhoods are seldom exempt. Punching into my BlackBerry now, I don't really miss the rotary phones of my adolescence, although some days I do lament the wait for each dialed number's trip around the wheel, a circular route of pause and connection in which I once had time to think about what I planned to say, had time to hang up without fear that Caller ID would betray a change of heart. I sometimes miss the creak of the rattan chair seat beside our family's single telephone, my long whispered conversations with friends, my father's monthly threat to install a pay phone booth in our front yard. All back in those pre-voicemail and cell phone teenage years when my anguish over a silent phone tiptoed around the possibility that only because I'd been away had I missed the call from a particular boy.

No doubt in future years, given the perennial threats to close the Deer Isle village post office, I'll walk to a roadside mailbox (if postal mail hasn't by then become extinct) and long for the time when the retrieval of mail in the village was a daily ritual, when communication came by way of not just a clutch of letters and magazines, but in the exchanges with fellow islanders. In the possibility of obtaining a recipe, passing along an invitation, seeing photos of a new grandchild, securing the recommendation of a tree-trimming company or a local seamstress to slipcover a favorite chair.

I don't want a return to the past as, listening to them talk, it seems some islanders do—wishing to have back the island of, say, thirty years ago, or moving further back still, to that of their ancestors, some of whom on Little Deer Isle, a local paper recently reported, greeted visitors with pitchforks. But, selfishly or unwisely, I do want many things about this place to stay the way they are *now*. Some days, as though sealing it into amber were a possibility, I find myself wanting to preserve the present.

And so I, too, wish. Which, perhaps, makes me a partner in collusion. Islanders nostalgic for a place that maybe never was but nevertheless has been lost, and newcomers like me nostalgic for a place that never was but seems to have been found.

*A*fter showering this morning, I say to Bob, "You know, these rocks don't have to stay here. I can move them."

I've been prompted into this offer by last night's phone call from my father. We'd just finished dinner and I was bussing our plates. Bob answered, and after a bit of small talk involving something with baseball scores, he said, "Yep, your daughter's right here. Be sure to ask her about the large rocks she's now putting in our shower."

Before passing me the phone, Bob said, "Yes, more rocks. Big ones."

And then, presumably after another of Dad's questions: "Oh, I don't know. Maybe for their weight. You know, in case a nor'easter tries blowing the house into the ocean."

"Seriously," I now tell Bob, "I'll move them."

"Oh no, the shower is *so* much better with rocks in it."

"Popples," I say, but go no further. I don't explain that what to him are rocks are in fact *popples*, a type of smooth, round rock common to our grinding, wave-tossed shores. Nor do I say how popples were once used to pave streets in East Coast cities. Nor how, even further back, they served a specific purpose, so much so that prior to a nearby island with a long, thin, cobbled beach "handle" being named Great Spoon, it was known on early nautical charts as Fill Boat Island.

Yes, popples gathered there were used as ballast.

*T*hinking about how the captains of those ships knew how much ballast was needed in their holds—enough to stabilize and help keep a steady course but not too much to weigh down, arrest movement—I'm reminded of the captain of one of the steamships that carried passengers to this island before our cable bridge was built. It's said that after safely docking at the wharf, a passenger exclaimed, "Captain, you must know where all the rocks are." "No," the Captain replied, "but I know where they aren't."

Daily I look out to the bay's watery expanse. I don't know where all the rocks are, or where they aren't. I do know, though, that there is one large boulder that, except for a few days each year, is concealed. I've learned where to look for it, and now know where, in a spring tide's ebb when water levels are at their lowest, I can walk to it. Exposed on a sunny day for a few hours, the boulder, when I splay my hand against its side, feels warm. Once, I felt invited, too, to press my ear there, hoping to hear some interior whiz and whir.

"Go inside a stone," Charles Simic invites in his poem, "Stone." Inside, he suggests, it may be quiet but it's not dark. A moon shines from somewhere, as though from behind a hill with "just enough light to make out/The strange writing, the star-charts/On the inner walls."

Read Simic's poem and it's easy to visual a rock cave. Read it to a classroom of youngsters, as I often have, give them a rock to finger, its heft to palm, and their imaginations may well transport them inside, into a cool quiet, even when, Simic warns, "a cow steps on it full weight." Or when, thrown into a river, it sinks unperturbed to the bottom, where "fishes come to knock on it and listen." We're drawn to such places, to the possibility of moonlit star charts. The unlikely places where things happen.

And yet, against my splayed palm, a large rock seems emblematic of stasis. I pick up a stone, feel its inert weight in my fingers. Looking at it, I see a portrait of permanence. But am I right?

"Rock here has no plan ever to be sand," Maine writer Charles Wadsworth once observed. A panoramic view suggests he may be correct. Were each convoluted inlet and cove stretched taut and measured, Maine's shoreline would extend more than 7,000 miles and yet possess only 60 miles' worth of sandy beach, a ratio that seems about perfect for those of us who love rock. Still, I'd never deny the allure of a stretch of sandy shore, how it invites bare feet. How it's more forgiving. Years ago, had I fallen on sand rather than slippery tide-exposed rock while hiking with a friend ("watch where you step," and, actually, I was), I might not have a sensitive, lingering lump on my knee. Had Theresa, a forester consulting with a client and, while practicing her trade, looking up, tripped and fallen on a bluff of sand rather than granite ledge, she might not have endured a skull fracture and such a long and painful recovery.

Sand, as we know, shifts. Dunes undulate. Here, small, sandy pocket beaches are bounded and created in part by rocky headlands that subdue wave action. These are places where lower energy waves cannot carry away sediment except in high wind and wave storms, in which case, pocket beaches become ephemeral, too. They may change or disappear just as their bigger, burlier cousins do, like those, say, of Cape Cod or North Carolina's Outer Banks, all highly dynamic beaches subject to constant movement and rapid, extreme change.

Though geologists identify our rocky coastlines as "high energy" environments, rock for the most part appears to stay put, as unbudging as some long-held grievances or beliefs. Or a resistance to change.

Here, we islanders so love our rock, it's likely that those homesick for things "the way they used to be" might well hold concrete to blame for unwanted change. While local granite could've been used in the construction of our island's cable bridge spanning the Reach and connecting us to the mainland, it wasn't. New York's Triborough Bridge boasts Deer Isle granite, but our bridge, completed in 1939, came decades after cheaper and easier-to-transport concrete forced most Maine quarries to close. And it's here at our bridge's concrete foundation where many have been quick to lay the blame.

"No other event has wrought so many changes in our lives, brought us so many benefits, and created so many new problems," observed the late island historian Clayton Gross. As though the bridge itself were a fault-line running the length of the island. But of course it's not a question of the material in the bridge's making. And to project with any accuracy how things might've been different had the bridge never been erected is now almost impossible. The bridge exists. We know where the rocks are. And nostalgia in all its yearning and bittersweet longing can't impede movement, hold back change.

Probably easier to resolve would be whether rock or concrete is more durable. I'm no engineer, but it's pretty obvious concrete degrades. At various times over the past few years, work crews have barged over their cranes to remediate problems with the bridge's foundation or decking, and for weeks, as traffic is reduced to a single lane, we nibble as close as we're ever likely to get to "rush hour" or "traffic jam." Likewise, back in my native Chicago, and threatening more than just traffic, aging concrete viaducts routinely and dangerously crumble. Each winter, as though shedding another layer of skin, they expose more and more skeletal rebar. Concrete sidewalks take a beating, too. Bit by bit, they disintegrate beneath an expanding web of cracks into which rain and frost seep and heave. Everywhere evidence mounts. There are places where things don't hold. Nothing is finitely, permanently, set in concrete.

Nor in rock. Just ask an experienced stonecutter, many of whom once thrived here, who is able to determine how grain runs in granite, like that in the island's old Settlement Quarry where after millions of years of tectonic stress, granite cooled and solidified, and fractures formed. He can speak to granite's perpendicular rift, its parallel lift. And thus how granite may fracture at right angles. But whether from massive natural events or man-made assists, fractures aren't all clean-edged. They're often jagged and gaping, like maws or wounds.

Fissures, on the other hand, appear less dramatic. Smaller, harder to detect, they lack precision, rarely possess a clean, clear edge. Typically preceding them is a natural, mind-boggling process—a first penetrating raindrop or snow-melt dribble that sets the whole thing in motion, assisted then by lichen's persistent gnaw and countless cycles of freeze and thaw. Myriad circumstances that might prevent the fissure's eventual widening and deepening are thwarted, until the riven rock is not so much cleaved as split, separated, nudged apart. Changed.

It's not unlike the way most sand gets made. True, explore in bare feet the sandy, shifting stretches of Maine's Popham Beach or the Cape's Outermost Beach and you'll likely forget you're walking on rock, unlike

Downeast Maine's Jasper Beach, its cobbled shoreline likened by one geologist to "walking on ball bearings." But your sand-burrowing toes are actually wiggling their way into broken down rock, including the hardest mineral-specimen quartz, that last-to-crystallize post-magma holdout which, closer to home, in a white unbroken band, puts the wish or the cow into a bowl of black, polished stones. Progressively in the rock-to-sand process, thanks to many of the usual fissure-inducing suspects along with acidic rainfall and whatever necessary chemicals various organisms exude, rocky particles become smaller and smaller. Wind and water get in on it, too, tossing against one another the particles that further abrade. Meaning a fissured rock, in the right environment, subject to an array of unpredictable circumstances, over what would have to be another one of those brain-synapse-busting computation of years, could eventually become sand.

Last week, going down to the shore on my exploratory expedition for shower rocks, I picked up a promising specimen, and before my mind kicked in and assessed aesthetics, my fingertips, the outermost edges of my body's bulk, once again told me with their particular knowing: this is rock. And, with the certainty of a steamship captain's knowing where rocks aren't, I knew, too, the rock's destination would be my shower floor. But I couldn't have told then, nor can I now, how that rock first made it to this shore or where its journey might yet have taken it if I hadn't intervened, arrested its natural, of-the-world movement.

Had a lighthouse keeper on Matinicus Island not kept such meticulous records over his many years there, we might not know that waves can move a granite boulder weighing approximately 100 tons a distance of more than twelve feet. A fact that maybe shouldn't surprise us. In wind-driven storms, waves can wallop with three tons of power per linear foot of shore. What such wave power translates to in the open sea I can't say, but I bet ballast in a ship's hold only does so much in keeping a course steady.

And yet we need, continually seek, ballast. Once, for years, come each November, I loaded a few large rocks into the back of my old Volvo wagon to make it less likely I'd fishtail on winter ice. I didn't know where the hazards might lie, but in storms, I chose my route carefully and navigated the best I was able. Until, in April, when the seasons again changed and spring advanced, I knew, with a certainty conferred on what was, really, so little, that it was time to unload my rocks.

Admirably, ship captains stopping at Fill Boat Island knew how much ballast was enough. Perhaps that's the knowledge I'm seeking, that balance between what weighs me down and what's needed for stability and steadying the course of inevitable change. A journey in which, along the way, even some wishing may be appropriate.

*T*his morning, over our breakfast coffee, I told Bob, "Okay, so I'm moving those rocks out today."

Deep into a newspaper article, he managed, "That's up to you."

"I just think it's best."

He lowered the paper. "Why? Because of the stain?"

So he'd noticed, too. Beneath the rocks, where our high-mineral-content well water is puddling and can't drain, a pale orange stain was spreading. Over time, it would darken, look like a patch of rust. So okay, yeah, partly because of the stain.

"You know, it's a good thing I love rock," I blurted, as Bob picked up our empty mugs and headed for refills. "I mean, rather than…."

"Rather than what?"

"I don't know…Sand."

"Well, yeah. That would be messy."

"What if I truly loved the landscape of a salt marsh instead?"

"Yuck. Mud." He set down my filled mug. "And just imagine if you loved rain forests. We might have parrots and monkeys all over the place." He raised his mug as if in a toast. "Instead, you love rocks. Believe me, I'm grateful."

I am, too. I've chosen well. My husband, this island, three rocks for my shower, and, now, a stunning day such as this one to return them to the shore.

Overhead, the sky is cloudless, and so clear and intense with golden light, I expect it to chime. I'm reminded of what poet Giuseppe Ioachino once observed about the light in Rome: "Look: it's splitting the stones."

Halfway down our stairs to the shore, I lower the canvas totes in which I'm carrying the rocks and pause to rest my arms. Spread before me is the calm, spangled sea, and in distances near and far, small islands, some of which, like treeless and barren Hardhead, seem to have derived their names from the suggestive shapes often given to rock. Closer in, among the large boulders increasingly revealed by the ebbing tide are gulls, a few crows poking in the wrack, and, further out, a resting cormorant with its wide, spread-winged cape. Everywhere I look along this mostly cobbled shore are stones and rocks in a seemingly infinite variety of sizes and shapes, whose activity seems to be their stillness, their steadiness and quietude, but each with the power to move me to bend, reach out, stoop for a closer look.

And how many, I wonder, are on their way to somewhere else, to being something else?

I hoist the bags and head for the shore. I can't remember exactly where I found each of these rocks, nor do I see any particular, perfect spot to place them. There probably isn't any. About a foot or so above the wrack line, I set the bags down. Reaching both hands inside, as though unloading ballast from the hold, I lift the largest rock. Speckled with pink feldspar, black mica and white quartz, it reveals part of the recipe in its making. Whatever else went into it, I can only guess.

I tuck it up in the lee of two large boulders then step back, assess the arrangement.

And right there, in all that inertness—change.

For years my belief has been that rocks represent permanence. That they don't change. But of course they do, and must, to become what they are here. It's not a specified course, the way, say, the earth moves around the sun. It's a process millennia in the making, and one that isn't over. Compared to what this rocky shoreline in some distant future might look like, today is a mere snapshot, already more obsolete than a Polaroid.

I decide to keep the three rocks together, as they were in my shower, and place them, abutted, in among the boulders. But how crushingly insignificant is my human hand agency. Long after my journey is over, these rocks will outlast me, however they may change and in whatever form they become. To them, my handful of decades doesn't even register as a heartbeat.

We are of the earth like stone, writes John Mansfield in *The Bones of the Earth*. And how we want to marry our short days to stone. But "stone is a ticking clock…a slow clock, slow enough to believe in its consistency." To believe in its permanence.

*B*ob and I are winding down a late afternoon walk on our road when neighbor Lew with his golden retriever sidekick on the seat beside him, brakes his pickup. "Hey," he says, "stop by. Come see what I found."

We detour down his drive and as soon as his house comes into sight, I spot his find—an impressive wheelbarrow-sized boulder of mottled gray and rose, intriguingly bumped and splotched like a piece of bruised fruit. Unearthed by his contractor while digging a proposed sunroom's foundation, Lew had him nudge it up against one side of the porch. Suddenly, his house, just built last year, looks anchored, tied to the land. As though it's always been there.

"So you're not the only one with new boulders," Lew says, as if we've been in competition over baseball trading cards and I didn't know it. And *new*, of course, being relative. Even the granite cellar stone he's using for his front step, the result of a swap somehow involving frozen turkey drumsticks, a story whose accurate version Lew's smile told me weeks ago I'd never get, predates both of us, even him, an island native son with generations preceding him here.

He's right, though. About my having boulders. Two summers ago, I arranged to have three feldspar-spotted boulders hauled to our house from an abandoned quarry and placed near our front door. The scrapes and dings of their transport have weathered over, and with a thick collar of sweet woodruff at their base and ivy twining among them, it almost looks as though the house had to be built around them. More newly acquired—a finest kind gift—is the boulder that Buster, a fellow rock-lover, surprised me with one afternoon last fall, delivering on his flatbed a dark oblong boulder with a white, unbroken band circling one end (an immense wishing rock!) and an irregularly shaped bull's-eye at its center. Positioning it beneath the trees at the top of the driveway was occasion enough for me to plant a new bed of ferns and bunchberry.

Our boulders—Lew's and mine—may help define our property and personalize our landscapes, but, older than any boundary, marker or deed, they belong to time, to a time before the land beneath them became property and property place.

"Okay, Lew," I concede, "I've got rock envy."

"I bet you do. This thing disappears, I'll know just where to look."

Leaving Lew's, Sam the retriever escorts us home as always, not turning to trot back until, as if it were her job to deliver us there safely, we reach our lane.

I love coming home at this time of day. The lowering sun is now due west, showing off its golden, skillful ease in finding and ravishing every branch of every tree overarching our lane. The light, as though spilled, transforms our way home into a path I'd be tempted to take, wherever it led.

With a nudge of his shoulder against mine, Bob says, "You know, I like your Buster rock better."

"I knew you'd say that."

"But I do."

I reach for his hand, my other hand inside my vest pocket fingering a pebble I keep stashed there. Above us, in these last hours of daylight, nattering birds have shifted into high gear. Rummaging in some old fallen leaves and collapsed bracken, a red squirrel makes a racket all out of proportion to its size. Sunlight through trees keeps tossing golden coins at our feet.

It's this. This, I think, squeezing Bob's hand. The certainty of our walking together on a sunlit afternoon. Of returning to a house in a place we both love. Recognizing the fact that we've got more years behind us than whatever number still stretches ahead and no amount of longing—or wishing—can make it otherwise. It's this I want to fossilize. The constancy of moments like this. Nostalgia's anticipated memories.

As we approach the house, Bob points to Buster's boulder and says, "So I'm guessing that's your favorite, right?"

"Well, yeah," I respond. "I suppose if I had to choose just one…." But truth is, I've already been through this exercise in my head many times before, and my favorite is a boulder back at the woods' edge where our lane turns in from the road. A sentinel I pass each time I return home. About waist-high and of no exceptional shape or color, it sits solo amid a stand of old spruce. A blanket of moss that's grown more luxurious with each season covers one side. There, improbably spanning its generous girth is a fissure. And in it, in that thriving moss, a spruce seedling has taken hold.

I can't say how many years this micro landscape has been in the making. Nor can I predict how tall this new spruce will grow or how deep its roots will sink. In my lifetime, I'll likely never know if, growing further into the cleft, the roots will push the boulder's two fissured segments apart. Or whether, growing out and around like an able hand's strong fingers, they will, if only for a time, help hold the pieces together.

IN CONCERT

"Why can't it just be quiet?" I erupt to my friend Kate who's come by for a glass of wine as another day of splendid weather winds down. We're out on the deck where we'd hoped to enjoy some long-overdue conversation and watch the sun set behind the Camden Hills. The light over the bay, though barely pinking up, is already coaxing from the resident bird life its familiar a cappella, the kind of accompanying music I'm convinced the sinking sun itself would request.

Instead, for the last half hour, pummeling the customary stillness and punctuating our entire conversation has been the piercing buzz and whine, the hard, wave-whacking slaps of two wet-suited Jet-Skiers in what appears to be a series of mind-numbing laps just offshore. Periodically, with revving engines, they move out, loop nearby Heart Island, and then return, as though they're messengers paid to deliver another example of enviable leisure-time entertainment. And lucky us, we've got ringside seats.

"Who are they?" asks Kate. "They don't look like kids."

"I think they're visiting someone on Pressey Village Road."

"So they don't live here."

No, and I suppose I could find solace in the fact that such intrusions on the water are rare here. Or that tomorrow morning, these enthusiasts, whoever they are, will likely haul away their Jet Skis, maybe to some lake where residents are more hospitable, less quick to brand such seemingly innocent fun as noise, and is certainly minus one sometimes cranky woman whose present reaction seems to suggest that here is an activity bordering on the felonious.

Kate has gone back to commenting on my garden, how lush it's

117

become. Customarily, any talk—better, any compliments—about my
garden and I'm all ears. But, still peeved, I'm simmering. As I am in a
movie theater where patrons often think they're back at home with their
remotes and bags of chips, their freedom to burst into dialogue or com-
ments at any time, and Bob, in that last-ditch tone parents deploy just
before their toddler explodes into a red-faced tantrum, urges, "Don't let
them distract you."

I blurt to Kate, "And why shouldn't it be quiet? Especially now, at this
hour?"

Sipping her wine, she looks up at the trees as though she may find
there an acceptable answer.

"Here's what I *really* want to know," I say, stabbing a finger toward the
water. "What's the point of those things anyway? I mean, really?"

I don't care if I'm being unreasonable or judgmental, or that I'm ele-
vating my quieter pursuits to something more worthy than Jet Skis. So be
it. Too often and for too long, we quieter folks have been under assault,
forced to dwell in the narrow chinks between the huge desires of those
seeking sound and speed regardless their cost. As though space and stillness were empty and, by way of some inalienable right, theirs alone to fill.
And just what red-white-and-blue rights, I want to shout at the foam-
spewing Jet-Skiers, extend to me or to the birds or mammals or whatever
glides and feeds beneath the churned up water whose home this is, too?

Should I be ironically or sadly encouraged that a recent study reports
the top neighbor-against-neighbor complaint isn't crime but noise?

Head bent, her long enviable hair cascading forward and making a
sort of screen that hides part of her face, Kate is studying her wine glass
as if, instead of pinot grigio, it held tea leaves that might tell her how
to respond to my puny and possibly misplaced tirade. I've always loved
her bubbly effervescence, her tendency to talk louder than necessary, no
doubt the product of coming from a family of nine. But now she's not
speaking at all, as if I were insisting on a total absence of sounds, her
voice included. I'm reminded suddenly of a sign I once saw posted on a
Quaker website: "In Case of Emergency, Please Be Quiet."

"Hah," I say, "listen to me." Meaning *don't* listen to me.

For all my reclusive habits, I also possess a loquacious social self who
can hold her own with lovers of chatter and gossip. Invite me to a cocktail
party and I'll not retreat to the corner where the least appealing bowl of
dip sits untouched. Pulling on that hat, I change the subject and ask, "So,
are you going to the Jazz Fest this weekend?"

Soon we're moving effortlessly from that weekend's schedule at the
Stonington Opera House to the upcoming opening of a new gallery in

the village. Then, as if our goal has shifted to curing the island's ills, we wind our way to conflict over school board issues and what might be done to offset rising heating fuel prices for fixed-income seniors in the winter months ahead. All the while, diminishing light and impending dusk have urged the Jet-Skiers homeward until, once more, to my ears anyway, a recognizable quiet has been delivered back to me, us, the quickening then settling birds.

*M*y family often complains about my hearing. Meaning, for example, in a house at night, with its normal hum and tick of refrigerator and furnace, I ask "What's that?" about a sound no one else notices. Or, in a new car, my ears alone are plagued by a mysterious rattle or squeak.

I can't say if my hearing is particularly acute. If so, perhaps it's compensation for my poor, corrected-since-the-fifth-grade eyesight, just as Bob's exceptional vision could in part account for his (by my standards) so-so hearing. Although in that, he and I may be typical. We female *Homo sapiens*, I've read, have a better-developed auditory sense. After all, we descend from the gatherers, the ones likely to keep offspring fed and safe, the quick responders to sounds of distress in the crib or a tardy teenager's key in the door. Our male counterparts, with their ancestral hunter linkage, require keen sight and spatial perception and have thus developed, it's been concluded, and mostly, I suspect, by men, a greater proficiency in driving, interpreting a GPS system, or reading the fine print of seldom-consulted instruction manuals.

Despite my family's assessment, I doubt my hearing is exceptional. What I do know, though, is that without fail and always on one of our first days back on the island, an exchange takes place. Perhaps it's on the deck in midafternoon as we're reading, or as we settle into bed at day's end.

"Listen." I nudge Bob and whisper, "Listen to that."

"To what?" His look is, understandably, wary.

"The quiet."

I'm sure I must be grinning, my arms open, at least figuratively, in wide embrace, in a Midas-and-his-gold moment when I want to scoop up as much of the treasure as I can. A gift of immeasurable value. The quiet, rich and full in itself.

*A*nd from which I must exempt the birds. That is, birdsong—or, as one urban houseguest assessed last summer, "What a racket!" when she stumbled into the kitchen at 6 a.m., looking as if the rowdy congress of crows on our lawn had in fact physically assaulted her.

Whatever the variety of species in the morning choir, whatever their tune or cadence, multiple variations of phonetic bird lyrics urging *"get up, get up"* erupt from forest and shore at first light. And here, in early June, that's not much past 4 a.m.

Peep, tweet, chirrup, trill. One note, two notes, three. Robins, jays, warblers. Flycatchers, nuthatches, chickadees. Squabbling gulls. Trunk-bonking flickers. Nearby, if I'm lucky, an impresario thrush flutes its ascending notes of impeccable purity, all breaking at last like struck crystal into cascading modulated harmonies, each ending ethereal, as though disembodied and assisted by a touched key or plucked string. Crows, too, are essential to the mix. Once, I believed that, in their raucous commotion and group commutes up and down the shore, their raspy cawing and rusty-hinged croaks had to be most feverishly pitched before the sun is fully up. But that was before I saw crows drive away a bald eagle hunting just off our shoreline, and, on Pressey Cove, flush a fox from the woods and chase it across the mudflats. I'm now convinced that anyone in need of a good guard dog might be better served by a murder of loutish, bullying crows.

As daylight asserts itself, the birds settle, their songs diminish, except perhaps in early season when males yet to hook up still advertise their talents by broadcasting ardor in endless refrain. The wind picks up and plays its music in the spruce limbs' *shoosh* or our big oak's leafy rustle, in a high tide's splash against rocks or the seethe of its retreat against a quickening onshore breeze—recognizable melodies and instruments, but forever changing in their shape and shift, push and pulse. In new worrisome numbers, the yammering red squirrels launch into the day, dash across our deck, their pattering against wood like a migrating herd of miniature wildebeest on a dry African plain. Putting out from harbor across the bay, distant lobster boats thump. The coffee maker burbles. As I clatter around the kitchen making breakfast, the phone may ring. Or Peter may arrive to finish hammering new boards as he replaces the garage's rotting trim.

But at first light, in the "racket" in which even crows get a pass, I lie still, eyes closed, and let my ears do all the work. I attempt to hoard the quiet, absorb it into my tissues, as though I can store it there like small pocketfuls of trail mix that later, far from here, feed a hungry hiker.

*N*oise. Most simply defined, it's a sound of any kind that's unpleasant, unexpected, undesired. As a word, it derives in part from *nausea*. And right there, the tip-off. Just what about nausea do we find pleasant? Still, identifying noise is sort of like attempting to define beauty. Noise, we might say, is in the ear of the beholder.

No doubt many folks would object to the charge that almost all of the world's noise is made by man and his machines. Or that—cue one grumbling houseguest—a plague of unwelcome sound rarely occurs in nature. And to be fair, the ears can be assaulted by what the natural world too often and mightily dishes out—like, say, the roar of a tornado bearing down. Even the noise-queasy among us must concede that some man-made sounds are not only unavoidable but often welcome. Hospital machines, for example, with all their incessant squawks, whirs, and beeps helping to save lives, not to mention the hurtling, siren-screaming rides that often precede them. Consider, too, how, with our violins and pianos, we're able to make sublime music. Let's not forget that with body alone, a gifted soprano's aria reaches for the heavens in ways that rival a thrush. And what in the natural world can best the first full-throttle cry of a newborn?

Most of us would probably agree that the shrill, grinding screech of a dentist's drill evokes discomfort by sound alone. Maybe we'd even call it noise. Elsewhere, there's much less agreement. Federal safety guidelines limit a worker's daily decibel exposure to just thirty 110-level minutes, but none are put forth for how long or at what amps that worker can later rave at a favorite dance club. Beethoven's "Ninth Symphony," cranked up to any elevated decibel level, may not be noise to the person for whom nearly muted rap is intolerable. No doubt objections to gas-powered leaf blowers wane a bit when it's our yard being cleared.

In *The Power of Place,* Winifred Gallagher points out the subjective and somewhat obvious: "Noise is any sound the individual listener doesn't like." My father enjoys television commercials at their ratcheted volumes, but I can't hit the Mute button fast enough. I object to the amped-up drone of overhead airport TV monitors installed at already fraught and noisy departures gates, but other passengers seem held in thrall by every word emitted via CNN as though such utterances were their last earthbound assurances before being lifted into the unbuttressed sky. Once, at an artist colony, the loud, thudding rock music a painter required to do her large canvases distracted this writer who needs quiet to hear the rhythms of her words. Generally, I dislike piped-in music at stores, and reject some marketing executive's notion that certain music propels us to spend. For one stressed grandma attempting to tick off another teenager's Christmas wish list, the blasting mayhem that passes for music at Abercrombie & Fitch gave me ample reason to flee. But I

have to confess that one Sunday afternoon in the produce section of a
Whole Foods Market, along with fellow shoppers of similar age, I welcomed the familiar strains of Bob Dylan and vintage '70s Motown—in
selecting music, someone had obviously gotten the demographics of the
customer base right. Bopping our heads, mouthing lyrics, we picked over
cauliflower, tossed kale into our carts, looking as though we might suddenly break into song or dance.

Certainly this island is not without its man-made noise. Here, the
usual summer orchestra of leaf blowers, weed whackers, power wash-
ers, jackhammers, and heavy construction equipment is translated into
piston-banging lobster boats leaving their moorings at dawn, rumbling
granite trucks, occasional shuddering dynamite blasts at nearby Crotch
Island quarry, whining chain saws, and throbbing generators after a
storm's blow-downs. And the late-night squealing of tires. In patterns
some call graffiti, others signatures, the laying of rubber tire tracks on
certain roads here is done by island youth who are known as "burners."
Such primal territorial marking can't be accomplished without standing on the brake and flooring the accelerator, melting rubber into pavement, maybe blowing out the rear tires or dropping a drive train, and
all at noise levels usually associated with NASCAR. But this isn't about
noise, say burner supporters, or even the potential danger to other driv-
ers on the roads. It's an island rite of passage, a handed-down tradition,
an artistic expression akin to folk art, and recently heralded as a cultural
phenomenon in no less than *The New York Times*. Still, I'm in agreement
with my neighbors. It's reason enough to keep this end of our dirt road
unpaved.

*M*y mother's early message about noise wasn't subtle.

"Be quiet. I can't hear myself think," she routinely hurled back to me
and my siblings from the car's front seat or while sitting at the kitchen
table with a late afternoon cigarette and cup of coffee.

By my unscientific observations, today's moms seem more immune
to noise. They may even be physiologically habituated to our culture's
ambient noise, to a chronic cranked-up amplitude of TV and video game
mayhem. When at last my stepdaughter shouts in the direction of the
family room, "Turn that down," it's possible my young grandson can't
hear her over his ratcheted up Nintendo, or that, in his eventual "What?"
he could as well be asking, "*What* noise?"

When noise is routine, there are fewer opportunities to listen to
quiet. But, in fact, we often refuse them. And reject solitude, too, quiet's

sidekick. We turn away from the reflection quiet often births, afraid, perhaps, we'll be ambushed by certain parts of our self that may show up. Or that we'll find ourselves in, as Plotinus called it, "the flight of the alone to the Alone." Noise and its myriad distractions shield, so that a dose of quiet may only translate as a painful pause before we're delivered back to friends and family, even strangers in a loud theater, a crowded shopping mall or pulsing stadium.

I'm reminded of the "time-out," that frequently invoked parental antidote to misbehavior, some of which is likely egged on by scheduling overload, lack of sleep or loud, continual stimulation. Children are sent to their rooms, and there, in spite of its being another place rigged with computers and TVs, the idea is to be still and quiet. To disengage. Defrazzle. How odd that time-outs are considered punishment! I wish they were mandated, as rigorously pursued as a daily run or workout at the gym. Better, as a friend once suggested, some legislator ought to propose a bill decreeing one day—just one?—as Day Without Noise. Yes, please, someone order us into a time-out.

Obviously, not everyone agrees. Here, for example, loving this island requires an embrace of its natural and inherent not-much-happens-here quiet. And here, too, in households and at gatherings, numerous are the attempts to fill, enrich, ignore, or even reject it. When defined as a lack of opportunity or exposure to experiences other than the familiar, the island's quiet may drive some of its long-time residents away. Visitors, too, wrestle with our brand of quiet. They arrive, marvel, soak it up, but readily admit they need only a small dose. Yes, there are those of us who visit and return, sometimes summer after summer, who may even try to figure out how to remain year-round. Vaster, though, are the numbers who agree, "Yes, it's lovely," but look stupefied when responding, "Me? Live here?" Their interest in visiting is more akin to the midwinter's trip to a beach resort where, as glossy brochures instruct, the idea is to "recharge the batteries." As if we were appliances that needed only a new filter or more efficient rinse cycle to clean out the sludge. It certainly seems foreign to me that a friend, an artist from New York City, once found it less frightening to walk the streets of Hell's Kitchen at midnight long before it became a desirable address than to walk in the woods at dusk where the quiet, he claimed, is "really creepy." To be more himself, he needed the buzz and hum, a 24/7 double-espresso jive. Which is not to say that from my wintertime perch in Chicago, I can't relate to local island friends, year-rounders who, come January, routinely head to New York or Boston for a "city fix."

As newborns, we enter the world and a hard *thwack* is one of our first welcomes. We answer with a lusty bawl. We let the world know with our loud hungering cry that we're ready for its rich cacophony and our mind's eventual natter and nag. But aren't we all born needing quiet, too? Remnants of our hushed, sloshing first world?

We each need to find a place—don't we?—where by choice we can be still, where we might hear the quiet center of our being, the voice within our thoughts. Some personal sanctuary or retreat. Be it an adolescent girl's wooden tree house perched above an alley, a stand of sheltering spruce near a crowded house, a muffled closet interior, an urban rooftop, a park bench at the farthest remove from traffic, a library or church, a patch of open meadow, a vacant lot, a dark room?

Almost daily, I'm reminded of how inordinately privileged I am to have this house, own this piece of land, particularly when so many people are without shelter of any kind. I'm fortunate to have found this island, its full and enriching pockets of quiet. Too few among us have the freedom or means to escape. Obviously, we can't all retreat to mountain or sea, pursue the path of hermit or recluse, run off to sanctuary or monastery. Or to a (relatively) quiet island in the northeast Atlantic. I'm damned lucky.

I envy those who've learned to meditate or find peace in some way, regardless their physical location. I empathize with those who, like me, never travel without earplugs or are tempted to spend money on expensive noise-cancelling headphones, whose idea of one form of Hell is to be sealed in an airplane where cell-phone usage is permitted throughout the flight. I come from a family of six who had to squabble over a single bathroom, share a clutch of tiny bedrooms and one TV, but I had a basement, a yard, a nearby patch of woods to roam, and a mother who needed to hear herself think. I was, and remain, lucky.

And as much as it's my gift to give, I now attempt to offer a measure of quiet to our grandchildren who visit us here. I try to redefine "time-out," redirect their attention to the wonders quiet invites. The yodel of a loon. The cheep of an osprey in its aerial acrobatics high above Heart Island instructing its offspring by example. A summer night's flash-lit, whispery walk to the shore, the emergence of bright bits of phosphorescence—"like stars!"—in still water stirred with a stick. A calm sea's quiet slap punctuated with the occasional *plock* of a mussel dropped by a hungry gull rising above tide-exposed rocks. The sloshing wade out to the rosy, coralline algae–spackled boulders revealed briefly at a low spring tide, or the hush in peeling back bladder wrack and discovering a sea star that without so much as a peep engulfs a sea urchin in spite of its spiny armor. Here, I have a chance to muffle the "Awesome!" evoked in explosive chase scenes on noisy monitors and screens and restore it to its rightful place.

*A*nd then rising above the jangle are those sounds as Proustian to the ear as madeleines to the tongue. Particular song lyrics or a melody do it for many of us. Hear a few phrases of what is vaguely familiar as lullaby and you might feel the rocking chair's rhythmic tilt and sway. Listen to a particular hymn or carol and feel again the hot, woolen press of fellow church members at a crowded midnight Mass, back when it was easier to believe in Santa or God.

Without fail, some sad band eking out another questionable rendition of "Feelings" spirals me back to my high school's Pops Are Tops dad-and-daughter dance and my awkward attempts to slow dance with my father in a decked-out gymnasium where no amount of crepe-paper roses could mask the sweat of the varsity basketball team's popular boys. To this day, any selection from the *West Side Story* soundtrack launches my return to my childhood basement rec room where, 33-rpm LP blaring, I strutted my stuff, as though, not Maria, I were a defiant Jet. And I ask you, my fellow time travelers in teenage heartbreak, who can forget what song was at the top of the charts when your boyfriend dumped you?

So many sounds burrow within our memory's quiet recesses. They emerge when we least expect them. Back in Illinois last November, battalions of gas-powered leaf blowers descended on our neighborhood, blasting their way across yards and parkway in a seasonal last hurrah. Just two days later, in typical Chicago fashion, several inches of snow blanketed the ground. I awoke before daylight the morning of the storm, after the plows had barreled through but before my neighbor's new yapping dog had cranked up. (Over yappers, I'll always choose loutish crows.) As I sat at my desk, the world seemed muffled, its gift of craved quiet so palpable it was as if a blanket had wrapped itself around me. Suddenly, unexpectedly, out of that just-before-dawn quiet, a snow shovel scraped against the sidewalk between our house and the neighbor's. Just like that, I was transported from desk to narrow twin bed. To the mornings my father awoke in the dark.

Even when the arrival of a new snowstorm meant another day without work on a construction site and fewer dollars in that week's paycheck, he left the house. He put his labor into the drifts. From the warmth of my bed and slumbering house, I listened to him scrape his way down the back walk to our driveway. There, soon, his truck idled, his only job on a stormy winter morning to save me from a cold walk to the distant bus stop.

Mankind's noises are, we know, mighty stuff, even its routine sounds, particularly when amplified by quiet. Likewise, the natural world is no slouch with its pervasive buzz, rattle and chuff. A chorus of rasp and whine, murmur and thrum, forever re-presenting itself with sounds that evoke, that arouse within us something visceral, sealing into our tissues a particular person or place. Or event.

Sounds like those of the sandhill cranes I once knew next to nothing about. How each fall, with scores of their kin, they wing their way south from Canada and the Arctic, often traveling up to 500 miles each day in dense, unraveling columns, in unfurling spirals and winding riverine patterns that make it look as if their job is to inscribe the sky, to calligraphically outline the invisible thermals while following interior maps we cannot read.

My introduction to sandhill cranes came through sound on a long-ago late autumn day in Illinois as I kneeled in the garden planting daffodil bulbs, and heard an unfamiliar sound overhead, a loud trumpeting trill, a rattling prolonged *kar-r-roo*. Each bugling call an insistent tug resounding in some deep inner part of me as though they were ancestral and piercing an ancient, dormant piece of my being awakened by sound—a sound I'd never heard, but remembered.

Tipping my head back, I scoured the sky. Except for a few wispy cirrus, the sky looked empty. But there, flying much higher than I'd imagined, was a distant, dark skein of birds. Their calling defied distance. It seemed too loud for the size of the bodies making it. As I watched and listened to their incessant trill—an announcement? a warning? the audible signaling of direction?—something inside me reverberated. My spine hummed. My rib cage expanded—as though I wanted, needed, to call out a response to one of the oldest flying creatures on earth, winged messengers whose ancestors stretch back to the Pleistocene, further back than my human mind could fathom.

For several minutes, it was as if the ground I stood upon rose. The cranes remembered their journey's markers, and the earth, with its long memory, remembered them. It rose into their wordless song that in the finest way had pierced a morning's quiet. A sound that is sealed in my memory. Imperishable, transcendent.

*B*ut sounds also terrify. Like those I've only had to imagine: air strikes and bombs detonating somewhere close, a tornado roaring overhead, or, on another in a long string of dark nights, the bedroom door clicking open then shut again and a floorboard groaning beneath heavy, frighteningly familiar feet.

Or like the concussive shuddering that shattered my sleep one unseasonably cold September night on the island, a blast and roar that rattled the windows, shook the bed. Fumbling for my glasses, no logic yet in sight and the last shreds of sleep yet to be ripped away, I wondered: How was it possible that a fast train was bearing down on our house? Or that a plane was about to drop from the sky onto the roof?

Suddenly, a bright light strafed the bedroom walls and windows, blindingly scoured the deck, garden and yard. And with it the snapped-into-place recognition: the engine and cranking rotary blades of a helicopter.

Inexplicably, one of the big elongated types used by the Coast Guard had swooped low over our house. Hovering above the bluff, its red lights pulsed. I pulled on my sweatshirt, hurried to the window and watched as the copter swung north, its downward-thrusting light beams blasting a swath of shoreline, setting ablaze everything it touched with so unnatural a brightness, the trees themselves looked stunned.

For several minutes, the helicopter, in all its thunder and blare, rose and banked, its sweeping, thrusting beam insistent, as though it intended to grab by the neck the shoreline's slumbering bayberry, its young spruce and rugosas, and shake out of them whatever they knew but about what offered no clue. At last, as the copter turned and headed out over the bay, it mercifully hauled away most of its throb and thud. But, as if I'd been forced to ingest it, my body still thumped, my heart banged.

At the window, home alone—Bob was back in Illinois—and hugging myself against the chill, I watched the copter circle nearby Heart Island and relentlessly jab its beam into the spruce-thick darkness. Though distant and muffled, the loud throbbing was still ominously present, until, in a final thudding bank and turn, the copter rose and sped further out toward Bradbury and Pickering Islands. Quiet began to reassert itself.

But so suddenly had the night, like me, been yanked awake, it was now unmistakably colder, darker. Just like that, robbed of all that is typical. The inhale and exhale of a still sea. The gurgle of the ebb. The drip and tick and pop of tidal creatures at home there. A feathery glide among the trees. In the underbrush, a startled scurry and retreat. The murmur and scritch, churr and creak. Night's symphony wrenched into discord.

A new, uninvited quiet had been thrust into the night that just hours before had ended a quintessentially gold and blue September day, its light, as if liquefied, spilling over the island—"like every clapboard just got a fresh coat of paint," my friend Bill had said of it. And perfect for being out on the water, I'd consciously noted while working in my garden and casting enviable glances at the calm and immaculate bay. A day so quiet and still that as a crow winged overhead, I heard the rasp of pinions against air.

In the palpable absence of the noise that had ambushed the night and seemed solely responsible for triggering whatever was happening and would happen next, I wanted to believe the helicopter was part of a drug bust, some federal agency's new crackdown on what newspapers had recently reported were large caches of marijuana plants being grown in camouflaged local woods clearings. But as the now distant, low-flying helicopter moved out over open water then looped other island shores, and the flickering lights of a small flotilla of boats crisscrossing the water joined in the choreography, a knot formed in my chest. I was witnessing a rescue.

Each year, there are drownings. Usually they involve a lobsterman or perhaps the crew of a dragger. Each tragic. Each a shock waiting to come ashore to family and friends, and, after, the ache, like rippling water, spreading into the entire community. Most times, these tragedies occur far from shore. There are no witnesses, even the few who, like me, watch rescue boats and helicopters from nearby safety. Who recognize that somewhere out there, a life's plenitude is slipping away, is beyond grasp.

For close to an hour, I watched the distant tableau. Our shore-facing windows with their expansive view of the bay and its far islands made of my vantage a kind of movie screen, albeit of scenes rendered mostly in silhouette and blinking lights. Beyond its edges the helicopter occasionally disappeared, then circled back into view. Boats glided in and out. As if all this were only being dramatized in a movie and someone had hit the Mute button. If only.

If only, I still sometimes think, the morning after the search-and-rescue had not dawned clear and bright, had not been quiet in its usual way. But, as was customary, clots of wrens nattered near my bedroom window. Crows, raucous in the nearby spruce, bickered. Worse, a cidery-hued light thick as syrup spilled over the calm bay whose only fault looked to be one of overly extravagant dazzle. Another gorgeous morning intent on its business, abuzz with energy, intently alive. In spite of whatever had happened. And all of it testifying to what I already knew: there is room in such beauty for terrible pain and grief.

Among the morning-after's first man-made sounds was my neighbor's call to deliver the news. A kayaker who'd left shore at 3 p.m., waved to her family and promised to return in time for dinner, didn't. A few hours later, a search began. About the time the helicopter and boats disappeared from my vantage point, her overturned kayak was discovered, and not much later, washed ashore on a nearby island, her body. Sad truths rippled out into the dark night until, for most of us, they crashed ashore in a calm morning's spectacular light. Susan, a widely known and loved summer resident, whose family had been coming to the island for decades, was gone.

There were, of course, and for days to come, so many particulars that in such aftermath fill the gaps, attempt to glue together fragments of what is known. A new kayak but an old proficiency on the water. A good life jacket but no cold-water gear. An outgoing tide. A stiff breeze that blew up in late afternoon. Strong currents in that part of the bay.

So much can't be known about what went so terribly wrong in fatally cold water, in a familiar archipelago, with land and its certainty so heart-breakingly within a kayaker's view. Imaginations blast open the chinks the known facts try with each telling to seal, all prompted perhaps by the recollected sounds of a recognizable and now gone laugh, of whispered intimacies, of a voice's lilt in particular words, favorite phrases.

But certain things about that night can never be known. Was there in the end a struggle or protest? Or, in slipping away, a silence?

On another night, this one in 1952, when John Cage's notorious composition *4'33"* was first played, what would I have heard then? Often referred to as his "silent piece," and named after the length of its three movements, the pianist played not a single note. Instead, assisted by a stopwatch, he signaled each movement by lifting and clicking shut the piano lid, turning and brushing open the score's note-less pages. Else-where in the hall, air vents likely hummed and ticked. At the rear, where the hall opened onto a forest, the wind blew through trees. Rain splat-tered the pavement, plocked against the roof. Some members of the audience began to nervously cough, shift uncomfortably in their seats. They whispered, muttered, sighed. Increasingly bewildered and indig-nant, many, with clattering footsteps, stormed from the hall. Had I been there, I wonder, what would I have listened to? What would I have heard?

It wouldn't have been silence. So prove the experiments that have shown how, even with the best earplugs or fanciest headphones, or in a specially rigged sound-proofed chamber, we are able to hear the hiss and throb, the hum and roar of our beating heart, our circulating blood. I wonder, too, if there's not some low-level but detectible ping of firing neurons, like a computer's hard drive storing a new batch of data. In other words, aren't we likely to hear ourselves listening?

"Try as we may to make a silence, we cannot," Cage himself declared.

He agreed with the many who believe that silence, when defined as a total absence of sound, does not exist. Instead, Cage aimed to redefine silence as the absence of intended sounds.

Like one of Rauschenberg's large canvases covered in white paint and seemingly blank but really a home to whatever shape-shifting and unintended shadows different light or conditions give it, Cage's composition is a sort of intentionally made silent frame filled with accidental sounds of the environment. They are the music. And, indeed, on another night without rain, performed in a hall not open to wind in the trees and with another audience better clued in, the composition of Cage's "silent piece" would—wouldn't it?—sound very different. Endless variations seem possible. In the absence of the intended dwells the presence of the ever-changing unintended.

Of course things do happen without sound. Or seem to, if experienced from a distance.

As in a tableau of helicopter and boats. Or in the moments after the phone rings and a voice on the line delivers from some distant place the news you want to refuse.

Some nights, I haul our telescope onto the deck, and far from the interference of ambient light, peer into the distant star-studded skies. Were it powerful enough, perhaps I'd witness a star's fiery implosion or the disintegration of a meteorite into bits of dust, each without sound to my earthly ears millions of light-years away.

For weeks during the Gulf War, I watched generals on television point at monitors, urging me to watch American bombs blow up bridges, roads, vehicles, and houses as though they were mere targets in the latest edition of some kind of "surgical strike" video game played without sound half a world away. Years later, over and over, my television screen filled with images of planes hitting New York's towers. Like most people, I witnessed those events from a distance, in images that needed no sound. But individuals close and firsthand, when recounting the planes' impact and exploding fireballs, often began with what that morning they heard. Others claimed that in the moments after, in spite of the loud, terrifying tumult and chaos, all sounds vanished, an absence filling with what for a time must've seemed like silence.

For the island family who waited on a cold September night, their rejection of a body's indisputable fact may have been a swelling whimper or uncontrollable wail. But I can imagine it soundless. How denial's cry launched into the night sky and lodged for a time between distant stars beyond our human ear's capacities, until, reentering the earth's atmosphere and rather than disintegrating out of hearing's range, it smashed back whole, a shattering roar no amount of silence, however defined, can absorb or deflect.

*T*he absence of language. Isn't that also what we often mean by silence? What isn't audibly voiced? The unuttered apology, proposal, or offer. The failed delivery of an outcome we'd prayed for. Our mind's booming blather that isn't made known through language. Or what of it has been silenced.

A long wordless pause in a telephone call is, we might say, silence. Or our reaction to what stuns: "I was silent. I couldn't speak." On a September morning, what I didn't know about the previous night's search-and-rescue attempt bordered on what seemed like silence until my questions found answers in my neighbor's spoken words.

Though we wait for the sound of a key to probe the door and for familiar steps to echo in the hall, it's the recognizable greeting afterward that we most hunger for. One word. One sound. Ten thousand emotional inflections.

In *The World of Silence,* Swiss theologian Max Picard claimed that silence is necessary for language's birth. It's the source from which language springs forth, and to which it must constantly return in order to be re-created. Only in relation to silence does sound, most notably language, have significance. And language, we know, is powerful stuff. According to Genesis, God from silence *spoke* the world into existence.

As a toddler, my nephew was by no means silent. No slouch in the walking, gesturing, chattering category of miniature hominid, he busily and doggedly cruised through the physical world, pointing and assigning to everything the same name—his one-syllable, obsessively uttered word "dee." And though followed not long after with the more recognizable "bye-bye," an inkling of the verbal torrent soon to come, it was that first syllable approximating human language that spanned a wordless gulf, linked him to others of his kind, a little and not so very still or silent star in the human galaxy.

Also distinguishing him from the cats in the house or the birds on the yard's feeders that flew off each time he boisterously banged on the window, an individually achieved cause-and-effect he acknowledged with a merry clap, was his uniquely human consciousness. Watching him stumble and run, hum and howl, I wondered back then: So what is he thinking? Experts claim that what we consider human thought can't really occur until we achieve language adequate to make connections, to understand some of the often complex and ever-changing relationships in the world of our species. And to articulate such, if only to ourselves.

"Unthinkable silence," the phrase that's used. Not about pre-language toddlers, though possibly about a world leader who does not raise his voice against genocide, or the crafters of policy who don't address our march toward a climate-change crisis. Nor does it apply to my mother, who, through much of her last year of life, was silent. But not, I'm convinced, without thought. Rather, thought withheld. Not articulated.

"So what do you want for lunch?" I routinely asked after reading to her the daily menu options during one of my visits to the Arizona nursing home, in the room she rarely left.

From her cranked-up position in bed or from her wheelchair with its tray already snapped into place, she answered with a vacant look or shifted her gaze to something beyond me, across the room, vaguely near the window. She voiced no answer, not from a failure to understand, nor solely, I was convinced then, because she possessed little desire to eat. Finally she shrugged. Or said simply, "Soup."

To the social worker, therapist, and pastor, she had little to say. To my "Mom, should we try someone else?" there was no response.

Though multiple complications following her stroke made holding the nursing-home phone to her ear difficult, and, as she weakened, impossible, she refused the new mobile phone with its big easy-to-read numbers and lightweight earbuds. When I called, I couldn't speak to her unless my father was in the room holding his phone to her ear, in what, without fail, became monologue. Mine. Mostly, she just looked at us as we talked, her mouth sagging, slightly agape, as if she'd forgotten what it was for.

"Before words, before sentences, before paragraphs and parts of speech, there was only the sound of my mother's voice," memoirist Debra Marquart has written. Before the interruptions of the outside world. Before its recognizable consonants and vowels. My mother's voice. I was already struggling to remember the timbre and pitch of it when one day, on another of those mornings I could neither trick nor cajole from her more than a syllable or two, with my latest week-long visit to Arizona quickly winding down, with the spring daffodils beginning to bloom and the Prescott foothills starting to let go their chill, I wheeled her outside. I parked her chair beside a bench near the Center's front door. I adjusted her cap and tucked tight her blanket in the way, with life's customary reversal of roles, she once did mine. For several minutes, as had become routine, we sat without speaking.

"Listen." Her voice was faint. I leaned in. "Listen to that bird." She pulled her hand from beneath the blanket and pointed at a sparrow beneath the eaves of the entrance carport.

"Oh, yes," I acknowledged, "a sparrow."

"Sounds pretty. Like spring."

"Yes, Mom. Spring." I took her hand, once so accomplished with needle and brush and now so idled, its covering of skin so tissue-thin and horrifyingly bruised by IVs, it looked as if, from some dark spill, patches of black and blue endlessly seeped.

Together, we watched the sparrow busily flit and flick, putting finishing touches on a nest. Occasionally pausing, tilting its head, as though assessing the results and, apparently, pleased, the sparrow emitted a brief, bright, self-congratulatory chirp. Watching, head back, mouth open, my 78-year-old mother resembled a kind of young bird herself. She'd become so thin, was so easy to lift even by the slightest built CNA, I could imagine her bones as hollow. What of her hair remained was not much more than down.

In the parking lot, a car door slammed. A van door—*swoosh*—opened, and then again—*swoosh*—clicked shut. Behind us, footsteps clacked against concrete. When the foyer door slid open, a vacuum's whine leapt forth like a fenced-in dog glimpsing an open gate, then quieted as the door sighed shut. Somewhere in the distance, traffic hummed. Nearby, among the dogwoods, other sparrows chittered. But for us, there was only one.

For days, I'd worked so hard to fill the space between us with her words, the articulation of whatever she was thinking, feeling, wanting. But, perhaps, whatever words her mind had shaped, had risen to her tongue from silence's deep well, had seemed to her inadequate. Unnecessary. None could fill the gulf separating us. Between where I was and where she'd retreated.

I'd been so quickly convinced that a kayaker would do whatever she could to upright her vessel, to struggle to reach the safety of shore before hypothermia immobilized her limbs and pulled her head under. But it took me so long to recognize my mother had abandoned recovery. She'd given herself over to the cold water.

Maybe the words I'd been seeking from her were mere camouflage, and necessary only to me. I'd needed them to hide what I, like my father, wished not to see. Or hear. The silent after.

I know from the hospice folks who helped my mother later, and from volunteer training I've done with them since, that it's widely believed our ability to hear is the last of our senses to go. And so to patients we talk, sing, read aloud. But it was *my* hearing that had been the problem. For too long in my mother's final year, I didn't hear her. I didn't recognize that in her silence, she was listening. Listening for what, I can't say. I don't know. And maybe she didn't know either. Maybe I should've asked.

But on that day, in the sun's warmth, as we listened to the cheep of a busy sparrow, in the wordless space expanding not between but around us, I learned that for all our good intentions, words do fail. Sometimes they become just noise.

I didn't need them, hers or mine. Not that day, as I sat with my mother, my first instructor in quiet, who, I'd almost forgotten, needed to hear herself think.

*A*t last the work is done at our end of the road. No more grating, dumping, rumbling, whining, shouting, beeping, grinding, screeching. Potholes have been filled, the gravel surface graded and raked, the new culvert dug, the road section subject to washout widened, the fallen trees limbs chipped and hauled away. Blissfully, as though on cue, John and his crew have wrapped up whatever at the nearby Dalton's required chain saws and a chorus of hammers and power drills.

The usual quiet has settled again like a welcome coverlet against a night's chill. Late afternoon and the sun has sunk a bit lower but is still warm on my back and arms as I put the finishing touches on my too-soon-to-slumber garden. I bend and stoop to trim, prune, stake, to prepare for a last dressing of compost. In the weeks ahead, I'll erect the deer fencing and rig up whatever I think this winter will keep voles from nibbling the trunk of the new red maple sapling planted just weeks ago. My spade tings, my shovel scrapes. Shears snap and clip. Were this a musical composition attempting to frame unintended sounds, I'd put down my tools and embrace what is unique to the afternoon but is nevertheless familiar: the nearby plethora of buzzing bees plundering the snakeroot's blossom-packed wands, the muttering crows paddling the air overhead, a morning shower's last drip plocking from awning edge to wood-planked deck.

Silence? Perhaps not. But a familiar and longed for quiet loud in its pronouncement: the seasons will soon irrevocably shift.

Already the red squirrels have revved up their pre-acorn-thunking frenzy. Muttering eiders are rafting up in larger numbers on the bay. The woodpile is stacked against the garage like neat rows of sentries guarding the periphery. Golden days have begun to taper off. The world slows. Ahead and too soon, the first frost, the harder freeze. The world closing in on itself.

There's always a particular hush in such waiting. And on the island, it's always seemed to me, there is so much waiting. For the seasons to change, the lobsters to shed, fog to lift, rain to fall, sap to run, frost to leave the ground, ice cakes to empty the coves. For the eaglet to fledge, the osprey to return, the power to come back on. For a lone kayaker to return.

Pausing in the wings, winter waits, ready for its cue. And, as though in preparation for the bluster and howl of its entrance in the next act, we've been given this hush, an anticipatory hint of snow's recognizable muffle after a blowing blizzard's retreat.

Not so, of course, in late spring's run up to summer, when days grow warmer and molecules accelerate and bang about, when gases and solids and liquids expand, elbowing each other for more space. When animals and birds, awakened from long slumber or in arrival and a bit bedraggled from a long and turbulent flight, are on the move. When frogs with their vocal sacks bulging take over the creeks, and spotted salamanders, at their peril and in spite of nightfall's cover, emerge from beneath leaf and log and creep across our road to the vernal pools where they spawn. When skunk cabbage uncoils, flings back its cowled hood, and things in the garden, almost imperceptibly at first, shift. For a time, it's quiet there as bulb and root dig in. Although, even at the height of summer's bolt and thrust, I have to confess my reputedly high-attuned ears can't detect the sounds unique to a riot of growth, not like those of the farmer who, standing in his fields at night, claims of his mid-August corn, "It squeaks."

Recently, I stumbled upon the words of Italian futurist Luigi Rossolo, who in 1916 wrote that the "much poeticized silences" of nature and country life are actually made up of an "infinity of noises," each with its own timbres and rhythms. Indeed, he proclaimed, without our fellow living creatures who vibrate and buzz, coil and unfurl, bulge and bleat, life in the country would be a "tomb without noises."

In harmony or discord, these are the sounds—or are they noises? and might I not just let philosopher or linguist dispute over it?—that belong to this place, to those who dwell here, sinking roots, building nests. Each being emitting sounds into space and time. Sounds that join one big cacophonous composition.

And go where? I have to wonder. Does it all rise? Swarm among the stars? And from up there, what is heard of us down here? A deafening crackle? The static of a radio frequency impossible to contain in a single bandwidth? A long uninterruptible hum, a terrifying white noise of monstrous proportion? Of hiss and spatter, clatter and crash?

Imagine if such storms of sound molecules were to vibrate, accelerate, expand, and in so doing, require more and more space. What then would happen to us? Beneath such crushing weight, wouldn't we perish?

Maybe to survive the world's noises and sounds, whether intended or accidental, spoken or inwardly nattered, sung or played or withheld, it all needs to rise, leave us, be lost to our ears. Absorbed somehow, somewhere. But then don't we need, too, some measure of rich and deep quiet, no matter how brief? Not just so we can hear what the world is newly offering up or figure out what it is we're listening to, or for, but to retrieve within it the people, places and important events that belong to certain sounds, and have shaped us.

That remind me again of who I am. Trill and scrape and a sparrow's cheep.

At last, as though in answer to a distant siren's call, I succumb to this fine afternoon's tug. I put down my pruning shears and stretch out on the lawn where a swath of sun looks its warmest. Overhead, the spruce limbs sigh in a freshening breeze. Nearby, a resident crow family erupts into a loud back-and-forth calling, some kind of argument in which the parents may still be dismayed by their newest offspring's lack of flying prowess. And though they keep on with their throaty croaking, their loud *caw-caw*, I'll concede it would probably be too quiet around here without them. Through the woods, I hear my neighbor fire up his mower. Somewhere out on the road, a truck rumbles past. Against the ground beneath me, my percussionist heart drums its persistent beat. Here we all are, on the empty score sheet another new day hands us, each of us individually and in concert making our music.

GUIDING ME HOME

$\mathcal{T}$he forecast had predicted a thunderstorm, possibly severe. But the morning dawned still and clear, awash with light. At noon, only a few fat clouds ballooned over the Camden Hills. Perhaps, I thought, we'd gotten a pass.

But as late afternoon tipped toward evening, and with what seemed like little warning, a black wall of incoming weather tore across the bay. I'd no sooner closed all the doors and windows when the skies opened. Shuddering gusts of rain pummeled the glass slider where I stood looking out. The wind ratcheted up, scouring the length of our deck, tossing chairs, boosting the table. Overhead, the besieged roof creaked and moaned.

Clearly I was being warned. Get away from the windows. Seek shelter on the other side of the house. But I was mesmerized by the malevolency unleashed from what had been a benign blue, by the now heaving ocean swells and the way, in shades of charcoal and slate, the sea and sky seemed to merge into something no longer liquid or permeable.

And, there was the wind. The swollen din of it. Deep sustained notes above the roof's complaint and the window's high-pitched rattle and thrum. And then, one loud sharp retort as though a gun had been fired close by and was somehow involved in transforming the deck's sun umbrella into a missile. Launched the length of the deck, it heaved up the table, smashed into a pair of Adirondack chairs, splintered their seats and broad arms, all skidding at last into a tangled heap wedged among the whipped branches of the climbing rose. And amazing, I thought at the time, how so cleanly, as if with surgical skill, the wind had uprooted the potted lobelia and my entire crop of basil.

I should've been watching the trees.

The spruce trees closest to the house, just a few feet from the glass slider where I'd become immobilized. They'd have instructed me that this was no ordinary summer storm. They might've succeeded in booting me away from the window glass sooner. But then I wouldn't have seen how the bullying wind stripped away pieces of bark like flayed skin, pushed and contorted the thick limbs as if they were just sticks in a child's game. Nor would I have seen the way, in flanking the house and its exposed shorefront expanse of glass, the spruce were taking the wind head on.

The first tree to go was the largest. After all the pitching and heaving, a surrender I didn't immediately register. So tentative at first—branch tips reaching out to the window, with no more, it seemed, than a polite tapping on the glass as if awakening someone from a nap. And then a sudden closeness as though offering for my closer inspection the green lichen splotching its trunk. Surely a splintering noise must've erupted when the tree broke through the deck rail, some kind of loud thud when other parts of it further up pressed against the eaves and crushed the flashing, all that immense weight coming to rest against the roof, the corner of the house. But I heard none of it above the wind's unrelenting howl. As if, in silent advance and so slowly at first not to be noticed, the spruce tilted, leaned, until trunk and limbs and a tangle of branches filled the expanse of what moments before had been a view of Heart Island and the churning sea. Suddenly, I was looking up into the tree from a perspective I'd never imagined. The way a bird might.

Convinced the cellar was where I needed to be, I turned away. But by the time I'd made the short journey down the hall, I could see more trees had lost their fight. Five spruce trees now sprawled across the deck, their weighty limbs jammed against the house as though such ballast had become necessary, would prevent me from being plucked away, Oz-like, by the wind.

Minutes later, it was over. The wind ceased. The rain stopped as abruptly as it had begun. Gushing gutters merely dripped. The sky lightened. As though it had thinned, the sea settled, again distinguished itself from the sky. Already, blue peeked through.

*F*rom my desk on the other side of the house, I look out to a small stand of trees and a strip of woods bordering our property. Just beyond the window are two old spruce trees, though it's easy to think of them as one, so closely have they become entwined. Many years ago, long before this house was even a blueprint, these two trees, mere seedlings then, emerged side by side. Simultaneously, their roots deepened, lengthened, re-branched. Over time, they competed with their growing neighbors but in a more proximate battle for the same light, the same drops of rain and snow-melt's ooze. Each withstood the wind, survived the seasons. And then at some point—as an accommodation? a necessity?—the trees joined. The trunk of the one on the downward slope grew up and around the other, its uppermost roots exposed above ground, thick gnarled arms that almost encircle the other tree's base. From there, for a good two feet up, the trunks appear almost as one, the seam between them so tight, I couldn't if I wanted to wedge a pencil between them. At this point, the trunks separate, but several feet further up, just where it looks like they began in earnest to grow apart but then had a change of heart, two big knots emerge. Over some period of years, here is where the trees touched, rubbed, abraded one another's bark until, through some convergence of factors, they merged, a thick-knotted spot in which it's easy to imagine veins coursing with sap, flowing from one tree to the other. Overhead, their branches spread, entwine. Together, they fill the vacant air above them, above me, this room where I work. In more human terms, they stand shoulder to shoulder, hands clasped, heads canted into the wind.

I could, I suppose, be accused of sentimentality in seeing the human in trees. But the perception of physical characteristics shared by trees and humans has a long history. According to Lisa Knopp in *The Nature of Home*, such perceptions led many ancient civilizations to believe trees had souls, were living, conscious beings that created the weather, gave voice to oracles, allowed crops to grow and women to reproduce. Later, she writes, civilizations believed deities more closely resembled the human body and weren't actual trees but resident spirits within them, with the ability and freedom to depart their leafy abodes whenever they wished. Though the direct links between trees and deities may have lessened over the years, trees are everywhere present—Moses and the burning bush, for example. Abraham and the oak. Buddha and a bo tree.

Of more recent vintage, Sarah Orne Jewett, in writing about a Maine maritime village in *The Country of the Pointed Firs,* saw in the great army of fir trees soldiers that "seemed to march seaward, going steadily over the heights and down to the water's edge"—a battalion that advances to greet and protect. Elsewhere, poet William Carlos Williams wrote: "… the wise trees/stand sleeping in the cold."

In literature and art, we're still in the business of finding the human in a tree, be it a face on a trunk or the toss of hair in wind-pitched branches. With mere adjectives we project onto trees our human emotions. As was evidenced, I can't help but note, by my long-ago leading role in our third-grade theatrical production, "Weeping Willow's Happy Day."

And so, perhaps, it wasn't overreach when, with post-storm amazement, I recognized in the minimal damage done to this house that the fallen spruce trees had not so much given up and heaved themselves at it, but in their final surrender attempted to embrace it, maybe even protect it. Nor was I the only person to tip my hat in this direction. The morning after the storm, Chris, an arborist and tree removal expert, came to survey our felled spruce. Walking around and among the thick trunks and upheaved roots, he shook his head, assessing the angle and location of where these immense beauties leaned against the house, considering, I assumed, whatever means of removal might be attempted, given such narrow access between fallen trees and bluff's edge and house. Instead, running his hand over the trunk of the tree that was first to go, he said, "Oh my, but she put up a wicked-good fight."

Even coming at it with scientific knowledge and years of experience, Chris appeared to see in the aftermath what I did. He appreciated the struggle. How it wasn't foolish to suggest our spruce trees were valiant in the way they held ground, fought the wind head on. How, when they were forced to surrender, they did so, but only with reluctance.

As though he'd joined me at the rain-blasted window, Chris seemed to see how the first tree—*she*—didn't so much pitch or fall as lean, slowly, against the deck and house, upending, but only in a final slump, her roots. As did the others soon after. One by one, they too surrendered to the storm's might, went down as they were forced to, but gently, kindly, causing the least possible damage. As old friends would.

"*B*ut look at your view!" my friends and neighbors declare as they peer out from the house at a new, nearly unobstructed vista. They see a watery expanse pocked with small islands and, on the bay's far shore, the distant Camden Hills tacking down the horizon.

When I look out at the prospect our spruce trees once framed, I see only that they're gone. One entire side, half the frame, is missing. I see absence. Of rustle and dapple, of enclosure and embrace. Of birds and squirrels, the seep of sap. Of needles pelting the deck. Five healthy spruce trees no longer part of what I expect, have come to know.

Gone now, too, is the hammock that swung between two of those spruce, long the ideal place to settle in the afternoon shade. There, beneath a broad canopy of rustling limbs and an occasional plash of light, Bob and Ben napped, Michael read, I daydreamed, Craig sought solace after James's death. A fixed place—or so I'd thought—that, with the screen and protection of branches, formed the kind of physical shelter that philosopher Gaston Bachelard claimed was a requisite for reverie, where dreams and versions of our self blur, expand, grow more distinct.

Over many years, I've been lucky to live with special trees, beloved trees with which I've shared the same molecules of air. The big buckeye at our home in Barrington, with its picture-book pyramidal shape, broad low branches, bright spangles in spring. The stooped apple trees behind the Indiana farmhouse where my grandparents traveled on weekends after my grandfather retired and before my grandmother was crippled by her stroke, a mere handful of happy summers. My childhood's shade-gifting elms on Oakdale Avenue ravaged one summer by Dutch elm disease, chainsawed and trucked off by city workers indifferent to how our neighborhood suddenly looked stricken, painfully bare, every flaw blazing beneath the unrelenting sun. For weeks after, in the altered light and temperature and shadows on my bedroom walls, I awoke confused, convinced in those first few minutes that I'd fallen asleep the night before in someone else's house.

But the most important tree in my personal pantheon has to be the scraggly crabapple in the yard of my childhood house. What it lacked in looks, it more than made up for with mettle and tenacity, talents I failed to marvel at then—how that tree survived no matter how many twenty-penny nails I hammered into it and in spite of an inhospitable position behind the garage, wedged between sidewalk, alley, and the steel drums where, in the early '60s, we were still allowed to burn garbage and leaves. I knew it only as home to my tree house, a simple, cobbled-together enterprise of scrap lumber and old wooden fruit crates possessing a direct lineage to my early, cruder shelters of abandoned appliance cartons or blankets draped over chairs and porch railings. There, many years before discovering Woolf's *A Room of One's Own*, I first experienced the yin and yang of safety and freedom, the joys and necessities of an unshared space. In solitude, I escaped chores, a crowded household, carrying with me an aching, inexplicable loneliness, a late summer afternoon's boredom, the worry over whether boys are ever attracted to a plainish girl with bad bangs and eyeglasses.

With word and image, I can attempt to paint my experience in that tree house. But, like the sway of my car on Route 175 as I approach the island for the first time each summer, much of my connection to that tree house is kinesthetic. It resides in tissue and bone, in the physical memory of the pitch and dip of wind-tossed branches, the fall of light and air on my skin through the small fluttering leaves I sat among. Memories retained not in the mind but in the body, like those the Heart

Island osprey must know alighting, wings spread, on the same stick nest she returns to each spring. Or those of the young jays in their first solo flights out and away from our now toppled spruce. What, I wonder, will the crows retain in their bones of our fallen trees, where in a foggy day's earliest hours they hunkered in the dripping branches, calling out in a raucous choir of rusty-hinged croaking?

"What Aunt Debbie needs at her house in Maine is a tree house," my ten-year-old nephew, Michael, proclaimed to his mother, pledging to commence construction during an upcoming visit, a zeal I don't aim to diminish.

And actually, he's tapped into more than just a childhood fantasy. The importance of trees and the essential vantage points they offer were long ago recognized by our hunter-gatherer ancestors. Yes, we've long been instinctively drawn to watery terrains. As Winifred Gallagher in *The Power of Place* observes, even if only choosing photographs and landscape paintings to adorn our walls, we're still pulled as though by tidal currents to creeks, lakes, waterfalls, the crashing surf—all good news for the seascapes proliferating on the island's gallery walls. But close on the heels of water's attraction, Gallagher claims, is a combination of meadow and treed savannah, ancestrally linked as we are to landscapes that offer prospect and refuge. Not only did our predecessor hominids want to peer out and gather information about the whereabouts of, say, sabertoothed tigers, they sought a safe, sheltering place in which to hide while doing it. Ever since, we've been genetically and behaviorally scripted.

Just in placing a bench in a quiet shaded corner of an ordered garden among spaced trees and easy-to-navigate surfaces, we still seek an ideal combination of prospect and refuge. Other examples abound. And many support the observation by Knopp that if "a setting is forested, we like open spaces in it, and if it's prairie-like, we like some trees." Or in Gallagher's riff, man is "the species who, where there are no trees, plants them, and where there are trees, cuts them down."

Now, where forces beyond my control snatched five healthy spruce trees that made of a hammock a refuge, I plan a new garden. I'll rototill, dig, plant and mulch, watch as whatever trees or shrubs I plant sink their roots—none of which in my lifetime will likely obliterate my new, enviable prospect. But unlike my friends, I can't see the new view yet. I see only the ghosts of old arboreal friends without hearts or minds or nerves, but who were—mea culpa for adjectives conferring emotion—vital and generous.

*I'*m a lucky one, I had to remind myself. The storm—actually a microburst, as it has since been classified—tore through the island's northwest corner and was so severe and fickle that folks on the southeast side of the island saw not a drop of rain while those further north and west of me had their house roofs pried off and wide swaths of their woods mown from shore to road as though an army of bulldozers had barreled through.

I was also lucky to be first in line with Chris and Ed, whose list of islanders requiring their services already ran long.

At 7 a.m., as promised, Ed rumbled down our drive in a vehicular hybrid of cherry picker, crane and flatbed. Typically used to hoist concrete foundation panels for big commercial buildings, this was the tool of choice for lifting five 50-foot spruce trees off and over my house. In its cab was an instrument panel arrayed with gauges and joy sticks. A young boy's dream.

As Ed sidled it up as close as he could to the house, Chris climbed onto the roof, up among the limbs of the fallen trees where more than half the spruces' height still reached for the sky but at an unfamiliar angle. Deftly flipping a few switches, Ed raised his crane rigged with a kind of sling that Chris, balancing up on the roof, began sliding beneath a tree trunk.

"We're going to have to lift up each tree and then cut it, probably somewhere just below the spot where it rests against the roof," Chris had explained earlier. "We'll use a sling to hold it. Otherwise, we just cut and let it drop and you'll have an awful mess of tree falling back on the house. Last thing you want is more damage....Oh, and," he added rather nonchalantly, "we'll need to lift each one up and *over* the house. No way we're going to get Ed's rig in on the other side where they fell."

The sudden screaming eruption of Chris's chain saw shattered the early morning's customary quiet. Rousted from their perches were the crows, who, in their proprietary patrol, had winged in for a closer look when the crane arrived only to discover that today, clearly, there were more peaceful places to breakfast. As Chris's whining saw bit deeper into the trunk, Ed incrementally raised the crane. Slowly, the sling lifted the cut half of the first tree up and away from the house.

For the next two hours, theirs was a brilliant choreography of chain saw and crane, though not without a few hair-raising moments. One tree nearly slipped out of the sling. Another, while being raised over the house, began to spin, gaining momentum with each revolution, all the while pointing downward spear-like and taking aim at the roof before finally being swung away from the house. Nor was the whole process without some pain as I watched such big, healthy trees being brutally cut and unceremoniously hoisted away.

Before morning's end, all five had been limbed, lifted onto a flatbed, and laid out side by side for a trip to the mill. And the upended roots that for so many years had hugged as best they could the thin topsoil over granite ledge? Those last parts of the trees to which Chris took dead-aim with his chain saw? I was surprised again at how shallow such roots were, on an island where most roots run deep.

"*O*ne needs to know the trees of a place," poet Wallace Stevens once asserted about attachment to a physical place.

Long a student of Midwestern oak and maple and other deciduous trees, I've had to learn conifers since coming to the island. Spruce, balsam fir, pine, hemlock. Also, the beautiful larch. A conifer but not evergreen, a larch, in a final golden blaze each fall, beguilingly drops all its needles, calling attention to itself, particularly if in a sunlit meadow.

I can now distinguish spruce by its square needles that can't be rolled between fingers and a fir's flat ones that can. Or the way a spruce's cones hang like beckoning piñatas at a child's party and a fir's sit as upright as attentive pupils at their desks. I'm learning better how to read the forest— not just in the identification of species but in the ways similar diameters of neighboring trunks say less about age than the fierce competition for the same limited moisture and light. Though I remain largely powerless in the damage they inflict, I'm better able to recognize the signs of budworm, witches'-broom, woolly adelgid, and the choke hold of mistletoe.

I also know where, close to shore, some spruce trees twist and bulge in fantastical shapes. Or how others, storm-bent, stoop like old men resigned to their canes but with quiet resolve get by. Others, lightning-gashed, testify to high drama and survival. And then there are those that balloon with myriad goiter-like globes, growths that I've learned are burls. Often created by storm-driven particles of salt embedded in bark, they're a reaction to stressful irritant, a response to challenge and change. Just as a tree's limbs adjust to prevailing winds, a tree's burl is evidence of an accommodation that allows it to survive. In the bargain, the burl's large knob or gnarly knot lends distinction to the trunk, makes of it a more interesting specimen in the way that the wrinkles and warts of our personalities in their growth and adjustments often become our most compelling features. Such trees are shaped by physical location just as we are shaped by places where we've lived, no matter how shallowly rooted or how frequent the transplants.

One of my favorite island hikes is out to Barred Island. The trail there leads through a dense maritime forest of spruce, balsam fir, a smattering of birch and maple. Carpeting either side of the trail are gorgeous swaths of various species of moss and lichen. Granite ledges bearing the gouge-and-scrape evidence of a glacier's passage 12,000 years ago are everywhere prominent. Because of them, much of the root structure here is so shallow it's visible on the surface. Networks of moss-covered roots, some as thick as a man's thigh, crisscross the trail. I like to think of them as speed bumps. They limit the length of my stride and set the pace of my walk. I'm forced to slow down, to better notice how such roots work to hold it all—moss, tree, rock—in place.

The forest the trail traverses is one of living and dead spruce. In some areas, the stands of trees are so thick and close a dying spruce is long supported by its neighbors. A dead tree may even for months afterward be propped up by the trees around it. Walk the trail on a still day, and in the wind's slightest movement overhead, you can hear where the trees lean against one another, bark rubbing against bark, a low keening.

It's unlikely many scientists support the notion that plant life possesses intelligence or emotions, but as Knopp recounts, researchers do acknowledge a type of chemical interplant communication. They believe warnings of insect infestation can be communicated from one tree to another. A Sitka willow, for example, when attacked by a siege of hungry bugs, communicates a warning to fellow willows whose response, by way of quick chemical modification, renders them unpalatable to the impending invaders. Studies suggest such warning signals may be transmitted in the air. So that, yes, isn't it easier then to believe a tree might shriek or wail at a pitch much higher than a microburst's howl? To believe that, unheard by my human ears, the first spruce to lean toward my house and let go, but only after vigorous struggle, did in fact wail in warning, in protest, and, finally, perhaps, in farewell?

Such a recognition, however, does make it more painful to imagine what might get transmitted in a forest when the first brutal hail of chain saws is gassed up and logging trucks rumble in.

*A*nd it reinforces how what's now a seasonal ritual isn't always easy.

Today, orange plastic ribbon in hand, I walk the woods bordering our lane. I've got some decisions to make.

Over the years here, I've come to understand that spruce trees are almost as likely to be blown down as cut down—albeit not usually with the drama and uber-efficiency of a microburst's assist. A number of factors work against them, most by way of topography, weather, history, and natural life cycles.

Early settlers who counted on farming cleared the island of most of its trees. Later, when they turned their backs on subsistence farming and their faces to the bountiful sea, trees, white spruce mostly, claimed cleared fields. Photographs, of even just a few decades ago, reveal some island landscapes virtually free of trees, or, in some places, richly endowed by hardwoods that were long ago crowded out by the rapid, unmanaged willy-nilly growth of white spruce. Today, few of the island's trees predate the years the woods were fields. And, sadly, many stands of white spruce that grew out of abandoned farmland are now approaching the end of their relatively short life spans.

Downed trees do, of course, cause damage, often much more than what our house withstood. They also block roads and take out power lines—not a mere nuisance in mid-January when winter winds howl and well pumps and furnaces squat silent in the cellar. Tangled among undergrowth like giant PickUp sticks, downed trees increase the risk of fire. They also inhibit new growth.

Today, the easiest part of my task—tagging what trees Chris will remove in the upcoming winter months—is the blowdowns. Without even stepping off the gravel lane, I can determine from a distance which of them are likely to block new growth and which, like an old birch that long before it went down was peeling its bark, will, in decay, add to the soil's nutrients, hoist a welcome sign to whatever crawly critters may want to claim them as home.

It's also easy from this perspective to see and thus better understand why, a few years ago, I resumed the task of forest management that the previous owners of these eight acres began after many years of neglect. In some areas where I've yet to tinker is evidence, to my eye anyway, of what resembles a type of climax forest. Here, where growth is dense and the crowded conditions competitive, the largest trees, many fast approaching the end of their life cycle, can grow no bigger. Nor can many of the newer, younger trees get a foothold among them. Plus they're all of the same species—white spruce, not surprisingly. Because these conifers so densely dominate, the deeply shaded ground beneath them is more or less barren. There's very little groundcover of ferns or other woodland plants more common beneath deciduous hardwoods. And, given the thick canopy and lack of light through it, there's little sign of new seedlings taking root. Without any disturbance, natural or otherwise, the same species and growth patterns will likely continue for decades.

And so it's here where I meddle. I stick my hand in to try to fix what predates me, what in large part human hands before me helped to create.

Not that the "fixes" are without their downsides. Literally. Take a few trees out, poke a hole into the canopy, increase space within a thick stand of trees, and you risk that the wind will find its way in among them more easily, cause more blowdowns of trees neither unhealthy or old and, in falling, take with them a few of their younger, even more robust neighbors. But the benefits, I've learned, generally outweigh the risks.

Leaving our lane, I step into the part of our property that, just a few years ago, bore the most drastic results of accumulated storm damage, of trees succumbing to old age and to disease that followed two back-to-back summers of tree-weakening drought. Here is where I started my management efforts, an area that for a whole year after looked to my horrified eyes like a clear-cut, only to be followed by a thorny sea of wild blackberry canes. But what experienced forest management folks counseled me to expect has happened.

Among the proliferating canes, numerous seeds sank roots after being dormant for who knows how long, spread and dropped by what and how I can't say. Soon, seedlings clamored for moisture and light. Outcompeted since by these seedlings' growth and by the younger trees once stunted when their old-timer brethren hogged all the light but can now bolt skyward, the canes have largely died back. Meanwhile, the free-for-all competition between spruce and balsam, birch and a few maple is playing out. Walking this area today, some of the new trees are already my height or taller. Calipers range from finger thickness to a couple of inches. I see where, soon enough, thinning may have to be done—more tinkering if the hardwoods are to have a chance. Bad enough that the deer find mini-maples delectable and utterly irresistible, but the faster growing balsam and spruce will soon outcompete and shadow the hardwoods, even the pair of highly desirable oaks that have hoisted themselves a few inches into the light.

Continuing on, I come to an adjacent stretch. Here, where clearing has been most recent and for some reason seems not to the berry canes' liking, is a mat of tiny trees measuring no more than an inch tall and, from a distance, resembles a groundcover of velvety moss. So far, this carpet of miniature green appears to be a mix of fir and spruce, but it's possible that here, too, other species hunker and by next season will begin to flex their muscles.

Beyond this patch of promise is where I've set my sights today. Unlike a savvy mom who's learned to prioritize, to know which fights to pick with her growing children, I arrive here with little certainty. Along with my roll of orange ribbon, I must carry with me a dose of hubris, what I've come to feel is required in such an enterprise. The dead trees are obvious. The ailing and infested ones only a bit less so. And then there are the hapless that, because of location, force me to choose.

Unwinding my tape and encircling their trunks, it's as if Chris is standing by, chain saw at the ready, and I'm directing him: "Okay, this one I'll remove. This one I'll leave." As though I were doling out sentences and pardons, condemning the spruce, sparing the oak.

*E*ssayist Mary Rose O'Reilly in *The Love of Impermanent Things* recently reminded me of Thoreau's notion that we need to know what kind of tree we are and thus can know what kind of ecosystem we require to thrive. If true, I seem to have gone about this enterprise a bit backwards. Having determined that this island is where I best thrive, I am now learning about its trees. I may even have to ask myself which tree in it I might most resemble. (Which leads me to consider the improbable: is it at all possible that Barbara Walters got her inspiration for her infamous and much ridiculed," If you were a tree, what kind would you be?" interview question from none other than *Walden?*)

No doubt many of us would likely jump at identifying ourselves with oak, that long-lived, shade-bestowing hardwood beauty. And while in my five doomed spruces' admirable struggle there's much to find heroic, traits I'd like to think I share, I know spruce trees elsewhere on our property are less inclined, or, being more shallow-rooted, are less physically endowed to put up a good fight. They're apt to shrug and topple over when winter winds blow hard. True, my canopy-opening forest management efforts may sometimes stack the cards against them, but numerous are the other reasons they're the species most frequently tagged with orange ribbon. Indeed spruce trees do as much to define this island as firs do Jewett's landscape, but, likewise, the often unwelcome proliferation of white spruce trees where other native species once thrived also makes spruce trees close kin to us folks who each summer lay claim to more and more of the island for our seasonal use, an issue I'm loathe to call more attention to.

To heed Thoreau and identify the tree that's most like me, I'll choose larch. Or, as it's more commonly known, a tamarack, and, on the island, even more place-specifically, hackmatack. Never mind that this conifer is commonly found in New England and that I, a Midwesterner, am a transplant. Or that, lithe of limb, with arch and drape, the larch resembles a graceful dancer. Forget, too, that I am only one gal among its legion of admirers and a recent acquaintance, a From Away late to the party. Though a conifer, a larch is deciduous. After a late show of color that marks the season's end, it drops all its needles. But to me, it isn't as if the essence of the newly bared tree has fallen away. Rather, it's gone elsewhere, like that of a departing migratory bird, until, come spring, its arrival is announced again. A cycle I understand and in which, a little, I participate.

Every autumn, about the time the larch is at its peak color, I return to Illinois. I reside there in a familiar landscape, within a community of family, friends, neighbors, and colleagues. Most days, it nurtures and protects. I'm propped up by its networks, like roots that radiate from a secure base. I embrace the opportunities there, the work, diversity, and pulse of city life that propelled me to it and which each fall compel me still. There, I embrace so much of what I left my childhood home to find, rediscovering only lately and with some surprise what has followed me, shaped as I was and remain by a red-brick ranch house on Oakdale Avenue, a neighborhood's gridded streets bordering a small swath of forest, a yard's straggly crabapple tree where an odd little tree house perched above an alley.

Late next May, I'll again ready myself for the trip back to the island. No doubt I'll still be painting into my mind's picture the five microburst-toppled spruce trees, their loss this season too abrupt, too soon, to have been fully absorbed. A picture in which there was no peremptory "Here is what will be removed, here is what will stay "—as though, even with orange ribbon in hand, I can strike such bargains. I'll still need more time to revise a familiar part of this landscape, paint over those fallen trees with absence. Trees older than me, trees I lived among gone now, gone like some of the people who appear in our photos back-dropped by those spruce.

Eventually the viburnum I'll plant there next spring will fill in what is now an unfamiliar gash. Elsewhere, I'll find a different pair of trees for the hammock, a different perspective from which to read and nap. Memory will be overcome. The picture in my head will adjust to what becomes newly present.

All over this land, trees of various sizes thrive. Some straddle property lines, a distinction as meaningless to them as to the fox or white-tailed deer who routinely cross over them or to springs or aquifers a drilled well draws upon. Tree roots snake across what on a deed tells me is mine, and limbs intertwine with those of trees sitting squarely on someone else's plotted property. Such distinctions register nothing. Nor does, I'm to believe, my joy in rediscovering here, decades removed from Oakdale Avenue, how essential is a walk among trees just steps from my door. I arrived here and it was as if the forest welcomed me back, an arboreal landscape inscribed in my tissues, and which, for too long, hadn't been recognized.

I don't know what will determine when or how much in which place—here or Chicago—I'll spend my time. I can't say now what might propel me to stay put on the island altogether and settle down over the roots I'm sinking into this soil. I'm still learning the trees of this place, still discovering answers. What here don't I have there? What in this place can I not love in any other? What to me matters most, and when and where? With any luck, in the years ahead, I'll still have the privilege of choice and the ability to choose. For now I yield to the pull that the away-from-here still exerts. For now I leave and return.

Soon, acorns will again drop from our big oak sheltering the house. Loosened by their own ripeness or with the helpful assists of red squirrels, they'll pelt the hood of my parked car, thwump against our house roof, and remind me once again of another season's end and of how much noise a small acorn can make falling, returning to earth, to where the whole thing began. In each the seed of possibility. Of another oak like the hundred-year old beauty that shelters this house, protects it against the wind's assault, paints its walls with dapple and shadow, extends to my body-memory its cool shade, its sounds of squirrel and crow, falling acorn and wind-tossed branch. This mother oak already secure in my pantheon of special trees.

One day in the upcoming weeks, the ospreys, in annual migration, will lift off from their spruce-top nest on Heart Island. Not long after, our oak is likely to fill with nattering juncos. The oak will be full; the spruce empty. Juncos. Ospreys. Each will, I hope, in its own way and time, return. As will I, by way of a journey that now, over these many years, in familiar landmarks and touchstones, is securely mapped in my head and heart.

A journey where spruce, occasional tamaracks, and a stretch of canopy-making maples line either side of Route 15 that leads from the bridge. Where, closer to home, more trees—spruce mostly and a few broad-branching oaks in fields, clearings and yards—border the road. And where, the final leg, our lane curves among and around white and red spruce, a stand of birch, a few young maples, and, of course, our oak. All along my route, trees guide me home.

AWAY

"Home is where you start from."

T. S. Eliot

TOUCHSTONE

"... and what could I say at all without my roots?"
Pablo Neruda

*C*all them the Leavers.

They leave what has been their only place. Is it as if they've left their skin behind? Like a shedder lobster that backs out of its shell? A peeling birch just before its fall?

They leave for the usual reasons: not enough affordable housing, satisfying work, stimulating opportunity. Still, some islanders consider it a betrayal. Love this place, they say, love deeply, and, at whatever cost, hold on.

Many who leave hastily return. They forsake the world's expansiveness and come back.

"Boston was too far," a neighbor confesses. As was Baltimore for another.

A young carpenter answered the siren call of Oregon one winter. New Mexico lured his pal. Both returned within a year, distant throwbacks, some might say, to a different generation. One that didn't quit, and didn't dream to leave either.

Leavers, even those who pledge early to escape, may love this place deeply, but love alone can't keep them here. They head out—to Virginia, California, North Carolina—and there they stay. Some of them, however it's measured, become successful, satisfied. Some live in numbingly similar suburban developments. Others swallow traffic and noise, concrete parking lots and strip malls because that's where the work is. Wherever they settle, they may strike a bargain, considering the trade-off for better schools, higher wages and benefits, more rungs in a corporate ladder, along with, perhaps, ethnic restaurants, entertainment complexes, a major league team, and a jolt of clattering stimuli.

But away, perhaps, no matter how keen the pull to such far-off places, they perch in the treetops, don't sink roots into what feels like unfamiliar ground. Retained deep within tissue and bone is the route back to a geography by which all others are measured. Where land and home wait.

*F*ourteen years ago on an early Sunday morning, Bob and I drove to the South Side Chicago neighborhood where I spent the first seven years of my life. I hadn't been back in decades. I'd long been convinced I had no connection to it. All that drew me that particular weekend was my wish to set there the scene of a novel I was writing. I was, I told myself, merely doing research.

The two-flat on 115th Street where I once lived had been razed for a parking lot. Nothing revealed that Pat and Matt's with its up-front cases of penny candy—Mary Janes, Wax Lips, sugary nibs on rolls of paper—and, in back, its smoky tavern lit only by revolving Hamm's Beer signs, had ever existed, nor the adjacent Italian bakery with its counters of stacked torpedo-shaped bread and glass jars of seeded, anise cookies. The vacant lot forever strewn with bits of broken bottles tossed over the fence by a few late-night and otherwise benign drunks, and its tidier corner where Mrs. Alekna kept a vegetable garden of strange greens and, one spring, a bleating lamb whose connection to Easter dinner I'd yet to make, had become a weedy patch of pavement offering no clue to its present purpose. Of much smaller surprise was how St. Anthony's, a hulk of a Catholic church more preposterous than ever in its scale and excess, still dominated an entire block.

Once home to a large number of second-generation immigrants, mostly Italians and a handful of Poles, ours was a neighborhood where struggle and strife were constants. On summer nights, husband-and-wife arguments, often about how to pay for what, routinely echoed from open windows and down narrow gangways, making them everyone's business. Yet St. Anthony's of Padua, in all its grandeur and pomposity, reared up, its massive reconstruction as much a monument to labor as to belief, an edifice eked out of meager savings pilfered from passbooks and dropped without fail each Sunday into baskets passed for such purpose down every pew. Lost to me then and apparently to most fellow parishioners was the irony that such a monument's patron saint had rejected his family's wealth, turned his back on its trappings and embraced the life of a poor Franciscan. Nor might it have mattered. In sheer size alone, our St. A shouted a loud and prideful response to St. Salome, the rival, mostly Polish parish that for too long had declared itself the area's most magnificent church.

On that early winter morning of our drive, I returned to St. Anthony's. I walked beneath the vaulted cobalt ceiling for the first time in nearly forty years. Much less dazzling than it had once been to a seven-year-old's eyes, the expanse of polished marble still impressed, stone touted to have been shipped from Italy, from villages and regions whose multi-vowelled names on certain tongues sounded to my young ears like music. I couldn't recall our church ever being so empty, so void of music or murmur that my footsteps echoed.

"Where is everyone?" I asked Bob, using the "church whisper" I'd once known so well here but which now, in an empty place so many years later, sounded as though I'd shouted into an amplified megaphone. From the racks by the door, where programs printed in English with a smattering of Latin had once boasted numerous Masses, he handed me what now, in English and Spanish, announced a single midday Sunday Mass.

In a neighborhood that years before had already tilted toward blight, the church was serving a new wave of immigrants. Likely some had only recently moved onto the adjoining streets, into tiny apartments and small houses of faded, peeling paint, where plaster Madonnas presiding over the porch or in a front window added a few bright blots of color to an otherwise colorless, still treeless place. Once a hub attracting and demanding attention, St. Anthony's church and its adjacent rectory, convent and school, all long absent their earlier luster, were striving to survive. They'd become a fragile islanded nexus in a sea of shuttered businesses, chain-linked overgrown yards with a few slumbering dogs and tangled bikes, numerous derelict boarded-up houses and apartment buildings, mere canvas, it seemed, to condemnation notices, graffiti, and—in the newest take on the neighborhood's rivalry—the slogans of one gang claiming dominion over another.

For a young girl, this neighborhood was once an island that seemed to consist of a mere three blocks. Of a bakery, a tavern, a church compound, a huddle of brick buildings with their backsides stitched together by sagging wooden stairways and porches. And where, from the front stoop of our two-flat that likely no current area residents knew had existed, and from which I was never to venture alone, I watched a stream of neighbors file in and out of the church and the school, and, from the convent, like a covey of waddling birds, the black-from-head-to-toe-garbed nuns, their hands thrust so deep into their sleeves that for a long time I believed they were only hiding the obvious—they had no hands.

Decades later, early on a Sunday morning in winter, those streets not only appeared empty but gripped by an underlying menace that made me glad I'd not come alone. Had I any questions about who lived on them now, there was no one to ask. We encountered no one who might've peered into our car windows and stared, wondering how and why we'd strayed here, why on earth I'd returned.

"What's that?" Bob asked as we drove away. Unbeknownst to me, I'd begun to hum aloud the invocation to the Patron of Lost Things and Missing Persons that I'd learned as a child—"St. Anthony, St. Anthony, please come down. Something is lost and cannot be found."

*T*ruth is, long before that drive, the place of my birth, my life's earliest compass, had more or less become lost to me.

In 1956, my parents and I were the Leavers. In a burst of postwar, I-Like-Ike optimism and promise, and as part of the movement that was stamping *suburb* onto maps across the country, we moved to Oakdale Avenue, south of Chicago. Home became a neighborhood of small lots with blocky brick bungalows, clipped lawns, little yards, some shelter-ing trees. Children spilled from nearly every house onto sidewalks and into streets safe enough to ride bikes with trading cards popping in the spokes, to play boisterous rounds of Red Rover and Kick the Can until dark drove us indoors, a modest neighborhood rich in its simple declara-tion: We are not two-flats or cramped apartments. And, miracle of mir-acles to our parched city-shrunk eyes, it was also a neighborhood with a narrow swath of woods and a string of vacant weedy lots yearning to become again prairie, all bordering a narrow river that for years I had no idea eventually broadened as it snaked its way east past grain mills and warehouses already being shuttered, past the Calumet region's stench-belching paint factories and sulfurous slag heaps. To me, for a time, it was a small slice of paradise.

I lived on Oakdale Avenue for nearly fifteen years, more than enough time to consider it my childhood's true home. And then, from the house that still inhabits me, that, eyes closed, I can easily map in my mind, from the neighborhood whose streets I can, in my head, still drive, whose hid-den wooded trails I can, in body-memory, lead, I left.

At first, the leaving seemed only temporary. I followed in the foot-steps of so many other new high school graduates. I went off to college, though my path and course of study—English at a state university—veered from the neighborhood's usual expectations of beauty or secre-tarial schools or the loftier ambitions of my cousin Bonnie training to become an airline stewardess. As the first college graduate in a family whose members didn't all possess high school diplomas, I blazed what for many folks is a customary trail. Venturing forth into what was certainly foreign territory for my parents, it was as if I were an early pioneer setting out to cross the unmapped plains. A journey that soon became less about what I was moving toward as, more urgently, what I was leaving behind.

My parents had fled the old neighborhood to a house and neighborhood I now strove to escape. From what had been their dream and hard-earned accomplishment, I only wanted out. Everything seemed to point in one direction: away.

Just weeks after university commencement, I was armed with a weekly paycheck and a lease to a shared apartment in the city, both of which at the moment seemed more important than my newly minted degree. After summers of working in downtown Chicago office buildings, of riding a sooty Illinois Central railcar, its splintery caned seats ruining countless pairs of hose, after glimpsing another kind of life and the broader opportunities amidst a city skyline that already pressed deep into my psyche, I left. My journey now pointed not just toward advancement and potential achievements and away from my neighborhood and the work examples my father and mother, my uncles and neighbors predicted for me, but, most important to me then, it supported what I'd so long believed—I was better than my neighborhood. I was not really *of* this place.

What I didn't bargain for was not being able to return.

Within a year of my moving out, I found myself demanding into the phone, "What do you mean, you're *leaving?*"

As my mother laid out plans to pull up stakes and leave Oakdale Avenue, I sat at my desk in a small office cubicle, employed in a much more menial position at an advertising agency than what I'd pumped it up to be when regaling my parents at their kitchen table, back when it had yet to occur to me that it wasn't as Left-Behinds that they'd been so easily—obligatorily—impressed. Or had pretended to be.

"But when are you going?" I sputtered. Suddenly it was as if all my parents' arguments had been leading to this singular decision, a point on which they finally agreed. An embrace of some unknown opportunity. A Grand Adventure that, married at 19, parents at 20, they'd been deprived. Never mind that they had two school-age kids in tow. "Oh, they'll be fine," my mother insisted as though talking about transplanted saplings sure to take root elsewhere. As though a childhood had never happened to her. "You know how kids are. They adjust."

With one sweeping decision, my parents became the true pioneers, trading in shading elms and green, pliant lawns for prickly saguaros and yuccas and sand. Exchanging relative certainty for who-knew-what.

My parents left the childhood place that was always to be the place I left behind. The home of my early years, of my adolescence and teenage angst. The place to which, during college, I only returned for summers and semester breaks because I needed the money working the registers at Gately's, my only focus trying to bury my envy of new friends back-packing in Europe or baring oiled limbs on Daytona Beach. My family left the red-brick ranch my father and uncles built, a synthesis of clipped magazine photographs my mother had transformed into sketches at our two-flat's kitchen table, a house she had dreamed into being. The house that I so clearly see now was also home to anxiety and old hurts, resentments and unresolved conflicts. To slow, silent simmerings that should have been more frightening and certainly more revealing than the quick flare-ups or booze-fueled eruptions.

Before leaving, my mother purged. She brutally scoured the basement and closet shelves. Though I wasn't there to witness the choices made between what was taken, what discarded, I returned on weekends to rooms stripped to their bones, mere vessels of what they'd been, now increasingly stacked with boxes. On walls where shelves and paintings were removed and had faded, it was as if ghostly writings had appeared, already the encrypted messages of former inhabitants. I didn't understand why so much was being jettisoned. Like the baby food jars of nuts and bolts so carefully assembled on my father's workbench, or the last and best of my horse figurine collection, or the stamped tin-covered light fixture that had long shed its golden light over our dining room table as if it alone could make of our Sunday afternoon dinners a Norman Rockwellian composition. Grim-faced and with a brusqueness that became more and more customary, my mother said, "We don't need it." As if she were pitching possessions from a Conestoga hub-deep in the mud.

Stacked in the basement was my pile to pick through, things I'd left behind but which now in a small shared apartment I had little room to keep. "It's now or never," she made clear in her refusal to haul any of it to a clay-tile-roofed house and a distant desert landscape in which I still couldn't imagine her beloved maple hutch and ladder back chairs fitting in. Now or never. In a battered box, I carried away a couple of high school yearbooks, some rubber-banded photographs and other memorabilia, trinkets that long since have mostly been dispersed or tossed.

For so long, I'd wanted to leave Oakdale Avenue. But how was it that I didn't recognize my mother's same desire? Or how much more leaving might cost her? Only much later did I wonder: Was her ruthlessness a response to regret over a decision set into motion? Was she bracing against a potentially overwhelming loss by shucking so many possible reminders of a former life? In what boxes were packed the secrets? The dreams and longings?

In 1972, my parents left the only house I knew. Yes, I had left, too. I had left them. But their leaving trumped all. Vanishing suddenly with them was any possibility that I might return. As if it were my lodestar, they were hauling away my option to sleep, if only for a night, beneath the roof of the house I'd long called home. On a midwinter morning, they pointed their car west, my father impatient at the wheel, his garage workbench, the pegged board where he'd hung his tools, the basement rec room that he'd paneled himself seemingly nothing to him now. My mother, shrill and nervous, refused to turn and look at her house again, her good-byes to those empty, echoing rooms already—hopefully— made before clicking the door shut one final time. In the back seat, about to leave the only home they'd ever known, to embark on a leave-taking they could neither influence nor change, my sister tried hard to absent herself from the reality of being uprooted from high school in her junior year, and my younger brother, looking dazed and confused, picked his fingernails until the cuticles bled.

Of all the many losses their leaving would later mean to me, I couldn't have imagined then the one with which I've only recently had to grapple. Those years in the Oakdale Avenue house, the first ten years of my young brother's life, were also the years in which I knew Joe best. So few years, a sad, lamentable pittance, but a precious gift nevertheless when held up to the years that followed, those of our deepening estrangement. In distant Arizona, a place to which I felt no connection, no magnetic pull, he grew to become the 45-year old man and father he was at his death. Whose dreams and fears remained largely unknown to me, the product of oth- erness and distance and a journey that began the morning they pulled away from the curb.

*I*n *Staying Put*, Scott Russell Sanders laments the disappearance of his childhood places—a farm in Tennessee buried beneath asphalt, a house and barn in Ohio at the bottom of a lake, their adjoining fields drowned by a boondoggle dam. All of it gone.

Unlike our two-flat on 115th, our house on Oakdale Avenue still exists, as does its neighborhood with geometrically-gridded streets running at right angles. Still hunkered on small lots are the snug brick bungalows, some now with taller fences and expanded garages, a few with new dormers and bump-out additions, all either better buffed or more negligently worn. The spindly saplings the city planted after a plague of Dutch elm disease reach above rooftops. Sun and shadow spangle the streets. But lots are no longer vacant, fields unpaved. The woods with its network of trails we neighborhood kids stomped into it have long been carved up by bland, look-alike houses linked by what had been the old Markham Drive extension, nothing more then but a rutted dirt track we rode our bicycles on. There's no clue that a crabapple tree ever spread its branches in what once was our yard.

Long after other neighborhoods have claimed me, Oakdale Avenue remains a physical place to which, unlike Sanders, I can still return, and, were I to feel such a pull, I might catch glimpses of my past. But all the families we once knew there are gone: the neighboring Wrights to Indiana, the Segala family to Michigan, and Lenny, who, after Ruth's death, was the last to leave, a process that years before had drawn away his children, my pals, to Idaho and New Mexico.

Oakdale Avenue is a body of space, a geography that, even without us in it, exists. But isn't a place, any place, also a province of histories, of what writer Tracy Seeley claims are "stories rooted deeply in deeply remembered soil?" And of the people whose stories they are?

Several years ago, my father made what became his last trip to our former neighborhood. At our corner, he slowed his rental car and strained to look at the house he and my uncles had built, to take in whatever changes the intervening span of decades and a racially changing neighborhood had pressed upon it. He did so through the scrim of hostile stares, the taunts of teenage boys gathered around a nearby car. He didn't stop, didn't get out. He knew no one.

Later, he told me, "It was as if we'd never lived there." Speaking in a tone that betrayed old hurts, he suddenly reminded me of how young he'd been that long-ago morning when my family drove off, and how deeply embedded were his grit and determination in leaving. I also glimpsed the years of broken promises and disappointments that followed.

Looking off, he said, "It was like we'd never existed."

*N*ot once did I consider going west with my family. Nor did I regret leaving Oakdale Avenue before them, that neighborhood where, particularly each midsummer at its entropic pinnacle, I dreamed of a future far away, waiting for my real life to begin, afraid that it had and this was it.

I was hurt, though, by their leaving, by their willingness to leave *me*.

And, I suppose, I was a bit afraid, too, of what their leaving might mean. But soon, after the initial shock and only with a little less solipsism, I became convinced my parents' leaving sort of "saved" me. Without them dwelling in the old neighborhood, I was freer to move on, and not be drawn back by duty or obligation. I was also spared explanations I'd for so long felt I needed, was compelled to give. To any inquiries about my past, I could now vaguely reply that my family lived in Arizona, a somewhat hopefully exotic notion if not for a widely held belief among my new crowd that the Southwest was a cultural wasteland of saguaros, sagebrush, and tobacco-spitting cowboys. Among my friends and colleagues from the city's Gold Coast and privileged North Shore suburbs of well-paid professionals and advanced degrees, places that were not just desirable and okay to return to but to have come from, I kept mum about my old neighborhood patchworked with backyard clotheslines declaring with work shirts and coveralls which trade or union claimed which house.

For years, I wasn't able to sniff out the many phonies and smug snobs I'd befriended, but was certain they could catch a whiff of taint, of my exposed, dangling roots. No longer was it enough to have left Oakdale Avenue. I repudiated it. If ever forced into talking about it, I denigrated. I disparaged even that which once I'd been so certain was special. As though attempting to amend poor soil with costly mulch, I booked expensive haircuts, bought budget-busting clothes, carried fancy luggage to my friends' lake houses and beachfront condos, Oakdale Avenue tucked deep inside like a small cheap souvenir, the reminder of a place I'd once merely traveled through.

Luckily, over time, it became easier to be grateful for my childhood place even while accepting its shortcomings, the stunted, narrow view I might've obtained had I stayed there. If I had not become a Leaver. And how, I wonder, can you ever weigh a place, even a loved place, if you never leave it? How, without contrast, can you know it? And yet don't I also find something admirable—maybe even enviable?—in the certainty of remaining in a place, a particular here-and-only-here where your life begins and ends?

*R*ecently, one of my island neighbors whose daily regimen isn't complete without a stop at the dump's Take It Or Leave It shed retrieved there a box of sepia-tinted photographs. Before transporting it to the historical society's archives, he plunked it down in Neva's Periwinkle shop. Several of us who'd only gone in for the morning newspaper soon found ourselves hunched over the box, our fingers turning black from the loose, disintegrating pages of someone's old album as we sought clues to tell us what we were looking at and to whom these photos may have belonged. Nancy, a long-time summer resident, recognized her house's exterior, its living room, the view across a meadow—"so few trees then!"—to Heart Island, but couldn't identify the people pictured there, whether they had ever lived in the saltwater farmhouse she'd bought many years before. But someone will know. Over generations, knowledge is accumulated bit by bit. The island abounds with natives who possess more familiarity with certain pieces of land than those a deed and tax bill say own them. People who've opted to remain close to where their forebears lived, to tend their graves, observe their rituals, thus embodying, they hope, their traditions and ambitions as well as their own.

Seventy-year-old lobsterman Leroy lives in the house where he was born. His grown son lives next door. Linda puts out the welcome mat at the house bequeathed to her by an aunt, next to her brother whose house was their late father's fishing camp. Their cousin, as a Leaver, departed the island to attend university, teach, and marry. Though he raised his children elsewhere, he returned full-time after retirement, bought back his family's farm, and now resides in the rooms where his mother was born. In recent years, home for his offspring is California, but they've bought a house adjacent to the farm and each July make the pilgrimage back.

Elsewhere, mobility is the norm. American families routinely spread out across the country and are brought together as mine sometimes is in intense moments at airports and hospitals, weddings and funerals. A family's glue, its "daily enactments," as writer Deborah Tall called them, is strengthened through telephone calls, text messaging and e-mails, common experiences shared less in one physical spot than via fiber optics and finger-tapping digital connections. Like seeds tossed to the wind, friends and family live at great scattering distances from one another.

Mobile, we're likely to move from coast to coast. Many among us follow a familiar route: starter home to dream home, condo to retirement complex. In moving frequently, we learn to travel light and fast. More of us opt now for cremation, for being consigned to urns, as though, notes writer and funeral director Thomas Lynch, the aim is to be more portable for those who live after us and who, with ever-increasing velocity and frequency in movement, seem intent on trying to outrun their own mortality.

But with such increasing mobility, don't lives become fragmented, split into pieces like the broken branches and splintered limbs a storm heaves onto lawn and roof? When, often, the remnants of shared experience can't be gathered back up, reassembled? Only the memory of it. A mental reconstruction. Wedded to movement, we become the wind in the branches rather than the rooted tree.

Of course, in spite of fierce attachments, not of all us *can* stay in one place. We must go where the work is, or the promise of it. Ailing and frail, we must follow our children to wherever they're attempting to sink new roots. To survive, the perspective gained from staying put, of getting to know your neighbors and the land upon which you raise your young and bury your dead, where you're attentive to the forces that usher the tides in and out, can't be sustained.

And maybe the modern world, increasingly so, actually reflects what is a multi-millennial history of movement and migration, of essential journeys and wanderings not stigmatized into mere rootlessness. And, in many cases, is none the worse for it. Marked from its conception by myriad journeys, this country is a tapestry intricately woven with banishment, oppression, persecution, forced displacement, restless movement, exploratory curiosity, economic necessity, and capitalistic opportunity. It's a warp and weave of Plymouth Rock Pilgrims, American Indians, African slaves, Gold Rush prospectors, pioneers, Dust Bowl fugitives, oil drillers, any number of wartime profiteers, and late twentieth-century techie gurus drawn as though in worship to Silicon Valley. Mobility, at the core of our national identity, is often essential. When sinking roots isn't an option, isn't a way ahead or out. When salvation and success may lie just across a distant river, over the next ridge. Or on the other side of an island's bridge.

The fear of being trapped, particularly in "the sticks," of being on a dead-end road going nowhere, is real. And staying put in one place, as much as it may be a measurement of stability, can also be viewed as unambitious, a life lacking in adventure or stimuli. Of being stuck. Mobility itself doesn't guarantee success, but neither do our ties to one place have to mean being yoked to drudgery, bound to one's lot with small hope for betterment. Still, the messages often are: Move on. Move up. Don't be the last one left behind, waving at everyone else as they depart.

Mobility can threaten rituals, disrupt established traditions. But such fears can also exaggerate attachment, tilt toward sentimentality, cement a place into rigid intolerance and exclusivity. A fine line is often drawn between tradition's embrace and its stranglehold. A line that can blur or become more distinct.

A few years ago, two talented high school seniors, working with the island's Opera House Arts' Imagination Project public digital studio, produced a 24-minute documentary film, *Island Prom*, about the long-held custom of inviting community members of all ages to the junior prom, a cross-generational interaction increasingly rare in many communities. In an interview following a screening at the Stonington Opera House, the budding filmmakers confessed that at the project's outset they'd been convinced such a tradition, complete with red carpet and master of ceremonies, might well be considered hokey when held up to a larger world beyond the island's shores. But any original intention to give the film a satirical edge evaporated as they followed the year-long prom planning, extensively interviewing past participants as well as the third generation Grand March caller. Their skilled portrayal unearthed powerful attachments and a new-found respect for a tradition unique to their childhood place. Notably recognized in screenings elsewhere, the film also caught the attention of judges who awarded *Island Prom* the Grand Prize at the 30th annual Maine Student Film and Video Festival held in conjunction with Maine's International Film Festival, citing the filmmakers' honesty of presentation, their ability to capture their subjects at ease and to portray the sheer joy of the event. Soon after, both young women went off to college. They joined other young people who leave the island, some of whom blaze a new family trail not unfamiliar to me, and where, perhaps, away from family and home and a place's influences and expectations, their perspectives, aided by art and age and distance, expand.

Without traditions, without shared history and meaning that comes with time and commitment, attachments to a particular place aren't possible. We have human roots, wrote philosopher Simone Weil, by way of "our real, active and natural participation in the life of a community. In it are preserved particular treasures of the past and certain particular expectations of the future." And yet, leavers or not, the blood of vagabonds, of boundary-pushing pioneers, the merely curious and the economically-pressed, courses in our veins. We have an itch to wander.

Hop on a plane, and far from here we may have to wrestle traffic on city street or highway. Perhaps we belly up to another recognizable franchise restaurant or to the shopping mall where we eat our fill of whatever the TV ads and a perceived status tell us we need to acquire. But we can also expand our horizon within a museum or theater. We study and learn about what, from our childhood's first ground, we perhaps never dreamed, or, by working beside someone unlike our neighbors at home, we put a face on what we'd long feared. Whether we flourish or flounder, we relish—even need, often in life-altering ways—our freedom to wander. It helps makes us who we are. Indeed, our appetite for movement seems deeply embedded in our genes. In part, it's what got many of our immigrant forebears to these shores, and may even have been the impetus behind our earliest ancestors hauling themselves up onto two legs— just to see what's further down the road.

Yes, staying in one place, we risk being stuck. But wander and we may, as Tall warns, "fail to be a citizen of any one place."

Maybe it's only true nomads who come closest to accommodating both movement and attachment to place, as Sanders suggests. Nomadic travels harness inherent restlessness and reconcile the desire to rove with the need to settle down. Australian Aborigines, for example, so masterfully chronicled in Bruce Chatwin's *The Songlines,* may appear to wander, but they are clearly not rootless. Unlike vagabonds, notes Sanders, Aborigines wed themselves to one place and range over it widely, with gratitude and care. Their vast movements, driven by hunter-gatherer necessities, are not random but deliberate. The knowledge of the land their nomadic pathways crisscross is meticulously passed down through generations, an accumulation carried in stories and songs particular to each place. Rootedness is not to an abstract idea but to a place, or places, each necessary and known within cyclical, meaningful journeys of leaving and returning.

Achieving such balance between wandering and staying, venturing and returning, of seeming boundlessness and restriction, has, of course, some tricky parts. Venture where and for how long? Learn and experience what? How return and when? And might not the returning part of the journey be most crucial? Having a place to return to, within which to incorporate the journey? A place of constancy and duration and rooted community. A place where things hold.

A place that, though I may leave it, remains.

I can't go home again. I can't return to my native ground, to my natal 115th two-flat. It's gone. Oakdale Avenue, the hospitable oasis my family once knew it as, is gone, too. Like Sanders, "If I'm to have a home, it can only be a place I have come to as an adult."

And I've come here. Or should I say, I return here.

Ever since we bought our house here nine years ago, I leave the island in October, return in June. I relive the act of leaving, but from a place I'm able to return to. Like all places, the island is subject to change. Its history is not static. Its stories are still being written. I've had to say good-bye to so many people who have forever left it, this place reshaped each year by leave-taking, by what was and can never be again. And how, truly, can a place become home if in it we have not suffered loss, if in it we've not had our hearts broken?

To lament the loss of childhood ground is not an attempt to reclaim childhood, the lithe limb and unfurrowed brow of youth none of us can have back. An adult as sensuous child can't go home again. Were my Oakdale Avenue backyard crabapple tree still to exist, and if these aging muscles were willing, could I, shinnying up among its highest branches, truly relive in my adult body the blood-coursing thrum of my early years?

Still, just as, when looking into the mirror some mornings, I sometimes discover a teenage girl who each morning fought a stubborn cowlick and who secretly admired her own blue eyes, the childhood place of my formative years is retained deep within. And aren't we all naturally drawn to such places, if not physically then mentally, if not by love or desire then by curiosity? Or necessity? Such ramblings help us know—learn—who we are. In Sanders' words, we forever bear the impression of our "first ground."

I'm no longer the young woman just out of school, the Leaver with her future spread before her and still taking shape. I'm not the young woman who, with her foot on the accelerator toward a singular if still amorphous destination—Away—had little interest in returning to the place she knew best, the place she's no longer embarrassed to claim. It took years to understand the obvious, to recognize the ache—how you can lament the loss of a place you wanted to leave. And not just the physical place, but the act of returning to it. Of being *able* to return.

Maybe it's why I envy people with attics, the real and imagined attics I've often pictured in houses all across this island—with dusty heaps of mementoes belonging to families whose childhood place has not been lost to them, with cobwebbed boxes stacked beneath bare bulbs with pull chains, their contents not endangered by now-or-never demands. Here, I live among people so deeply rooted, some of them have never filled out a change of address form or packed into a moving box so much as a cup. And for whom the familiar two-liner often circulated here—"Have you lived in Deer Isle your whole life?" "Not yet."—is no joke.

Wherever I've freely wandered and no matter the satisfactions I've obtained in doing so, it turns out I've longed for a place, a touchstone to pull me to it, that declares to me, not by virtue of where my parents or siblings put down stakes, not through mere circumstance or chance, "This is home." A place that whispered, "Welcome." And with each year's successive—nomadic?—ritual of leave and return, says, "Welcome back."

The local lexicon may brand me a From Away. More accurately, perhaps, at least when leaving, I become an Away From. From a place in which I hope to shape a future, and have begun to create a past. A Here that has redefined Away.

"Before any choice," writes Tall quoting geographer Eric Dardel, "there is the place which we have not chosen, where the very foundation of our earthly existence and human condition establishes itself. We can change places, move, but this is still to look for a place...a *here* from which the world discloses itself, a *there* to which we can go."

One day, possibly, my nephew Michael, recently transplanted to Wisconsin by way of his father's new job, will return to his childhood place in Illinois. He may drive the length of Edson Avenue, park in front of the large house built after the sweet stone-and-stucco cottage-like house of his first nine years was demolished by the developer who bought it. Perhaps, unlike my father, he'll get out of his car. Who will be there? What will greet him, remind him of his first ground? Will he glimpse in his mind's eye the card table in the driveway from which he displayed his "bone collection," bleached bits of seabird skulls and fish vertebrae collected from our island shore, to any neighbors with a willingness or kindness to stop and look? Will he recall the bright blue-roofed "fort" at the yard's rear, beneath the big willow that swept its arms over many a sun-spangled summer afternoon?

In one of my last conversations with my brother Joe, who still believed until the end that he'd recover or obtain a transplant and become strong enough again to choose where and how to live, he said he'd move. He'd leave Phoenix, a place he no longer recognized, that years before had ceased being the undeveloped desert and mountains of his youth, a landscape he'd grown to love. Not so far away, parts of the Four Corners region lured him. Even so, he claimed, Chicago would always be home to him, the red-brick ranch on Oakdale Avenue, that neighborhood we shared for all too brief a time and that became lost to both of us. Long before he became lost to me. It's the only place where I can with personal knowledge and specificity situate him—playing hockey at the vacant lot flooded each winter by a friend's dad, a fearless four-year-old goalie among boys twice his age, and as equally defiant on summer afternoons when, with countless Golden Books, my chore was to read him into naps, and the only eyelids that drooped were mine.

My brother was taken from his childhood place. He crossed the continent, attended a new school, fished in the canal on late afternoons with his pal Scooter, knocked out his front teeth on the sidewalk of the first house my parents eventually bought, kept a desert tortoise in the yard, cultivated cacti with a passion that would put some botanists to shame, worked, married, had two children born to that desert landscape, and yet Chicago, its microcosm of Oakdale Avenue, persisted.

Love, detest, or try to remain indifferent to it—from one's native ground, from those roots, we seldom shake free. We are always going back even if we wanted so desperately to get away.

IN THEIR HANDS

*"Humans became intelligent creatures
because they were given hands."*
Anaxagoras

*"Humans were given hands because
they are intelligent."*
Aristotle

I. His

In spite of his quick wit and humorous stories, the lobsterman I've
gotten to know in recent summers is easy to embarrass. So let's call him
Bill.

About sixty, Bill's big in manner and broad in girth. Even in the tranquil kitchen of a mutual friend where we first met, he looked burned
and blown, his red, deeply etched and repeatedly cooked face quick to
announce: here's a man who's spent his life outdoors. But it was Bill's big
slab of a hand held out in introduction that seemed to me most familiar.
In its thick, blunt fingers toughly ridged with calluses, scars, and nicks,
in its rougher-than-sandpaper grip, I met hard work and physical labor.
I glimpsed "getting by" come winter. And waking before light, year after
year, with little complaint.

I can't claim kinship to Bill, nor to any lobsterman. No one in my
family relies on the sea for his livelihood, faces the obstacles that such
work in cahoots with Mother Nature routinely dishes out. I possess no
personal stories of survival in a life-threatening oceanic encounter, nor
do I participate in any of the more mundane experiences universal to
fishermen. There's not a seafaring bone in my body. And yet, in the work

169

ethic of the best of the lobstermen, in their going at it day after day in spite of physical discomfort and tough conditions, these "cowboys of the sea" connect me to the "working stiffs" of my family. To its carpenters, bricklayers, welders, steam fitters, cement masons, heavy-equipment operators.

In Bill's hand, I recognized my father.

*A*ll through my childhood, my father rose long before dawn, even on the many Chicago winter days when temperatures were too cold to pour concrete and held no promise that any side jobs might come through. During my high school years, from the bedroom I shared with my sister that was closest to the kitchen, I'd listen to him percolate the coffee, crack open the newspaper, his stockinged feet whispering against the floor. Like the father in Robert Hayden's poem, "Those Winter Sundays," my father in the "blueblack cold" with "cracked hands that ached/from labor in the weekday weather/made banked fires blaze." Only then, "when the rooms were warm," after he'd "driven out the cold," he'd tap on my door, murmur my name into the dark.

For years, I didn't know how to be grateful. I was often clumsy in the minutes we sat together in the kitchen. I wasn't sure what to do with my embarrassment when, out of love and a father's diminishing sense of usefulness, he offered to drive me to the bus stop in his dinged truck with its front door's hand-painted sign proclaiming to the world his name, our phone number, his job as a cement mason. On mornings too cold to refuse his offer, he'd encourage me to wait inside his idling truck until the bus came. But I almost always slipped out, hopefully unnoticed by the girls from another part of town—Doris with her science-teacher father, or Becky, whose dad, a manager at a printing company, wore a suit and tie. And worked in a real office. Climbing down from my father's truck, books hugged to chest, I barely waved good-bye.

I was still years away from discovering Hayden's poem, and how, in my first reading, I was propelled to the dictionary by the usage of the poem's last surprising word. In my desire for escape from my father's truck, "What did I know, what did I know/ of love's austere and lonely offices?"

I've never seen Bill fish—his traps are set miles out from the other side of the island. I have to assume, though, that his hauling maneuvers would be similar to those of my neighbor Mike who fishes just off our shore, so close that when the shedders come in, I can easily watch him—how he circles a buoy, throttles down, coasts alongside, deftly pulls the line over the pulley that runs into the hydraulic pot hauler, hauls in the dripping warp line, and, moments later, wrestles the trap onto the starboard rail. Without a wasted movement, as though this were a timed pit stop at the Indy 500, he pops open the trap's door, flings overboard the crabs and other unwanted critters who've wandered into the trap. Just as quickly, he tosses away some lobsters, too—the "shorts" and "berried" V-notched females—before gauge-measuring any of questionable size and banding the keepers. Even more speedily, he sets a new bait bag, heaves the trap overboard, guns the engine, and races to the next trap.

How many times any lobsterman repeats these maneuvers depends on how many traps he's set—the maximum by Maine law is 800—and whether he fishes with each buoy line rigged with a single trap or on strings of pairs. Time after time he'll go through the same tissue-embedding choreography and it might look as if his repertoire were a single dance step, and of a mind-numbing sameness. But chances are the terrain his mind roams is vast—Where has he set his traps? And where—soft bottom or hard?—should he move them? How can he avoid water too deep for the amount of warp line or tidal current so swift it'll pull his trap buoys under water? Is it time to switch bait? What's the boat price per pound at the Co-op? Geez, what's fuel got up to this week? Factor in, too, how many times his traps break the surface empty, or worse, are lost to storm or tidal surge or because a careless boater's props cut the lines. While many of us may struggle to squeeze our cars into a tight parking space or on a rainy Interstate pass an eighteen-wheeler heaving spray against our windshield, a lobsterman, caught in the plunging sea of a storm only briefly heralded on radar, can likely steer his small boat safely back into harbor, and, as though born to it like a pelagic guillemot to the deep sea's pitch and roll, almost make it look easy.

When I watch Mike or imagine Bill, I'm not witnessing wage-earning employees of some conglomerate's subsidiary. These aren't "knowledge workers" in a technology-rigged office even though their knowledge is broad, possibly life-saving, and often independent of electrical gadgetry. And when their workday is done, there's little question what's been produced. As he pulls away from the Co-op's scales, Bill knows immediately the results of his day's labor. Men like him are competent in ways foreign to most of us, including my father, but who, I'm convinced, is cut from the same cloth. Like Bill, he's no stranger to manual labor. And just as Dad knows his way around a toolbox, I suspect Bill does, too.

Even at 80, Dad still balked at calling a repairman from any of the trades, although his crawling around under one end of his house to investigate some potentially faulty wiring had become out of the question. Even before that, though possessed with a willingness and an amply stocked workshed, he'd been frequently bested by complicated instructions and the often requisite, single-purpose tool he didn't own. For Dad and us aspiring Do-It-Yourselfers, as I discovered yesterday while attempting to change the bulb on an outdoor fixture but didn't possess the necessary miniscule Allen wrench, the message is: no one is really expected to want or be able to assemble or fix, to lift a hand or have at hand a toolbox generously equipped. It's a message delivered and mostly heeded, even as we become more and more dependent on the tyranny of our power-driven and cleverly camouflaged machines. Our culture tells us: Toss out, don't fix. Buy, don't make. Replace, don't use up.

It wasn't always this way. Once, we were expected to know and do, at least in my neighborhood. At my public high school, the automotive, machine, and wood shop classes flourished. Industrial Arts, Vocational Ed—all part of the parlance then. Perceived as avenues leading to a good living and alternatives for kids disinclined or ill-equipped for college, such classes were also billed as enrichment courses. At least one shop class was required of all male students, regardless your proclivity, your test scores and college-prep tracking, no matter the advice of parent or counselor. Similarly, we gals had Home Ec classes. In them, we studied food pyramids and sewed aprons, usually with lopsided pockets— few future Martha Stewarts among us—those aprons the equivalent, it seemed, of the cutting boards the boys toted home, each inexplicably made in the shape of a pig. While some moms held onto those cutting boards or the likewise ubiquitous shop-made birdhouses, few aprons survived, as, increasingly, daughters were pointed, even the college hopefuls, toward Typing I, the "just in case" fall-back position.

Beginning in the late '70s, shop classes began to disappear, thanks to budget cuts and efforts to steer kids away from blue-collar "dead ends." Some shop tools grew obsolete. Nearly artifacts now, those lathes and band saws offer few clues as to how they work or what they're used for, unless you're inclined to surf that part of e-bay. Here, on an island rich with a fishing and maritime heritage, the high school's marine trades program is often threatened by budgetary cutbacks amid the state's demands for standardized test scores and the prevailing notion that high school graduates ought to be college-bound.

Meanwhile, fewer and fewer of us know what it feels like to make or fix something. To have an inert chunk of metal or block of wood jump to life beneath our hands. To hear the sputter and then the roar of an engine we've coaxed back from the dead. Many of us have lost the feel of a tool in our hands, that heft and weight, its purpose clear. Even in the kitchen, we're often challenged. In the late eighteenth century, James Boswell reminded us "no beast is a cook," and labeled *Homo sapiens* "the cooking animal." A noted anthropologist has suggested that our ancestral discovery of hoisting meat over fire made us more human than language. Yet today, even as cable TV is swelling with an astonishing number of cooking shows, fewer of us plunge our hands in and prepare our own meals. While watching competing chefs go head to head, we're likely to be cozied up on our sofas, plates of microwaved take-out or processed food before us. And while we viewers may well buy all the advertised shiny gadgets, we seem less inclined to get off our bums and into the kitchen to actually use them.

Truth is, most of these food shows, or the myriad offspring of PBS's "This Old House," are more entertainment than how-to. It often seems that watching them, we're supposed to feel we don't know enough or don't know the right stuff. That it's all beyond our grasp. Sort of in the same league as those bottom-of-screen warnings in car commercials with professional demo driving—an equivalent "Don't try this at home."

Of course, if we don't know how something works, if we can't fix it ourselves, someone else is in control. We become more dependent. Over this past year, Bob and I had a new radiant heating system put in. Now when I go into our once familiar cellar, I feel like I'm in a foreign land, wandering among an unfathomable network of tubes, levers, manifolds, of computer-controlled settings on a compact boiler. About car engines I may know little, but I grew up with a father who was mechanic to his own cars, and mine. I hardly ever needed to lift the hood. I still don't. Bob isn't a genius in this area either, but he's the one who typically checks dipstick and reservoir. Recently, though, consulting with one of our island mechanics attempting to fix a malfunctioning wiper on my rear cargo door, I looked under the hood of my fairly late-model car and was reminded how much more it resembles computer than engine. And so different an animal that it requires diagnostics and special tools, ones my mechanic didn't possess to fix what he acknowledged was a simple problem.

You'd think more emphasis would be placed on self-reliance. But that requires—doesn't it?—an engagement with material things. With wood and wire, concrete and pipes, food and fabric, our hands perhaps dangerously linked via power saw or blowtorch. It demands a useful and at least somewhat skilled knowledge of how to make or fix things. But for many years, it seems fewer and fewer job descriptions emphasize the creation of tangible goods and useful services. The job market's tilted toward the importance of intangible information and away from materiality. Where, for example, the word "harvesting" is more frequently applied to, say, data and the Internet and can only figuratively suggest the dirty fingers or sore back in gathering what with hands is sown and grown or is hauled from the sea.

Scientific theories abound that the human brain evolved as a consequence of tool use, and that the hand's subsequent refinement—into dexterous fingers and the opposing miraculous thumb—led to further development of the brain's circuitry and, ultimately, to spoken and written language. Young children in their first months use their hands as a stand-in for language. Later in their development, they seem naturally drawn to making things with their hands. In his early years, my nephew Michael collected sticks. Obsessed with them, he stacked scavenged sticks of various sizes in the yard and at the side of the house. He sneaked them into his bedroom closet. Broken stick bits he'd stuffed into his pockets gummed up the works in my sister's washing machine. While visiting us on the island one summer, he scoured woods and shore, constructing mobiles, "bows and arrows," various contraptions he affixed to his stick-made "forts." Later he turned to Legos and KNEX. Later still, using Instructables, a how-to-do-it-yourself website, he was still "building" things. We trusted then and still that college is in his future. Maybe he'll be drawn to architecture or engineering, work to which, at the final material product in which he's played a part, he can point, recognize, find satisfaction. Not completely unlike, I have to assume, the electrician who flips a switch or the auto mechanic who turns a key and the results are immediate, known. Or like—and this is certainly not in the same league as, say, the cardiac surgeon who's able to tell a mother her son's surgery was a success—the power line repair crew aloft in their cherry pickers who last winter, after a big storm knocked out power for three days, were cheered by folks on this road as if they were returning royalty.

The assumption is my nephew will move toward the mental challenges of white-collar work and away from the "mindless" routine of blue-collar manual labor. But one error there, as Matthew Crawford in *Shopcraft as Soulcraft* points out, is the automatic mental vs. mindless assumption, the notion that manual work is absent of cognitive demands. He cites writer Mike Rose who observes that when it comes to the trades, we're given "the muscled arm, sleeve rolled tight against biceps, but not thought bright behind the eye, no image that links hand and brain."

Fact is, Crawford claims, more and more mindlessness is making its way into the white-collar office as we ride a rising tide of stifling clerkdom. Of paper shufflers morphing into computer tappers. Of a numbing maze of indistinguishable cubicles, often with all the drudgery of the assembly line—even among those corporations who, sniffing out greater profits, have latched onto the cachet of *hand-made*, offering, for example, to the deep-pocketed among us, a Hastings bed with a whopping $18,000 price tag.

I'll let the experts decide, but it's possible and the current economic downturn suggests it, that skilled labor may be tipping the scales for more folks. A good livelihood's economics and intrinsic satisfactions may be winning out over an increasing number of office jobs requiring little judgment or deliberation. Not too long ago, even *The Wall Street Journal* hinted that the future of the "knowledge worker" displaying his handiwork with computer and PowerPoint might not be as "open" as once thought. Or, said another way, more open than the message long delivered to a potential trades apprentice—become an electrician and always be an electrician, a plumber a plumber. Work in a trade, the theory goes, and you're less likely to learn new things—but try telling that to the auto mechanic who now lifts the hood on a computer or a plumber going into the basement who once had only to search for a simple thirty-gallon water heater. Or the retrained manufacturing worker who's learning new skills in composites and precision machining, the power pole climber who's got his eye on wind turbines, the boatbuilder who unrolls a set of plans for a "green" lobster boat.

Without question, manual labor is awash with mind-numbing drudgery. Especially for the less skilled, it's as built into the assembly line as some of its belts and hydraulics and an alarming obsolescence. And yes, lots of manufacturing jobs have flown from our shores, but so many of those have been stripped of all cognitive elements and judgment-making decisions, they would hold little appeal were it not for a wage-earner's increasing servitude to mounting personal debt and an economic climate in which any job is prized. But is this the case with skilled trades? Folks who do not assemble, but make? Who don't add a part but fix?

*S*o here's a story from the same party where I met Bill.

After his truck repair, a young local fisherman hands a check to Ron, one of the island's mechanics, and says, "See this check here, Ron? See how nice it looks with that sailboat, that blue sky and water? In fact, it's so pretty, you ought to frame it and hang it on your wall."

"And about how long you think I should keep it there?"

"Oh, I'm thinking until about Friday."

This, too, I recognize. The held checks and Friday paydays of my youth. The stretch of making do. Just as the past can be so effortlessly romanticized, it's easy to forget hardships or struggles. Or to perceive that somehow manual labor, in all its best guises and particularly when chosen from among many possibilities, spells a "simpler life" with fewer demands or needs. But this kind of working with your hands is not about taking up woodworking in your garage when most of your office colleagues choose instead to tee up on the back nine, though surely a craftsman in a rigged-out shop is a fine thing.

Like my husband and me, a lot of privileged folks are able to spend summers on the island. In increasing numbers, we are retiring here. After making money elsewhere, often in offices, board rooms, or lecture halls, we might do things with our hands, tinkering around the edges of what we think defines manual competence. Recently, an island friend's begun to keep a few chickens in her yard, another's growing vegetables in twelve raised beds, another has begun to braid rugs. One fellow I know, after taking a class at The Wooden Boat School, is making his own skiff, and another can't wait to arrive here each summer if only to split wood with, as it turns out, a machine designed for such purpose.

Maybe their interests in coming here and the desire to stay bear similarities to many of mine—a love for the island's natural beauty, an appreciation of its community, the pace and peace. But as I stand at my window this morning and watch Mike haul out his traps to move them into deeper water, evidence the shedders are on the move, another reason why I've settled here becomes obvious to me: it's also because of Mike and Bill and Ron. At least in some small part. Why it is I feel comfortable here. Who it is I recognize.

In this place where I feel most at home, I live among people like my father and uncles, the men in an unequivocally blue-collar neighborhood I was so eager to leave and reluctant to return to, and, for too long, was too embarrassed to claim. Here, unlike all the other places I plunked down since then, and in part due to its small geographical size and, though bridged, an island after all, I live more intimately with Bill and Ron and with women like Diane or Tilly, who still bear all the nicks and scars of years packing sardines at the island's long-gone cannery. They're my neighbors and friends, fellow committee members and volunteers. Folks for whom, when assistance is needed, I readily show up as they do for me.

After years of working hard to put distance between me and my heritage, avoiding hammer or drill as though, were I to pick one up, I'd discover my hand might feel too comfortably fitted around its grip, I've wound up here.

II. Hers

My mother had a hand in it, too.

Dad made things work. Mom worked to make things. Often she shaped them from seemingly nothing—like Peter Pan–collared dresses and flounced skirts transformed from remnants foraged at the yard-goods sales tables.

She also worked to make things beautiful. A notable and somewhat singular achievement in a family whose women were more apt to translate the combo of home and beauty into cleanliness, a determined, sanitized tidiness. "A well-kept house is a thing of beauty" should have been needlepointed and hung on someone's wall.

But a home is more than a place of function, of where things work. And here my mother excelled, the much-needed antidote to Grandma B's zealous, scrubbed applications of Pine-Sol and Fels Naptha, and to her credo "Everything has its place and you'd better never move it"—as evidenced by her polished hallstand that for as long as I can recall was home only to the rotary phone and a small cut-glass dish, presumably for candy but always empty, and, atop the Magnavox, a porcelain angel of such stern visage that "guardian" had to mean serious business.

What my mother created in our home she probably wouldn't have called beautiful. More clearly she suggested that whether in a person, a landscape, or a charitable act, true beauty only happens with little effort or intentional tinkering, and her house-beautifying efforts were conscious, and, I believe, intended. They were also improbably accomplished in jam-packed days lacking any extravagance of money or time—an enviable accomplishment amidst caring for four children, cooking, ironing, spending hours at her Singer sewing, patching, and mending, doing loads and loads of laundry (behind every cement mason in possession of clean-kneed workpants is a sturdy washing machine and a woman familiar with Clorox and scalding pre-wash soaks), and, on weekends, padding my father's thin Friday paychecks by waitressing at Louie & Mario's. Any creative effort all but seemed like another task on a long list. But I'd like to think that making things beautiful or pleasing to the eye—or, as I see it now, feeding the eye—was not only pleasurable but equally important as, and possibly the necessary counterpoint to, the task I recall most clearly: Mom at the dining room table with papers, stamped envelopes, and rubber-banded bills spread before her as she ticked off each cancelled check, reconciled down to the last penny. This was her semimonthly project—an attempt to get nearly everything paid, as obvious a struggle as if it were physical, and one that only at our peril we dared to interrupt.

For years, I took for granted my mother's aesthetic efforts, not recognizing them as talent until I saw in my high school pals' eyes an acknowledgment that our red-brick ranch, even though similar to theirs in modest size and single bathroom, was different. In our rooms, no kitschy knickknacks collected dust. Instead, interesting flea market finds were put to good and novel use. Seasonal displays of dried flowers and milkweed pods, of forced forsythia and pussy willows flourished. In spite of their cabineted plenitude, revolving arrangements of culled-from-yard-sales milk-glass pitchers and Blue Willow platters were often set out with a minimalist's restraint.

I didn't know much then about tableaux or vignettes. And I can't say if my mother thought of such things, or if, in her displays and arrangements, they were what she attempted to create. But across time, I have come to recognize that her efforts, those fixed moments of her attention in which objects framed, set apart, or juxtaposed were honored, as was the home she helped make for us, must've nurtured her in ways I couldn't even guess at then. And while she and I might not have talked much about beauty, nor about style or taste, I now know she helped shape what and how I see. She didn't have to instruct: "Take notice" or "Pay attention." In the best ways an apprentice can learn, like a journeyman at the side of a master electrician, she demonstrated by example.

Probably nothing singled out my mother more from the other moms than her basement "workroom"—a small space carved out of an area shared by my father's workbench, the laundry chute, and what must've seemed to her an endless stream of dirty laundry we thoughtlessly dropped from the floor above as she, attempting to be worlds away, sat before an easel and dabbed paint to canvas. While I was in high school and already focused on the exit toward college and a life beyond our neighborhood, my mother attended a series of Tuesday night art classes at a local community center. Here, certainly, was a means to a more educated hand but also, perhaps, a proclamation to her family that, as no mere dabbler, she possessed serious intent—and not totally unlike, perhaps, my pursuing at age forty, after years in the business world, an MFA in creative writing.

At first, my mother mostly painted still lifes. Later, portraits. Landscapes were few and often lacked depth and detail, as though by talent as much as choice, her focus was close in not pulled out or away toward distant possibilities. For a few summers, she participated in small, outdoor suburban art shows, her oil paintings displayed on portable pegboard stands my father made. Some paintings sold. Occasionally, she earned a portrait commission. She was still young enough to look good in a trim sheath she made from a Vogue pattern, her hair swept up in a French twist.

Recently, I was freshly reminded of all this when a cousin I'd not seen in decades, after learning of my writing and my sister's drawings and watercolors, said: "No surprise you girls took after your mother." The surprise was mine, his linking my sister and me to our mother in such a way and so many years later. But to him and most of my family, Mom was no mere hobbyist. She was the Family Artist. And we, he made obvious, had not fallen far from the tree.

I once overheard my mother call herself the equivalent of a "Sunday painter." Maybe so. But for many years, she diligently pursued her paint-ing, even after moving to Arizona when, with half a continent between us, I was already living my Life Elsewhere in a downtown Chicago apart-ment.

Even at such a distance, I knew from my visits there that over the years, in various houses in the desert southwest, she transformed spaces into her "workroom," until, in what was to be her last house, a small spare bedroom contained an easel, stacked canvases, some empty frames, cof-fee cans of stiffened brushes, tins of dried watercolors—all of which, not much more than a year after her stroke, she abandoned. One day, without fanfare, she retreated to her chair in the corner of her drawn-draped liv-ing room where, increasingly, she'd been spending time, having already ceased to take much interest in that last neighborhood, its people or gar-dens, not even her own yard where quail bobbed down the hill to eat the corn my father tossed toward the fence line each morning. In cave-like retreat, it was as if she'd strapped on a miner's light trained only on mys-tery paperbacks in her lap, or, just a remote's click away, reruns of *Law & Order.*

*U*nlike my sister, I never specifically asked my mother for any of her paintings, even though art hangs on my walls, work done by others and about which she never inquired, none of it like anything she painted for so many years. But I do have one of her last watercolors, a surprise gift that arrived one winter afternoon several months after her stroke, at a time when she must've felt she'd begun to master a bit the switch from her shaky, stroke-affected right hand to her still steady but untrained left hand—an accomplishment I see so clearly now and so deeply regret was given way too little praise. Painted in that workroom she was to abandon not long after, her watercolor is a muted, somewhat gauzy-toned landscape of sea and coast, a lighthouse silhouetted against a stormy sky, an imagined distant place she'd never traveled to or seen, but that I, so far away, presumably had.

It's said imagination is one of our most human qualities. It liberates us from the limitations of matter, time, and place. But mind alone can't paint or write. Notwithstanding Descartes's "I think, therefore I am" that privileges mind over body, we are, as embodied conscious beings, connected to the world through our corporeal senses, all of which in some way "think." Our brain inhabits our head but reaches out to our body, perhaps most critically to our hands with which, in their silent wisdom, we reach out to the world. Or as neurologist Frank Wilson in *The Thinking Hand* claims, "Brain is hand and hand is brain, and their interdependence includes everything right down to the quarks."

The hand helps release what the body knows. What the mind imagines. With pencil or brush, our imaginatively powered hand grasps immaterial thought and transforms it into concrete image. Bridged, head and hand span distances and time, and, possibly, alter reality.

Be it in a far-off vista or an arranged still life, the artist looks outward and inward. A painting is both an expression and an excavation. It contains a part of the maker and her mental world as well as the objects or landscapes in a real or imagined world. When my mother finished her small watercolor, what, I wonder, did she see? A hand-rendered image on paper? The image she'd constructed in her head? Or, when dissected with the mind's eye, the reminder of the hand's failing? Or of how her imaginative powers could not transform her reality?

How hard it must've been for her—to retrain her body, to pick up a brush with her unstricken left hand and go against the flow of decades' worth of bodily knowing and muscular mimesis. And yet for a time, she was compelled to do so, even if her frustration and disappointment were great. What the mind imagined, the hand could no longer satisfactorily depict. Only in her mind's memory was skilled hand able to lift brush to paper or canvas. A necessary link between a maker and her work had been broken. The union of mind and eye, hand and brush, gone. She snapped shut the paint tins and retreated to her armchair.

But I have this small painting, her brief—too brief—triumph.

*O*n a late Thursday afternoon, as each new summer session winds down, there's an open studio walk-through at the island's Haystack Mountain School of Crafts. In a natural setting of old lichen-splotched woods and moss-cloaked glacial erratics, several architecturally distinct, low-slung buildings hug huge granite ledges that slope a long way down to Jericho Bay. The setting is stunning, as is the view, but when "thick o' fog," as in certain summers it often is, you don't see much. Sounds, however, intensify. Even before entering a studio, there's a fire's roar, a whirring wheel's hum. A chorus of rhythmic taps, slaps, whines. Of hammer, loom, and saw.

Here, faculty and student craftsmen, each unique in talent, technique, and vision, create and learn. Knowledge is passed on, often in demonstration by hands trained for specialized tasks. Manual skills that begin as bodily practices are coupled with an understanding of materials and developed through training and experience, imaginative powers and individual vision. The objects made here are often both beautiful and unexpected. Of clay and metal, of glass, fiber, and wood. Or sometimes, like Michael's sticks, of materials scavenged from nearby forest floors or rescued from the dump in ways similar to how my mother once cruised alleys, one day hauling home a filigreed coat rack that, after a thorough polishing, revealed its bright brass, what to her eyes had been hinted at from a tangled heap of trash.

At Haystack, the metalworkers, often with hands as nicked and scarred as those of the island cannery's women, don't so much bang into submission a hunk of metal as coax from it a particular bend or graceful arch. Improbably, by exhalations blown into fists clutching the end of a long blowpipe, a blob of molten glass swells, its sinuous curves breathed into being. Like a writer bent over a desk, her body still except for the hands, a potter brushes glaze onto an unfired pot. Each represents a collaborative interplay between head and hand. Each begins in uncertainty, that part of the maker's journey similar to a writer's embarking on a new essay or poem.

By my last count, there are at least eight galleries on this island, and numerous individual artist studios. In summer, there are First Friday openings, group show monthly rotations, art classes at Sea Mark. In addition to its summer workshops, Haystack hosts lectures, artists' slide shows and demos, a year-round community exhibition space. This island is home to artists and accomplished craftsmen. To kilns, darkrooms, printing presses, to sheds equipped with tools to cut granite or hammer steel.

All of which I need. What fine crafts historian Sandra Alfoldy on a recent visit to Haystack referred to as "mindful hands and handy minds." It may have been what my mother would have wanted or needed, too. To live among artists of all stripes, bump shoulders with the creative makers of image, object, and word. Of what comes from familiarity with material or subject, from shared knowledge and acquired skills, all honed with practice, repetition, time. What would my mother have thought of Haystack had she, pre-stroke, been willing and, after, able to travel? Would she have recognized her need, or mine? A need that I'm freer and more privileged to pursue—a path that, perhaps unknown to both of us, she'd long ago helped send me down?

Did she ever recognize herself in me? Surely she did in my sister who is successful with pencil and watercolor, wood block and silver point. But a link between my making and hers, her painted images and my words?

My mother held brush to empty canvas. I press pencil to blank page. Such tactile connection is, to me, necessary, how the pencil's drag against paper slows things down, leaves more room for the unconscious to enter, allows for more space between hesitation and assurance. Before certitude solidifies. Sometimes, my hand seems untethered. It leads me into unexpected places. Or coaxes a fluent, possibly even inspired flow so that, for a time, head and hand are in seamless collaboration.

As with painting, the act of writing, of *drawing* out, gives shape to a world of space and matter. It concretizes thought, reveals internal images and emotions. Using words—a type of tool?—I span distances and time. I shape and make, imagine, retrieve, reconstruct. Doing so, whether at my desk or, wanting a different slant of light, spread out at the dining room table, I'm transported, hopefully, to places that satisfy and surprise. Much as I want to think my mother was for many years.

For a long time now, I can't help but notice how my hands have become so similar to hers—the long thin fingers with small nail beds, with trimmed and clean but never polished nails. Twin ridges of prominent knuckle bones. The pentimento-like emergence of pale-tiled sun spots. Knots of branching blue veins. And the way, entering another decade, my hands' thin covering of skin is, as hers was, more easily bruised. In tasks I learned beside her—ironing, say, or tacking up a hem or whisking an egg with a fork, I see my mother's hands. And I see them now as I write this, pressing lead against the page.

Brush and pencil are, I'd tell her now if I could, bridges between head and hand. Between mother and daughter.

III. Theirs

First Friday in Stonington has lured several of us to the southern tip of the island. Outside three galleries, colorful nylon flags flutter in the onshore breeze. Music wafts up from the Seasons waterfront deck. It's not yet dusk, but Harbor Café's weekly Fish Fry has already tempted early diners and day-trippers winding up their visit. Many of us have come to town as much to chat with friends as to see the new art hung in the galleries, much of it by people we know. But suddenly, it's as if the real show begins.

On the street running parallel to the harbor, cars slow, pull over. People get out. I, too, cross the street near Town Pier with its unobstructed view of the harbor. We've all been spontaneously struck by, even felt compelled to exclaim aloud over, the light, the sudden and exquisite spill of warm light coursing down over the granite-rimmed harbor and the pastel clapboard houses with their brightly planted window boxes stacked atop the corseting hills behind which the sun will soon set. Here's a light capable of doing extraordinary things. And it's the moored lobster fleet in the harbor that seems to have been singled out for special treatment. The descending sun's last light lavishes the sides of boats with a rosy hue, a type of gilded enameling reflecting off the expanse of still, slate-colored water. Is it too over the top to suggest that here is a type of benediction? At the very least, it seems a kind of quiet, hushed honoring. And how fitting now, at the height of the season when hauling is at its go-for-broke busiest.

Just this week, Mike, chasing after the hard shedders, moved all his lobster traps into deeper water and I'm no longer able to see him from our deck. Now, just a local boy with a five-trap recreational license putters out in his skiff. Earlier today, though, even he was a no-show. Instead, heading into the bay from an overnight anchorage in Northwest Harbor was one of the large three-masted schooners that transport vacationers to various ports along Maine's coast. In size and nobility, few other crafts can match these carefully restored beauties. Only rarely do they come in so close to our shorefront. Usually I see them silhouetted in the distance, their tall white sails in angular contrast to the humped, dark spruce islands and far-off Camden Hills. They're a magnificent sight, as are, on a different scale, the sleek racing sloops that compete in the annual Eggemoggin Reach Regatta, particularly when their bright spinnakers billow and fill like colorfully plumaged birds about to take flight.

But no boat arouses in me more appreciation than the tough, open lobster boat. The kind that the late Mike Brown, local newspaper columnist and lobsterman, may have had in mind when writing "The character of a boat starts early." (Like, I wonder, a young daughter's?)

I love the blunt-nosed profiles of lobster boats, their high, hard-working bows and wide, stable sterns, their efficient amidships wheelhouses. To me, these are "real" boats, the heavy-boned workhorses built for endurance as opposed to slender-legged thoroughbreds with enviable looks and bursts of speed. A calm harbor pierced with a fleet of anchored lobster boats is more attractive to me than a flotilla of rigged sailing vessels or powered leisure craft with lofty flying bridges.

And this evening, the day's last light is bestowing its luminescence on the flanks and bows of each of these forthright, blunt-profiled beauties, all of which, as always, are similarly swung about on their moorings in the direction the prevailing wind and tidal currents demand. To me, it's so arresting a sight that I can easily forgive the summer tourist who, as though such a phenomenon was the result of intended effort, an obliging attempt at picturesque symmetry, was alleged to have crooned, "Oh, look. How nice. All the lobstermen park their boats in the same direction."

Come dawn, though, any such romantic and generous sentiments are quickly doused by a piston-firing, diesel-engine-revving fleet sprung to life. The chorus of visitors and even some recent newcomers swells with disbelief: "Do those lobstermen have to leave so early and make all that racket? How are we supposed to sleep?"

At dusk, though, complaints are few. Especially tonight as we look seaward, rapt and hushed by a transient light that has already begun to fade, become a remnant of its former self before the sky darkens and we're left with what we carry in our heads, in whatever nooks and crannies our memories lodge. As the last light candles the placid harbor, I can't help but think the moored lobster boats look like a herd of sturdy animals quietly grazing a meadow. Rugged workhorses that in just a few hours will be back in the traces, waiting for knowing hands—like my father's—to skillfully guide them. It's a scene my mother might've painted.

UNEARTHED

*N*o more towering tomato plants threatening to topple. No mounds of bolting butter-leaf or vines of peas impossible to untangle. I've yanked out the plushy sage, confined all herbs to pots on the deck. My garden, like Grandma B's, is one of beauty not utility.

But even flower beds can heave stones.

*I*t's hard not to make mistakes. Or confuse synonyms.

Earth: solid ground beneath my feet, the terra firma home of my temporal world. Soil: the Earth's top layer, favorable to growth. Dirt: long have my fingers dug into it. But after, always, the washed hands, smoothed hair, the tucked-in shirt.

*G*randma B's house was quiet. As though in it there had never been any children. So many breakable things within hand's reach. And in drawers, like archaeological relics, special things saved for an unspecified event or purpose. In closets after her death at 90, tidily stacked boxes of tissue-wrapped dusters and nightgowns gifted her decades before.

Flowers also hoard. Especially the spring bloomers like tulips and narcissus, their bulbs buried deep in November with dollops of bone-meal and faith. Come May when blossoms wither, the bulbs store whatever the yellowing leaves make for them in dying. A deep warehouse of replenished energy saved for the following year.

Or, as poet Theodore Roethke proclaimed: "Deep in their roots all flowers keep the light."

*G*randma B loved her garden, was repulsed by dirt. But for her no robust scrubbing. No sudsy lathering beneath a long, hot shower. Her baths, such meager things—a couple of inches of tepid water drawn in a cold porcelain tub.

And secondary, like all things, to a tongued daily communion wafer at St. Peter & Paul's, the parish to which, I was made to understand, she *belonged*.

*O*nce, I tried to grow tomatoes. But after a season of ravenous hornworms and powdery mildew, of diligent feeding and hoeing that only produced sunscald in a hot spring and watery pulp in the rainy summer that followed, I abandoned my ambitions for the easier fecundity of cherry tomatoes which, by the time September rolled around, had worn out their welcome.

Now I discover how tomato plants seem able to show up anywhere. Evidence abounds. Among the barrel-potted zinnias at the post office. As the uninvited partner to my bee balm. Even at the cove's distant sandbar, a lone cherry tomato plant scraggily fruits forth. All far from their greenhouse ancestry, the tilled, loamy beds where they got their start.

Though they've long been banished from my flowers-and-shrubs-only garden, I still love the names of tomato plants I bump into at the local nursery or while thumbing through gardening catalogues on a snowy January afternoon. Sugar Pearl and Red Currant, Big Beef and Giant Syrian, Bella Rosa and Orange Pixie. So many speak to taste, size, gender. And, as though attempting to satisfy all three: the ever-popular Sweet Baby Girl.

I love, too, the irony: how hybrid tomato plants, due to all their tinkered-with vitality, must be staked, tethered, caged, or contained. They cannot bear the weight of their own fruit, all that desirable, nearly wild energy.

*S*ome flower specimens from my youth stand out. Orange spotted tiger lilies growing along the white fence in my childhood backyard on Oakdale Avenue. Fragrant Peace roses in mulched beds, crepey fist-sized mounds of peach against red brick that even commanded my father's attention. Diminutive deep-blue violets hiding out beneath the elm trees as though, already too short-lived, their aim was only to escape notice. Bright snapdragons with mouths that gaped open when your fingers knew where to press, and where presumably the smoke issued forth. Towering hollyhocks hogging the show at the back of Grandma B's small yard, shielding from view the alley and garbage cans, the driveway where on rare afternoons Grandpa B tinkered under his Pontiac's hood.

Why, in my garden, do I grow none of these?

*S*o much threatens to take it all under: canker, wilt, mold, blight. Bacterial lesions, fungal infections. Also grubs, whiteflies, Japanese beetles, leaf miners, thrips. And Pith Necrosis about which I agree with writer Andrew Hudgins—were this not the name for a fatal condition hollowing a plant's stem, it would be perfect for a story's swarthy villain.

So many threats. And necessities, too. Like rot and decay, what, like filth, can attract swarming flies. As requisite to a garden as dirt. As necessary to a fully lived life as what it can never be rid of—its soiled bits, messy parts, the later laments.

*E*nclosed by a fence, contained within trimmed, meticulous beds, Grandma B's yard was almost precisely squared. But at its clearly defined edges, it forever threatened to sprawl, jump the borders. Despite her efforts, it was not immune to armies of ants routinely marching into the soft petal-folds of velvety peonies, nor, come July, to the frenzied bees, their bodies wallowing in pollen as they plundered the white lilies.

*W*e gardeners nourish and nurture. We cultivate and develop. As though, troweling among the sweet william and veronica, we are parents.

Parenting. Is this a word my mother ever knew, or used?

Or was there some other 1950s-speak, a Doctor Spock-ian terminology that might've gotten thrown around with me, the loquacious early achiever, the lauded Family Star and (no doubt) insufferable Smarty Pants. The first child after the death of a premature three-day-old son. And to boot, Grandchild Number One. For four years, until a sibling's birth nearly kicked me from my throne, I was the garden's lone exotic specimen, receiving, like a lavish shower on a dusty afternoon, unabashed adoration. Encouraged and sanctioned, gifted with a family's expectations that—and why not?—I'd want to be just like them. But perhaps they, like me, had yet to understand: expectations are both support and what is pushed against.

"*A*n environmental value requires its antithesis for definition," claims geographer Yi-Fu Tuan. The virtues of the countryside, for example, need an anti-image—the crowded city. A Maine island of familiar landmarks requires the anonymity of suburban sprawl. The permanent opacity of rocks on a shoreline is better defined by the fleeting transparency of evanescing waves.

I needed the city's brawl, its brash "downtown." How it pointed away from my childhood's stranglehold of neighborhoods identified by parish boundaries as rigidly as if they'd been staked and fenced. I cut the cord, embraced dirt and mess, men and bars. As though I'd found tomatoes everywhere. Big Boy. Better Boy. Easy Girl.

I needed—then and now—all those years in the city's enlightening and grimy corridors. Would I, without them, have recognized my need for this quiet island where I've come to settle half the year? Isn't it possible that without Husband One and Husband Two, I wouldn't have possessed the wisdom to embrace my current husband of twenty-six years? A man who surely, according to Grandma B, my mother nodding approvingly, saved me (even if too late not to remain childless) from my wild and nearly calamitous past, neither of them understanding his had been similarly colored, a shared attraction that drew us together. And still does.

But what opposing force to that which I assign Grandma B and carry in my head propelled her to drop to her hands and knees in her pristine living room one holiday afternoon and allow my teenage brother to pretend to straddle her as though, with her head thrown back and wildly grinning at the camera, she were a spirited pony threatening to bolt? In the background of the documenting photograph are laughing, clapping family members, most of whom, unlike me, never jumped ship. Behind them squats the recognizable Magnavox with its doily-centered ceramic Madonna and the revolving brass clock enclosed in a glass dome as though in a terrarium encapsulating time, and on the wall above, as in every room, a wooden crucifix. It's all there, in a recently unearthed photograph. Of an occasion I know nothing about. Of an energy and grin I didn't think Grandma B possessed. "Because," they charge, "you didn't stick around."

*W*ere it possible now, I would lead Grandma B into my garden, point and say, "See? Like yours. Flowers." Still, after all these years, pointing away from the garden I loved best in my youth—the kitchen garden of a small Indiana farm my family visited for too few summers.

Possessing to my young eyes no link to the disciplined rigors of the kitchen, it was a garden neither enclosed nor meager, but sprawling, unruly, almost sinfully abundant. A bonanza of engorged, cracked melons oozing in the sun beneath a cloud of bees. Filet beans like groping fingers lunging past their chicken-wire cage. Zucchini languishing in the heat and each day growing larger, alarmingly swollen, as if their only purpose were to loll against a Chevy's waxed hood waiting to be noticed.

In my current, dedicated-to-flower-and-foliage garden, would Grandma B notice how well-mannered a specimen I am? Of compact habit, not given to sprawl nor needing much staking. With flowers that are pretty but not flamboyant or lavish. Adaptable. Easy.

*M*y garden is no formal affair. There are no clipped boxwoods, no meticulously symmetrical beds. I don't lavish time on tea roses. The color palette is cool, my aesthetics basic: taller spires at the back, diminutive mounds in front. Green and silver, lacy and coarse-edged foliage texture the mix.

But I do seek form. Some kind of order. I like the suggestion that things will last.

Sometimes, I follow the directions in how-to books and on seed packets as though they were tableted commandments. And when, in violation of my carefully made plans, the results I desire don't develop, I attempt other means to impose my will before recognizing, once again, what a puny match I am for the laws of nature. In the garden there are no catechism-like certainties.

Grandma B's garden certainties seemed simple: flower or weed. As clear-cut to her as Catholics or non-Catholics.

On the right side of that divide: *our people.* And of them, another certainty: the married possess a chance to ascend to Heaven. The divorced do not.

*W*orking in my garden in the afternoon sun, I try to transform propagate into proliferate. I transplant liatris to a sunnier spot and move a mound of coral bells to where, beneath the hydrangea's canopy, they can sprawl in shade.

I change what I can. Feed the plants. Amend the dirt. From parched soil, I've learned, anything can blow away.

In Grandma B's parish there were always a few families with so many children. They assembled at Sunday Mass in the frontmost pews, the backs of their heads lined up like peas prodded by a dull knife into a row on a plate. As linked as a rosary's strung crystal beads. Among them, hollowing out like stems attacked by villainous Pith Necrosis, a few thin, sapped women.

We were told: "The family who prays together stays together."

We learned: not always.

*B*ut let us not spill the dirt. Let's withhold dirty secrets. The unspoken warning when visiting Grandma B: Don't mention the narrow dormered bedroom at the top of the stairs, with its spartan twin bed and tucked-tight sheets, no matter how many times I sneaked up there on stockinged feet, stood at the threshold and peered in. As if into a type of diorama that, for all its accurate detail of polished oxfords in the corner, of ticking Westclox alarm and brown Bakelite radio on a dusted bureau, hinted at little life. Never refer to Grandpa B's increasing absence in photographs or family gatherings. Don't acknowledge what is never said. What's never talked about—like the War. Like the other woman.

"*M*y garden is going to hell."

So laments a friend about late August's dreaded sprawl, a time when the garden is months removed from its initial harmony and growth, its early seasonal attempts to show off, attract. Weeks past its fervent and near singular purpose after blooming its fullest: to burst, split, disperse, all seeds dropped, blown into air or carried off, before, soon, all is spent, crisped, sunk into collapse. When whatever form we tried to shape into those beds lets go, the order lost.

No gardener I know works harder than my friend. Singlehandedly, she rototills new beds, edges them with granite cobbles and small boulders, shovels loam by the truckload, pitchforks mineral-rich rockweed from the shore onto the back of her pickup and transports it to her perennial beds each autumn. She divides, transplants, feeds, prunes, wheels heaped garden carts to her compost pile, digs out shrubs taller than she is. Still, she calls her garden a "pleasure garden."

*W*e make choices. Not in everything we remember or can't. Not in all the ways we can change but won't. Not in wherever our minds might take us as our hands dig in the dirt or reach into a lilac hedge and lavishly clip.

And how could I not remember Grandma B's lilacs? That huge hedge of them overarching the walkway flanking the side of her house. A natu-ral arbor that spilled forth in June with unexpected luxuriance, especially when drenched by a soaking rain. Already back then, those lilacs, as effu-sively perfumed as some of the veiled and hatted ladies at Sunday Mass, seemed to me a kind of old-fashioned flower. But how I loved them, and the way that, for a few short weeks, several cut-glass bowls of purple brimmed atop Grandma B's TV cabinet and dining room buffet.

One afternoon, I peeled away from Grandma B and my aunts clat-tering in the kitchen. Clearing lunch, they were already planning sup-per. For years, that didn't seem strange to me, their going from one meal to planning the next. As if, for all the world's unspeakable hurts and in spite of whatever else might get doled out to you, there was always food. The planning, preparing, serving of it. Even in the cleaning up after, they seemed to say, there was always this. Already I was being welcomed into their midst—expected, actually, to join in—to plunge hands into filled, sudsy sinks, make countless trips to the fridge with a stream of covered bowls. In that hive of purposeful insistence dwelled a sustenance that to my eyes and ears lacked hunger's urgency, that possessed little fervor or zest. But, of course, to their hum and buzz, I was only meant to respond "let me in," not ever dream "get me out of here."

Although, a little, into that collective, I'd been pulling up a chair. Over coffee in Grandma B's kitchen, over the news of a neighbor's death, a woman who I only knew didn't belong to the parish, I listened as Grandma B declared, "She had so little."

Heads nodded. Hands lifted cups to lips.

"No," my aunt corrected, "she had *nothing.*" More head-nodding, long wordless moments, not of lament but acknowledgment. An unspo-ken recognition. As if having nothing were some sort of badge of honor. As if nothing were everything.

But on this particular afternoon, there were also Grandma B's lilacs. In the dining room, I stood before the buffet and leaned in, stuck my face into their fragrant wands, and deeply inhaled.

"So you like those, too?"

My aunt, dish towel in hand, had come up behind me.

"You know, these are one of your grandmother's only indulgences."

Here was news. Big news. Not in the way my aunt's smile and raised eyebrows seemed almost conspiratorial. Not in the way such a look hinted at a possible selfhood that might question, might traffic in free-dom, and, as I was to later learn, indulge. Nor that here again was some evidence about Grandma B I'd overlooked. Lilacs weren't nothing.

That afternoon, in those days when I didn't have to dust off my

Baltimore Catechism, I could only marvel—Indulgences! And incredulously wonder: how were lilacs on a par with carrying food baskets to the poor at Easter or, after Confession, racing through rounds of the rosary to shave off five- or maybe ten-year increments from Purgatorial punishment? How to explain it?

How else but to see that there could be in beauty, purpose. A usefulness. Beauty *and* utility.

I don't prune in late August as I do in June. In early summer, my intention is not removal but alteration, as though I am attempting to trim a bonsai, that miniature specimen of order and containment, snipped and shaped and encouraged into new direction, into a reflection of what a particular plant species was intended to be but is transformed by limiting scale, controlling shape. Nor in August do I permanently sever. Even if it might appear that way. When, among dwindling phlox and salvia, I reach with shears toward brown stems, spent blooms, the curled and crimped leaves all as surely "gone by" as any split and rotted, draining pulp of tomatoes, its final puddle of shrunken seeds sinking back into the dirt.

"Each thing an end of something else," wrote Roethke. And it's true, among the press of late summer's buzz and whir, long after another season has determined if my perennials lived up to my expectations back in snowbound January, there is a certain pleasure in letting nature take back the garden. A different kind of cutting the cord, like making peace with the messy past.

But even here, in the northeast Atlantic, far removed from my native Chicago, where Zone 5 tilts toward a harsher 6, there are multiple microseasons, one crop of flowers giving way to another. Crocus to daffodils. Lilacs to lilies. Roses to asters to, finally, mums with their compact blooms and sturdy stems that, like chard or kale in the kitchen garden, hold the door open until frost blackens and winter winds howl. In each, I'm given the chance to assess. To move, transplant, cut back. To stake what threatens to collapse under its own diligent weight. So much of what I do is create new spaces where things fill in.

But that's the way with gardens, no? Always evolving, the creation of what we cultivate, husband. A construct of the imagination, a complex synthesis of sensibility and desire, past experience and personal choice. A measurement not just of skills but time.

Even in January, the growing season isn't really over. In roots and bulbs buried deep below ground like the hidden past, flowers are keeping the light.

EDGES

"Where's the barge?" I ask Buster, who strides across the lawn, hitching up his pants with each step. Though it's still early, I'm out on the deck, a second cup of coffee in hand. For the past half hour, I've been scanning south beyond Bradbury and Pickering Islands to catch a glimpse of Buster's barge slapping its way across the wave-tossed bay.

This is the morning I've been waiting for. To see how, after timing the tides just right, Buster will nimbly nudge his barge against our shoreline. "It's the final step," he's assured me, in what began two years ago when a chance confluence of events—big northwest winds, a full moon's tidal surge, a week's worth of record-breaking rain following the spring melt-off—claimed a chunk of the bluff bordering the bay. Not far from my house, thirty feet up and clear down to the shore, a broad expanse of sodden dirt, vegetation, large boulders and three full-grown spruce trees was shorn away as effortlessly as a knife cuts through cake. Never had I been as envious of friends living on the southern part of the island with its unbudging granite ledge.

Since, volunteer grasses and wildflowers have attempted to make the exposed wound look less painful. The spruce trees, remarkably dumped in a nearly upright position on the shore, tried to survive the tidal seep of salt water into their remaining roots. But with each storm or surge, more needles browned, bigger branches dropped, their prognosis increasingly grim. Worse, in cracks and gullies carved by each heavy rainfall, erosion persisted. One day, I had to believe, my garden, this deck, perhaps my house itself would be jeopardized.

And so, Buster.

For days now, once I reluctantly accepted that a swath of our yard

193

would have to morph into a heavy-equipment track, Buster's been haul-ing in truckloads of pebbly fill to build up the steep cutaway, scale back the shorn bluff's nearly 90-degree perpendicular drop. More dramatic have been the thundering loads of big boulders he's unceremoniously dumped from the top of the bluff in loud, bone-clattering cascades onto the shore. Rocks that he's assured me are up to the task of becoming an armoring barrier at the bluff's base.

"I laid them all out at home first," Buster explained. "In my door-yard." Proof once more that Buster's a careful planner, but reminding me, too, that in this neck of the woods, dooryards usually mean more than neat flower beds and a patch of mown grass.

Today's plan: Buster, assisted by Alden with his excavator down on the shore, will set the boulders. Instead, tipping his chin seaward, Buster says, "We can't get the barge here today. Wind's kicking things up wicked fierce."

"So tomorrow, then?"

"Nope. Can't use the barge here tomorrow. I'm moving a house up to Bold Island. After that, I'm fixing to haul roofing shingles to Great Sprucehead. They say big rains are headed this way next week. Tides'll be working against us then, too." As I'm thinking lunar phases and weather forecasts surely trump barge schedules, Buster says, "Excavator's on its way."

I nod, uncertain what that means. In fact, I'm still puzzled over how all the pieces of this project fit, how a jumble of boulders is going to be transformed into whatever will hold back Penobscot Bay's undermining wave action and demand of it a respect for borders. Buster's not offer-ing any explanation and I'm not inclined to ask the obvious questions. Blanks, however, quickly begin to fill in.

Piercing the morning's quiet, an engine rumbles. Gears grind. Low-hanging branches snap and crack. Alden's arrived and he's trailering a yel-low Caterpillar excavator way larger than anything I'd anticipated. With pivoting cab, articulated arm, front bucket, and huge treads—do I even use the right terminology?—it's the kind of machine that, to my eyes, digs foundations, builds major roads. It does not park in my driveway.

With a wave in our direction, Alden deftly hauls himself up into the excavator's cab. A roar, a belch of thick black smoke, and slowly he backs away from the trailer.

Over the shudder and clank, Buster shouts, "We're taking her over the edge."

This I definitely hadn't imagined.

I step aside and give Alden a wide berth as the Cat crawls painfully close to my hydrangeas. It bites deep into what's become such a rutted, cleaved terrain, it's hard to believe any of it will ever look remotely the same again.

For the past few days, I've watched Buster confidently back his dump truck to the bluff's edge. I held my breath each time the heavily-loaded truck bed rose into the air and the weight of the shifting boulders lifted the front wheels off the ground. A delicate dance that big Buster with small levers and gears executed with precision and balance, until, in a swirling eruption of dust and noise, the boulders, like thunderous marbles, rolled down to the shore. Each maneuver had been admirable, often surprising. But putting this clanking beast over the edge and ensuring from this steep slope its safe arrival on the shore is in another league altogether. Or maybe I've just not spent enough time hanging out at construction sites.

At the bluff's edge, Alden throttles down and lowers the excavator's bucket. Giving the Cat some juice, he eases forward. In small, short bursts, he inches further still. And then further, until half the Cat's length is suspended mid-air. Hovering, the excavator tilts. Had I thought to freeze this moment into a photograph, it would later justify my belief that Alden and the heavy Cat are about to pitch forward in free fall and tumble end over end into the bay.

Instead, the bladed front bucket, now extended, digs in. A certain and possibly even catastrophic downward momentum is blocked by Alden's expert clutch maneuvers, a measured dig-and-ease. The burly, belching Cat begins slowly, almost delicately, to descend the steep slope with the minced steps of a diva on a red-carpeted runway. At last, Alden reaches bottom, and up top, I hoot my approval. Buster signals a thumbs-up.

For days, I've wondered how a barge would maneuver its way to shore. How close it would get at a quarter-moon low tide. How an excavator would disembark, possibly into water. And after, what path it would take over felled spruce and heaped boulders to work on what, at high tide, is a narrow strip. Instead—over the edge—I've had this.

*E*dges. This island has a mess of them. Many are indistinct. They blur.

While walking the shore as the tide ebbs, as I slosh my way among the vast fields of rockweed, bladder wrack, mussel beds and legions of periwinkles, among exposed barnacled boulders, myriad crevices and tidal pools where, for a few hours, sea stars and limpets and sea urchins are seemingly inert, it's hard to say at what spot exactly I've gone from land to water. Where is the demarcating, distinguishing edge of what

Rachel Carson called "the primeval meeting place of the elements of earth and water?" Where is, as Walt Whitman wrote of the seashore, "… that suggesting, dividing line, contact, junction, the solid marrying the liquid…"?

For no two successive days at the same hour is the tide line precisely the same. What's observed as an edge today is tomorrow erased, smudged. Children who visit find such daily revisions magical. They're naturally enthralled by how the water retreats, how it rewrites the shoreline, exposes tidal pools where they poke and pry. Places that with the incoming tide disappear. Like them, I love these mutable edges the tides make of our shoreline.

Nor am I alone. Taped to my refrigerator is a photograph taken when friends and I boated to Butter Island for a picnic last summer. In it, everyone's walking the cobbled beach at low tide. Like a flock of seabirds foraging what for a time is the edge, we're all looking down, open to discovery, wanting to be surprised. We bend and reach out toward the shore's riches, each of us searching for what peculiarly to her will become treasure. That afternoon, the landscape's mutable edges had knocked on our doors, invited us out to play, just as, on many mornings, I put up little fight when the shore's siren call lures me away from breakfast dishes, an unmade bed, the unrevised draft of a poem waiting on my desk.

Of course, this island has its distinct edges, too. Unambiguous places where crossing over from land to water is indisputable. If I were to lean over the side of our island bridge spanning the Reach's watery expanse or teeter at Town Pier's end, risking a plunge into the icy Atlantic, I'd know the edge is certain, definite.

Now, erosion seems to have redefined our bluff as a distinct but unrecognizable edge—this familiar spot that almost daily has drawn me to it in the nine years of owning this house and from where, presumably secure, I look out at the sea, the distant horizon, and whatever weather's being blown in. From such perspective, what's become familiar and known to me are jutting granite ledges, jagged outcroppings, numerous offshore islets and distant larger islands heaped with immense boulders, spiked with thick dark spruce, and all punctuated with deeply indented shorelines of niches, fissures and crevices where life forms teem. Each feature possesses a particular beauty but also makes this a landscape that comforts, a topography partly shaped by having been at the edge of an Ice Age glacier and, still proudly wearing its old battle scars, survived. Rugged ridges and half-submerged ledges appear impenetrable. Outcroppings boast they'll not yield without a fight. More than distinguish or give form to open water sweeping toward the distant horizon's thin, porous rim, they corset immensity, frame wildness. It's here, in such a limned yet expansive and fluid landscape that I often experience a type of bounded *un*boundedness. And on a scale I can more comfortably relate to.

Which is not to say I don't feel puny at the ocean's edge. But it's a different kind of puniness than when I'm out West visiting family in the Colorado Rockies or the Arizona high country. There, in palettes that don't favor green, that often tilt toward dust and scorch, there's little to suggest the gentler curves and kinder elevation of the bay's domed islands or Blue Hill's blue hill. Magnificent certainly, jaw-dropping even, but the mountains of the American West have long seemed to me—and is this part of their attraction to others?—impossibly huge, especially indifferent. I might think they were thumbing their noses were it not for the sense they'd already turned their imposing backs to me.

Not so long ago, on a family visit, both feet firmly planted a safe distance from the edge, I stood atop a canyon's rim. After several minutes amid that gasp-inducing, undeniable grandeur, I found myself wanting, needing, to reach out and touch something familiar—a tree, a fence, my nearby sister. I'd become momentarily overwhelmed. Was it because of my proximity to a distinct, unequivocal edge, or by how far I was from any landscape in which I felt anchored? I didn't know how to look, or where. Invisible to my eyes were what in the canyon must be nooks and crannies, burrows, caves and hidden nests, all the inventive, unknown-to-me critters and plant life that go with *butte, arroyo, gulch.*

Like a visitor to a hostile country, I wasn't invited by this landscape toward a closer, come-hither intimacy. I looked, admired, was immensely grateful for our planet's gifts, but I didn't feel connected, drawn in, claimed. How high up I was, and yet I didn't sense I'd find it easier to feel closer to anything that might reside in all that sky. And surely, when viewed from such a mountaintop and so far from any tugged sea, the moon had to be up to a whole different kind of business.

After several moments, I gratefully stepped back.

*W*ith its tightly gridded streets, its small yards of tidy lawns and small postwar brick bungalows, my childhood's suburban neighborhood south of Chicago, just out of—just over the edge—of the city, seems an unlikely comparison to this one in Maine. But it too was a kind of island, one with distinctly edged physical boundaries—Sibley Boulevard often busy with trucks hauling their loads from the South Side mills on one side, a network of freight-train tracks on another, and bounding it elsewhere a stretch of woods and the curving Little Calumet, which, by the time it wound into our neighborhood, was a narrow, sluggish river with pea-green water of dubious quality. Along the river's elevated shore grew a forest of high, rattling, amber-colored reeds that we neighborhood kids hacked down and hurled as spears or gathered into what resembled to our eyes the tribal huts we'd seen in old issues of *National Geographic*. There, on many long summer afternoons, our singular aim, it seemed, was to reinvent ourselves. The younger girls pretended to be horses, whinnying, flinging their ponytailed heads and clomping the winding paths, while we older ones furnished our huts with dried leaf beds, moss pillows, and floors of stacked sticks, increasingly mindful with nascent adolescent stirrings like sap awakened in trees, of the sweaty boys who clattered among the reeds in boisterous renditions of Swamp Fox, or threatened to be cruel to turtles and frogs. Together, we harvested thick cattails and, as if they were stogies, lit them with matches filched from our folks.

No early naturalist, I didn't scramble down the river's bank and poke around in the fetid mud at the edge. Likely, I feared there the near certain eruption of mosquitoes or a possible encounter with another river rat like the dead one my brother, to my mother's horror, once carried home. Back then, my interests lay elsewhere—in books, dance, and, more and more, my new solo imaginative roamings in a backyard tree house.

Mostly I thought of the river as less a place of potential mystery and discovery than as one of the demarcating boundaries that enisled our neighborhood. Beyond the river's defined edge I seldom ventured, not even in midwinter when we skated its frozen surface or, atop our sleds, careened onto it. If the push-off was strong enough and the spot of take-off high, I'd skim across, my sled bumping against the opposite, elevated wooded shore. But even if my sled running tips buried deep into the opposite bank's frosty, weedy hummocks, I didn't attempt to clamor up the other side, avoiding it as though it were a wall with electrified fence. I couldn't see what resided beyond its trees or the small ridge beyond, but little tempted me. The neighborhood's older kids unspooled stories of nebulous teenage gangs armed with rocks and fists, though it was our protective parents and neighbors with night shifts and self-proclaimed dead-end jobs who, with threats and few details, drew an unambiguous, thick dark line. They warned us not to cross over, not to check out the other side, the translation of which I partially deciphered later at a racially integrated district high school where such warnings lost much of their punch.

At the river's edge, I, a dutiful first-born, obeyed. I hopped off my sled and hauled it back. My tame, timid self was also already in bud, the chicken part of me prone to see threat at the edge, not thrill. I was still years away from cars, boys, college, work, from an essential curiosity firing the engine that eventually drove me beyond the neighborhood's borders to the choices I later made once those seemingly fixed boundaries of river and highway, of class, religion, and limited education were more clearly understood, less severely constrained. At the river's edge, I'd barely begun to creep toward an understanding that some seemingly hard-edged borders are in fact porous. I was still decades away from needing to step back from a canyon's rim or from discovering a flood tide's daily transit, its possible message-in-a-bottle evidence that some other life existed elsewhere. And further away still from this island, this house, this view, and a collapsing bluff's threatening edge.

I carry a thermos of lemonade down to the shore for Buster and Alden. Long an admirer of competence, whatever the field or endeavor, I pause on the steps and watch the team work, Alden maneuvering his big Cat, seemingly with as little effort as I require pushing buttons on a blender, Buster using hand signals to show which boulders go where, like the mastermind of an important experiment for which he alone has the formula.

It's obvious the placement of rock is calculated, not random. Nor is it being done freehand. Though he's redefining some of the shoreline's edge, Buster follows what's been determined by the tides. He's using the high-tide wrack line the way a wallpaper hanger might employ a plumb line. But even less so than if it were the wall of an old Cape with its settled, comes-with-age sags and slopes, there's nothing straight about how this final product will wind up. And that's the aim. Even if shoreline permit requirements weren't so strict, both of us know that attempting to determine the edge by creating a new one is out of the question. We're not about to wrest control from the sea. Whatever we do here, it has the last say in where the edge will be.

Once again, I find myself asking: Who am I kidding? Again I fret over how much I'm spending. Am I, I wonder, paying for nothing more than the opportunity to fool myself into thinking this attempt to control erosion is anything other than temporary, and that somehow I have a hand in halting whatever passel of elements might once again collude?

As though sensing my skepticism, Buster steps away from the dust and clatter to join me. Alden goes on hoisting boulders from heaped piles and, with the finesse of a jeweler setting gems, places them into the increasingly apparent band of armoring support at our bluff's base.

"This is quite the project," I say to Buster.

"You think?" To put me at ease from the get-go, he made it clear this job was not the first of its kind he's tackled. Nor the biggest. Wisely, he attempted to minimize any hurdles.

But the challenge, I want to say to him, isn't with you.

For all my unease and uncertainty, Buster still appears to possess little. Thanking me for the lemonade and rejoining Alden, he calls out, "Don't worry. This'll do the trick." It's the closest he's come to a guarantee.

Meanwhile, just steps away, the noncompliant waves toss their insistence ashore, their reminders that at the sea's edge, disorder lurks, frisson thrives.

*S*cientists have long confirmed that it's in places where one thing ends and another begins that the greatest potential for change resides. Within our individual anatomical geography, for example, intense energy concentrates at the edges of our skin, in its proliferation of nerve endings and in the membranes of cells in our vital organs. In such places, things are more likely to happen.

And so, too, in the world around us. On the shore, at its shifting tidal edge where two ecosystems abut, life is always in flux, a literal back-and-forth movement ecologists refer to as a pulse. Unlike a distinct boundary of, say, the forest-meeting-field "abrupt edge" familiar to birders, the tidal edge is a zone of transition between land and water communities. A margin where tides cyclically ease out and inch back again.

Along a stretch of shoreline not far from where Buster and Alden masterfully heave and shape, juniper and bayberry appear to grow down to the water's edge as though pulled as we are to dip a toe into the sea. But to survive, they must keep a safe distance above high tide's reach. Among hardier sorts are beach plums. Their roots can take some of what high spring tides toss their way and so can comfortably creep down over the shore's rocky edge and extend tendrils into the tidal margins as we do our fingers checking a bath water's temperature. Here, too, sea lavender adapts. For a short time, crows cross over. At low tide, they wing down from their dry spruce-top perches and bump shoulders with gulls plundering the exposed rockweed.

But none of them, and certainly not Buster, Alden, or I, can call the tidal zone home. In a place where two worlds meet and overlap, where water in swirls, slaps and surges presses up to land then retreats to expose mounds and rocks, holes and tracks, only true edge species can survive. Uniquely adapted to fully inhabit the tidal margin, not just dip a toe in or survive an occasional plunge, edge species twice daily belong alternately to water and land, to life between two distinct communities.

Below the wrack line of an ebbing tide, just steps from where Buster and Alden are busily working an edge, a giddy amount of activity is taking—must take—place as one ecosystem shifts to another. Among the green crabs scuttling for cover in the rockweed, among the calcareous-tubed worms sealing their entrances with gill filaments as securely as if they were double-bolted locks and the periwinkles retreating behind closed operculums like afternoon nappers drawing the blinds, a staggering number of changes and transitions are taking place, each as complex and common as my taking a next breath.

I routinely walk this sloshing margin abuzz with energy, churning with change, and I will again once Buster and Alden complete their loud and intrusive clank-and-grind task. Outfitted with a walking stick and comfortable shoes, inhabiting my dreamer self in a seemingly aimless meander or my productive writer self who needs to hear the rhythm of new lines in her head, I hike the wrack line or wade out deeper and bend over the exposed tide pools. With my body of specific weight and scale, with its arteries and muscles, its inner and outer edges, with corporeal senses that enable me to feel the Atlantic's icy grip around my ankles, to inhale and touch, listen and look, to be open to color and swirl, hum and chuff, and even with my clicking mind I've hauled along, too, I'm not equipped to permanently dwell there. Unlike a true edge species, I can only for a specified time remain.

The resident of one element, I can cross a threshold when for a time borders relax and edges blur, but I can't stay—no matter how much I might wish it on an afternoon inching its way toward autumn, when I'm lured by the sun's unexpected warmth and want to linger, prone, on a warm granite ledge, to chance there again another encounter as happened last month. Then, in wordless marvel, I watched a mink in its sinuous up-and-down arch probe its long neck and stubby-faced head into some nearby rocky recesses. Two warm-blooded creatures, residents of one world, one element, we'd each crossed a threshold, our purposes on a sun-drenched point different but related—the drive to fill a belly, a hunger to plug the hole a death had punched into the heart. In the margins, borders relaxed. At the edge, we mingled. But only for a time.

Down on the shore, Buster and Alden maneuver with dexterity and admirable ease, as though perfectly equipped to work in the shifting tidal margins. They look at home. Soon though, there'll be no denial. An incoming tide will force Alden to park his Cat in the narrow strip of land above the wrack line, tuck it up as close as he can and hope salt water doesn't seep into its cab.

In spite of tidal shift and change, so much on the shore seems certain, and expected. But so much, of course, isn't. Nor is it atop the bluff. There, the perspective's been altered, changed.

*I*n a way, this bluff has always been a distinct edge. Even before a chunk of it was sliced away, I knew that if I were to step from the bluff and what back then seemed softer-edged, I'd go down scrambling, my feet seeking purchase part of the way but ultimately tumbling if not plummeting down to shore, several hard, possibly bone-shattering bumps along the way. Still, it was an edge where I could solidly stand as comfortably as I wade into the tidal margins on the shore, as upright as the rooted spruce trees that once grew here.

The bluff's sudden collapse changed that. The ground that seemed so solid beneath my feet was, it turned out, unstable. Signs had been few: some exposed roots, a couple of cleaved, narrow gullies where rain runoff coursed down. The spruce appeared secure, as did the clutch of small boulders poking through dirt. After, I couldn't help but think I should've known something was going on underfoot, that I should've been able to feel the hidden underground spring that we discovered had been persistently undermining all of it, and after, had to be factored in along with the more obvious spring melt, tidal surge, and record-breaking rain.

Since then, I've become more keenly aware: instability doesn't belong to any one landscape or place. To any singular experience. It's everywhere. In a sense, we're always on an edge.

And being on an edge can be a good thing. Numerous were the winter days I hauled my sled to a frozen river, and there, teetering on the bank's edge, I willingly, gleefully, pushed off. But uncertainty at an edge can keep us away, hold us back. Or it can be what draws us close, invites us to cross over, even if venturing to the other side of the river and beyond the borders of an enisled neighborhood may take years. Often we're on an edge and don't know it. And there, regardless how we got to it, we're apt—maybe forced—to make choices.

I had no choice one afternoon earlier this year. Before the phone rang, I had every hope my brother would get well. After, there was none. Joe, my 45-year-old brother was dead. That day, I hadn't known I was poised at a canyon's rim. But from there, a single phone call pushed me off. Without choice, I plummeted.

Now I know that no ambiguity resides at the edge you cross when someone you love dies. Having been spared for so long, I now understand how distinct the border is between unknowing and such terrible knowing. Perhaps, other than death itself, no edge is less murky, no boundary so clearly drawn as the precipice you stand at when someone you love is here, and then, as though he's stepped off, is gone.

Since that afternoon, I'm still learning, best I can, how to be an edge species. To dwell in the margins between the shifting edges in a sea of grief. A place where the rise and fall bears little resemblance to a tide's cyclical certainty. Where at any time tidal surge can threaten to take you under, sweep you away. It's a place where those more familiar with this kind of knowing have told me I'll adjust, adapt. Unlike the dutiful child on a frozen river who jumped off her sled and pulled it back without attempting to check out the other side, I have no choice.

Our bluff was changed by forces beyond my control. And now it's been altered again. It's been bolstered, built up, and now adequately drains. But again, it might collapse.

I must remember: *bluff* is both noun and verb. Geographically, it's a steep headland or promontory, a physical place. But it's also a means to deceive, mislead. To bluff is to deter or intimidate by a false display of confidence. Like the way in a card game, a good bluffer will bet on a poor hand, withhold on a good one.

Were I the betting kind—but haven't I already placed my bet with the check I handed Buster?—I'd have to wager this bluff will, in my lifetime, hold.

And isn't that what we do every day? Bet on the ground holding? Wager we'll survive? Newly diagnosed with cancer, my neighbor, before departing the island mid-August for a rigorous round of chemotherapy and radiation, planned next summer's garden. Just last week, another woman friend, bald, between treatments, still fighting her cancer's recurrence, walked into our island bank branch and signed documents for her new house. Maybe from some similar place, my brother summoned what he needed to go on, betting on the transplant that might've saved his life. After diagnosis, all of my brother's remaining life was lived on an edge.

This event here? It's such a puny wager, really. The bluff will hold, or it won't.

*T*here'll be no barge. Again. At least not for me. I have to go off-island soon, and I'll miss seeing it haul away Alden's excavator when the tide floods later today.

"I need a high tide so's to tuck the barge up close," Buster explains. "The wind's aiming to kick up some by afternoon, but I don't expect it'll amount to much. We should be able to get her in and out of here."

We're standing on the shore, and the air this early in the morning is still. But there's a chill in the air. All week, autumn has been issuing whispery warnings. Just two days ago, I woke, listened hard for the Heart Island ospreys' high-pitched cries, and hearing none, knew they were winging south on their long, treacherous journey. Soon music of another sort will fill in, the muttering of eiders rafting up, and all the other seabirds who, bags packed, fly down from the Arctic to overwinter here. Not that the season's tilt has prompted Buster to pull on a sweatshirt or windbreaker. As I tug up the zipper on mine, he seems quite comfortable in his short-sleeved T-shirt.

He walks over to the new armoring boulder edge, stoops, takes a closer look at the stacked, interlaid rock, the matting behind that over time will disintegrate as grasses and other volunteer plants take hold. He straightens, pats a large boulder as if it were an old acquaintance. "Yup, this ought to do you," he says.

"You and Alden did a great job," I say. "It really looks like this'll work. Time will tell, I guess."

"Sure enough. Mother Nature has her own mind about such things."

I gesture toward the stacked boulders. Though admirably placed to look as natural as possible, they still look to my eyes painfully raw, the shoreline imposed upon. Even in its quiet repose parked up from the tide's reach beneath some arching branches of old bayberry, the indispensable Cat with its heavy haunches pressed into the cobbled shore looks like a snoozing prehistoric beast. Where earlier it sputtered and clanked, rocks have been heaved up, scraped. And the part of the bluff itself, with its new built-out gentler bulge rather than its sheer cutaway face, still looks with all its newness like a wound, the scar tissue yet to form. It stands out in stark contrast to the rest of the shoreline with its spruce, bayberry, rugosas, and richly vegetated undergrowth. I know the answer but can't help worrying aloud, "Will it ever look natural again?"

"Oh, sure." Buster, usually wary, tosses me a bone. "That part I can guarantee. Plant a few more bayberries. Give the seed mix you tossed onto that new part a chance to grow. Who knows what else might pop up next spring. The birds and wind will give you a hand with that. And the rocks here?" He points at the cobbled shore beneath our feet, at the scraped and scratched evidence that something unnatural occurred. "Don't worry. A few weeks' worth of tides'll clean these rocks right up. Besides, there's plenty more where they came from. Couldn't stop them from coming ashore even if you had a mind to. These here," he gestures out to the bay, "bet they rode over from Camden."

I, too, look west, over the expanse of ocean between us and the distant horizon's Camden Hills, trying to visualize all the rocks already tumbling beneath the surface on their slow, tide-assisted trip in our direction. It's sort of like trying to see in my mind's eye the ospreys on their journey miles from here. Hard work, picturing what is not—or no longer—visible.

As Buster and I climb the steps and walk to his truck, he assures me that from his barge this afternoon he'll take some photos, evidence for the permit folks that all was done in compliance. Regulations for shore-front work along the Maine coast are understandably strict. Our permit was issued for erosion control. *Control.* An almost laughable concept when it comes to the unpredictable heaving Atlantic and the howling winds of future storms. And an even crueler notion when it comes to so much else.

Hopping into his pickup, Buster sweepingly gestures toward the bluff. "So keep your fingers crossed. You got a good chance."

As Buster drives off, I turn toward the house to collect my keys, wallet, the food cooler, a sweater and slicker, all that I think I need for errands that require a trip to the mainland, another crossing of the bridge, that distinct threshold between there and here. Now that all the ospreys are gone, I'll miss out on the possibility of seeing the pair that this summer declared a bridge tower home. On an off-island trip just a few weeks ago, I watched one of them lift from nest into flight, its white undersides luminously sunlit, and, for a time, whatever edges a concrete-and-steel bridge help define seemed porous.

Crossing the yard, I stop. For the first time, I see that just a few feet from where Buster's dump truck and Alden's CAT claimed a wide, deeply cleaved trench, where grass once grew, where a storm plucked three full-grown spruce trees from the abutting woods and opened up the canopy to sun where once was shade, a transition is already taking place. Where the hay-scented ferns are pushing from the lawn's edge into the forest, where a carpet of woodland plants that began last year to creep toward the filtered light, but now, exposed, may blanch beneath hot afternoon sun, and where the sun-loving gooseneck loosestrife I don't want to invade my perennial bed but yearn to have for vases in the house may now thrive, the edge is being redefined. I see how naturally, over time, more growth will fill in. How sun and shade will adjust, mingle, and for a time, intermix. Such a margin is already evolving. Maybe it doesn't possess the ecological pulse of the shoreline's back-and-forth movement, but the subtle shifts of light and wind, of tossing branches and slow-growing roots suggest movement of a different sort is afoot.

From here, I can see that beyond the bluff, the tide is still easing out. Exposed already by small but unmistakable increments are what a high tide conceals—the barnacle-pocked boulders skirted with rockweed, swaths of violet-colored mussel beds, periwinkle-spattered rocks, a small sandy strip, the easy access to tidal pools the ebb has yet to fully reveal, and further south, those unmarked, secretly held places of sand dollars and sea clams. All are parts of what has become a recognizable and cherished landscape. Though that's changed now, too.

Yes, in the distinguishable ridges and bold outcroppings, in the distant anchored islands, each the product of volcanic eruption, glacial upheaval and major ice-melt, there are, still, some of the same old reassurances. But solid ground is always in some way tentative, isn't it? Even in bedrock, nothing stays the same. The contours of the land alter continually, are constantly revised. New occurrences throw off our best calculations. The sure bets.

Rather than return to the house, I feel dragged to the bluff's edge like a gambler to the poker table. There, like Alden aboard his big Cat, I creep forward. I inch my toes past the lawn, past the exposed dirt and seed. Past what is becoming the new edge.

MESSAGES

*T*ake Notice.

That seems to be the message our new roadside color palette is broadcasting in the ditches and culverts, the spendthrift fields and meadows ablaze with saffron and gold. Gone is the green wonder of June and the pale lavenders and purples of early summer's wild phlox and lupine. Even the white and rosy-pinks of the rugosas are behind us. Now it's about dazzle. As though it were possible for the eye to store all this brightness. Just as it seems possible when we stretch out on a beach in August, that our bodies, like solar panels, will recall such heat when winter winds howl.

This is the boil-before-the-simmer palette. When key players are goldenrod and tansy, those "rumpy bunches," says poet Mary Oliver, and "little towers soft as mash...full of bees and yellow beads and perfect flowerlets." They're also what, in my first years on the island, long before we had our own house and garden, I walked the roadsides for, filling whatever pitcher or mason jar the cupboards of a rental cottage offered. Punctuated with a few stems of Queen Anne's lace and meadowsweet, those bouquets seemed to me just about perfect.

I know now that these roadside beauties are too often brushed off as weeds and sneeze-bringers, as invasive bullies banished from our yards. Goldenrod especially unloved, except by bees somersaulting among its wands, their bodies furred with pollen, and by butterflies—monarchs, yes, but also clouded sulfurs and small coppers, chosen, it seems, for their suitably monochromatic hues alone—and by, says Oliver, "the rocky voids filled by its dumb dazzle." Maybe goldenrod, no longer touted as a wound-healer, diuretic, or treatment for gout, is merely misunderstood. No weed, it's a member of the aster family, cousin to that more refined, decidedly more welcome golden beauty, black-eyed Susan, but which, too often, bumps shoulders with the wrong crowd. Meaning allergy-sufferers need to pin blame where it belongs—on ragweed, a bullying opportunist that shows up just as goldenrod takes its seasonal cue.

More benign-seeming is tansy with its flat-topped button blooms, an oxeye daisy wannabe minus an Elizabethan collar of white fringe. Once considered a medieval medical treatment for expelling intestinal worms, and later, when brought to our shores, declared a perennial herb essential to the kitchen and necessary for colonial gardens, tansy's current dubious status is as one of North America's most invasive plants. Best then that tansy dwell in fields and roadsides, the bright follow-up to loosestrife, an equally land-grabbing sidekick that this time of year has lost most of its punch.

If I were a painter in late August (a lack of talent against which I still chafe), I'd not reach for citron or butter yellow. What's demanded are cadmium and sulfur. To depict what, on their airy backbones, goldenrod and tansy toss with exuberance, and at a time in the season when even the waxing moon in its slow ascent, as ripe and full as an apricot, ambers. We've come full cycle from the paler yellows of forsythia and daffodils, of marsh marigolds and butter-and-eggs, those cheerful messengers even in the coldest, wettest spring such as this year's, when August's tomatoes and cicadas seemed but an unimaginable dream.

Soon, my eyes will shift upward to the trees, to the kindling that signals more obvious changes are about to take place, to the color wheel tilting again, this time toward scarlet and orange, then the reds and russets of what falls away, to the endings such shifts say are near. Of things deepening into brown collapse, into what can never forever be ours.

Now, though, maybe the no-Midas-with-his-gold gifts being freely offered by goldenrod and tansy are meant to help us forget all that, regardless of September's pulse of urgency, like that of shorebirds fueling up in the marsh or in whatever's begun to stir the fields like incipient panic in a crowd.

In this imperfect world, important messages are often simple. Yesterday I hiked an island path flanking the remnants of an old rock boundary wall and crossed a meadow where stands of second-growth spruce increasingly encroach but was once home to an old farmstead with pruned orchards. There, I didn't confuse windfall with jackpot, with "sudden money," not even some unexpected happening that brings good fortune. But so hand-in-hand do windfall and September clarities arrive, it's as if those freely offered apples, true gifts of the season, were more like golden reliquaries that are not just a part of but responsible for this scrubbed and almost touchable early autumn light. "Rivers of windfall light," as Dylan Thomas celebrated in "Fern Hill."

Apples fall as they must. Out of the necessity of ripeness. They plunk onto a path, beside the roadway, into the grass of a going-by meadow, worm-eaten, possibly smashed, fermenting and abuzz, but no matter how blemished or misshapen, they juice the soil, sweeten the earth. And just as certain as the apple cannot return to the stem, we cannot halt the advance of colder nights, nor can we contain and stopper the bottle on this cidery, here-then-not windfall light.

It's the season of falling. Another inevitability we cannot shake. Like "we all fall down" the final line reminder in, of all places, our toddler-hood's sing-songy classic. But it's also the season of cherishing light. Of dropped apples in our path, each one a windfall. And of bright roadside beauties. Bright beacons in fog, plumed torches beneath a darkening sky. As unstinting with their gold as the fragrant roses their sweetness. Never does it occur to them that they might be something else. They never expect to be asked about happiness. Nor do they ever question what comes next.

WITH OPEN EYES

"*B*ut *where* is the soul?" I demanded of our nun in Wednesday afternoon catechism class. I had a vague notion it was somewhere near the heart, but I wanted specificity. I wanted to be able to locate it on the colorful anatomy charts my science teacher, standing before the dusty chalkboard, rolled down like window shades. As though one of those charts' clear overlays could reveal the soul as it did each organ mapped within our bodies, among a network of complex muscles and tendons and sprawling arterial highways, each part of us identifiable like the smallest speck of an island on a nautical chart. Such a question was, I suspect, tantamount to questioning the soul's existence. I may as well have challenged the presence of the Holy Ghost, or of Purgatory, that stopover where I'd been told the souls of even the most obedient and devout among us must often await a further purifying tune-up.

Previously, before our move from a South Side Chicago two-flat to a house in a largely Protestant suburb, when my family lived in the shadow of St. Anthony's church and convent, I routinely draped a pillowcase around my head, tied beads around my waist as though they were a rosary, and pretended to be a nun married to God, a seven-year-old's commitment more to costume than to sacrifice or belief. Excelling at memorization, I recited each new prayer with speed. The words, disengaged from actual meaning, rotely slipped past my lips as though through cogs in a well-oiled machine.

But then, some troubling news. In the run-up to first Holy Communion, I learned that we'd each been corrupted by Eve's sin of disobedience. Like that of all the apple-eater's offspring, mine was a blemished and corruptible soul. Through no fault of my own, and at birth no less, I'd been launched onto the narrow path between salvation and damnation. The least I might ask for then, given the stakes, was the specificity of the soul, some physical evidence. "Show me," I insisted.

For all the good the tension between grace and damnation, between love and wrath, might eventually produce, it can be a terrifying enterprise for a child. Bad enough that at some early age we cross awareness's threshold of our own extinction and, once crossed, can never go back. Thrusting upon a child the knowledge of a damaged soul and the possibility her life might be about to end, that she could be snatched in the night, this very night, regardless the next day's birthday or holiday, its field trip or championship game, can do more than disturb sleep. Scary visions of a hairy creature beneath the bed might well morph into a bearded man in long robes who is sure of foot in spite of the night-light's small flimsily-lit circle. Such nights cast long shadows.

From a perspective inching past late middle age, where the mere ticking of a clock can make some nights no less terrifying, I still can't point to any corporeal place where the soul resides. I do, however, find the contention of Plotinus appealing: "The soul is in the body as light is in the air." Or Plato's claim that the soul is the invisible essence of a person, or, less appealingly in *Gorgias,* that the body is the prison of the soul. As depicted by Peter in less constricting terms, the body is the soul's outer covering, its shelter or tent.

Turn on the television, watch the news, read the daily newspapers and soullessness is far easier to recognize. After twenty-six years of marriage, I look at my husband and see my soulmate, the familiar flesh-and-blood embodiment of vital qualities, numerous selves. But I can't see his soul in the precise way I demanded of those chart overlays. George Bush, upon meeting Russia's President Putin for the first time, claimed to have "looked into his soul." That's a talent I don't possess. I've long resided in the camp of Chekhov: "The soul of another is wrapped in darkness."

Long ago, regardless of any recited prayer, no matter my responses to questions posed by nuns or priests—Did I believe? Have I let God into my heart?—no place opened in my chest. Nothing poured in as I was sure it must, particularly if my soul resided, as I suspected, somewhere nudging up against my beating heart. But as a dutiful child who understood the unnegotiable outcome of Catholic sinners, I couldn't not respond.

"Do you believe?"

To the priest laying his hand on my head, I couldn't say no. Nor was doubt anything I felt able to articulate yet. Maybe, I reasoned, it was enough just to assume God resided within and that one day he'd make His presence known, like the way lightning bugs following long absence suddenly illuminate in bright bits a warm June night. Surely something as obvious as lightning bolts, heavenly harps or gauzy celestial light didn't have to be God's only accompaniments. And yes, I had to assume, too, that tucked up inside me was a soul, as secure and specific as the small blue robin's egg which deep in its nest had survived a plummet from our front yard's towering elm tree.

*M*ine is the only car in the small lot off Goose Cove Road. I have, I hope, the trail to myself.

This is among my favorite wooded landscapes on the island, a maritime boreal fog forest often shrouded by thick lingering fog and cool moist air. But today, in mid-October, on my last hike of the season, the sun is bountiful, the air dry and crisp. The light's clarity stuns.

Glacial evidence abounds here. On exposed granite are the remnants of scouring scrapes and gouges, cracks and fractures caused by the passage of a mile-thick ice sheet more than 12,000 years ago. Immense boulders—erratics—some the size of a compact car and now cloaked with moss, almost mysteriously appear. Though the soil cover here is thin, a forest of white spruce and balsam fir scattered with red spruce, birch and maple proliferates. Thick exposed roots protrude, spreading like webs over the trail. Lichen thrives, toadskin and rock tripe, a silver-green verdigris splotching boulders and ledge. Decades in the making, pincushion and reindeer moss carpet the forest floor, and, like luxuriant pelts, line the deep crevices of tumbled erratics. Even today's bright light filtering through the trees and the copious, pale strands of old-man's beard swaying from the branches can't obliterate this forest's primeval feel. Its quiet is punctured only by the scrapes my feet make when the spongy trail gives way to granite or by the creak when some leaning spruce trees rub together overhead. Occasionally, a sentry crow emits a guttural croak to his pals, who, stationed farther off, in similar but muted tones respond.

Walking this fine trail is treat enough. I could easily be satisfied and circle back, but my destination today beckons as the canopy thins, the light brightens, and the way ahead opens. I bypass the trail leg that winds up to a high granite ledge viewpoint blanketed with upland cranberry, drop down instead, and where the trails ends, clamber over some rocks. How odd to feel sand beneath my feet. Elsewhere on the island, beaches are almost always variations of cobbled rock and stone. Off to my left is Goose Cove, a small harbor, a smattering of houses hugging the shoreline. But I'm focused on what's straight ahead—tiny Barred Island, an iconic dome of pink granite crowned with spruce, which, as the tide drops, appears to rise from the sea. Between it and me is the bar, a finger of sand that's incrementally widened as the tide approaches its ebb. I have, I suspect, about a three-hour window before the bar is once again submerged.

Etched into the bar's sandy shoreline are some calligraphic scribblings made by gulls and maybe some plovers my approach has scared off. But no footprints precede mine.

The walk has been good. Carefully stepping over the trail's exposed, slippery roots slowed me down, settled my body into a rhythm. Now, barely midday, no afternoon offshore breeze has yet to stir things up. The gulls, without a reason to squabble, are busy gorging in the bladder wrack and rockweed. A few distant lobster boats slip across the horizon, their diesels barely registering. The sea is awash with glimmer, uncountable glittery eyes blinking in the sun.

I cross the bar, scramble over several large boulders, and pick my way across a broad expanse of granite ledge until I'm atop the small island. Venturing close to water's edge, I hop over crevices, find footholds on the smooth rock face until I'm on the islet's distant side with its view of nearby outcroppings and open ocean beyond. Here, above the splash zone, in a dip where two granite expanses meet as though hinged, is a favorite spot. I settle down onto it, lean against smooth rock thickly capped with crowberry, turn my face to the sun, and close my eyes.

*I*n *The Dream of the Marsh Wren*, poet Pattiann Rogers writes about the happiness she experiences when she watches someone sleep. Her joy, she says, arises out of "an awareness of the truth that the body itself is totally innocent, flesh and bone unquestionably fine, justified and without blame." In repose, the human body is "unbothered by greed or violence, deceit or guilt." If there is sin, she claims, it resides elsewhere.

Is that how I look now, stretched out on this ledge, even if I'm keenly aware of the sensations of my body—sun on my face, warm rock against my back, the crunch of matted crowberry beneath my head—as I try to will away thoughts of time, of the tide that soon enough will reclaim the bar, my path back?

There's no mistaking when my nephew Michael is asleep. At age twelve, he still sleeps with the complete abandon of his first years, his arms and legs flung wide to the night, the world outside his dreams. My sister has always experienced great joy in watching her son sleep, marveling at the trust he has in the night, in the security of his life beneath his parents' roof. In numerous photographs taken since his birth, she's documented his surrender to sleep. In them I see, like Rogers, the innocence of the body, this boy in his beautiful body, a grand and sacred gift.

A wondrous mix of leaks, smells, sloughing cells—our body. What many believe is the temporary, earthly abode of the soul. The ancient Celts claimed that immediately following death, the living must sit with the deceased because the body might become frightened when the soul departs. In other religious rituals, it's customary that the deceased, as emptied vessel, is laid out, a final gift to the living who find it necessary to witness the body in its final repose. The body of the dead who, we're to understand, whether final struggles were brief or long, is now at peace.

I open my eyes. The sky is startlingly clear, free of any summer haze, a blue so intense that were I able to strike it would chime. On the distant horizon, a dollop of clouds heaps up. A small raft of muttering eiders drifts close. A lone cormorant on a nearby rock has opened its cloak, angular wings drying in the air. Everywhere a clear and brilliant sheen. I tilt my head back and the crowberry scratches my neck. Above me are the pale branches of a long-dead tree, stark against blue, a stripped-to-its-basic-elements modernistic sculpture touched by no man's hands.

It's the body—the eye—that takes in twisted tree, cormorant, murmuring eider, the toss of waves against granite ledge, all this material evidence that could suggest something exists beyond such irrefutable presence. And, I readily admit, such creation is a sublime gift, however we've come by it, whoever is behind it.

Years ago, I discovered an odd kinship between these ledges of little Barred Island and the primitive backyard tree house of my adolescence. To that simple treetop platform of cast-off wood I carried youthful aches and yearnings—for a first bra, for more skill in my mother's hands as she trimmed my bangs, for the day when I might no longer need eyeglasses. There, I escaped household chores, younger siblings, erupting tensions between my parents, and nurtured what has become a lifelong need for solitude. There, too, in that place of light and shade and breeze through the branches, as I observed the busy flutter of nearby sparrows and a raucous jay, listened to bees plundering my mother's orange tiger lilies below, I began, without my conscious knowledge, to develop a keener awareness of and connection to the physical world. I gathered to me material and natural evidence that, in my experience, no nun or priest or catechism instructor celebrated fully. If anything, in the words and lessons of prayers and homilies, I'd been taught that there were two distinct worlds—the mundane, useful, and often beautiful material world in which, embodied, we live our daily lives, and that other better, perfect world for which our souls are meant to yearn. If Sister Mary Nicholas found much to reject in my question, "Where is the soul?" it's hard to imagine her outrage had I confronted her with Mary Oliver's "How can we not know that, already, we live in paradise?"

Not that I sprawled in my tree house and, like a youthful mystic, contemplated such things. I was no fourteen-year-old David in John Updike's story, "Pigeon Feathers," who questions his mother about the soul and declares, "Don't you see, if when we die there's nothing, all your sun and fields and what not are all…an ocean of horror?" Likewise, I bore no similarity to anthropologist Scott Antran, who, at age ten, as reported in the *New York Times,* scrawled on his bedroom wall, "God exists, or if he doesn't, we're in trouble." But in my tree house, distanced from the confines of any church or dogma, I began to absorb into my tissues some of what these many years later I've come to associate with the spiritual and sacred: quiet, solitude, stillness, a deep and abiding awareness of the physical and essential world, a profound creation. Up among those branches, I was being encouraged to open my eyes, to witness.

*M*y brother died with his eyes open.

After suffering with terrible illness for several months, but on the brink of what we'd hoped was a turn for the better, he collapsed in the shower. Tragically, it was my father who found him, who'd come by for a visit on the first day my brother's wife returned to work.

On a blistering midsummer day, in a bathroom darkened by blinds drawn against an early-afternoon desert sun, awful truths mounted—my father lost his youngest child, my sister-in-law became a widow. Her two young children were now fatherless. Joe was gone.

The news reached me here, almost a continent away, and instantly an afternoon's gloss, its sun-spangled beauty, was transformed into the unforgiveable. No longer could I see the day's slow downward spiral toward dusk, a sunset that may have been one of the summer's finest. The world was reduced to the phone against my ear, to every detail offered by anyone there able and willing to talk as they waited for the removal of my brother's naked body, which, I was to understand, had been carried from the shower and was now mercifully covered. Like the Celts, my family sat with the body. Joe's.

"His eyes were open." That singular detail was spoken aloud again and again, a mantra into that night and many days after. It's not unusual for the eyes to remain open in death. A host of physical reasons account for it. But it seemed to come as a sort of revelation to my family, a necessary comfort, and an answer to the needs of those who were just beginning to struggle with the permanence of mortality, of a loss not yet absorbed.

The eyes of the dead, Sherwin Nuland tells us in *How We Die*, are at first glassy and fixed in an unseeing gaze. Within minutes, they "yield up their sheen and become dulled...." They "forever lose their watchful light." And soon, as if a thin gray film has been laid down over each eye, no one can look within "to see if the soul has fled."

Even so, my brother's wife found comfort in Joe's open eyes. Here was a final gift—to see one last time his eyes that always, unmistakably, and now irretrievably, had been a startling blue. In them, she sought the tranquility that had eluded Joe for months. Whether or not this was the work of the body's endorphins, she, like my father, saw in Joe's eyes a release from pain.

And was there, I wondered but didn't ask, an absence of fear? Had something—belief, or the body's shutting down—protected him as death approached? Had I been there, gathering as they were the evidence each found necessary (like the mouth, the relaxing of muscles in death some in my family chose to read as a sort of smile), would I have interpreted my 45-year old brother's open eyes differently? As a last hungry look? As futile defiance? As shock in the suddenness of it? Or in final protest, one last fight against?

Clinical death is often preceded, Nulan reports, by a barely more than momentary period called the agonal phase, a sequence of visible events that take place when "life is in the act of extricating itself from protoplasm too compromised to sustain it any longer." Deriving from the Greek word *agon,* meaning struggle, it occurs in all forms of death, whether sudden or following slow decline, and even if, as the body shuts down, the person is too far gone to be aware of it. If Joe's open eyes related to that agonal phase, to his body's final struggle, only medical folks who later examined it could, with their scientific knowledge, say. Even so, who knows what, were this their brother or son, they might have chosen to believe.

Joe died in a cold, tiled shower, far from his beloved mountains and the Sonoran desert, at a remove even from his backyard with the kiva he'd hand-constructed and the cacti he'd lovingly propagated over many years. He was alone. Only after death could some of those who loved him hold his hand and sit with him on the nearby bedroom floor where he'd been carried. Only my father knows with certainty what my brother looked like slumped in the shower, his vital heart stilled, my father who now singularly and indelibly possesses that physical reality the rest of us can only, perhaps mercifully, imagine.

No one was witness to Joe's death, those moments of his naked-as-he'd-come-into-it departure from this knowable world. But those who gathered around him on the floor of a darkened room, awaiting the coroner's transport, attest to witnessing something else. Before them was Joe's lifeless but irrefutable and so clearly present body, the body through which we had come to know him. But now Joe in his purest essence was gone. For the believers, the soul had already traveled someplace else.

*N*ever. *Always. Gone.* Words a death redefines.

A death revises questions, too. "Where is the soul?" can become "Where does the soul go?"

On Barred Island, I prop myself up, look out at the open ocean, a vast and shimmering wave-tossed expanse. I know that somewhere distant and out of sight is land, a hard incontrovertible evidence. Of that, though I'm no geographer, I'm certain. And as sure as I am that a small flotilla of black guillemots now bob and whirr their stub-wings just a stone's throw from where I sprawl, I know, too, that beneath the surface, in this water's blue and silver translucence, creatures big and small jostle, each pursuing their hungers in ways science can explain. Though I can imagine its not being so. Meaning I can imagine the guillemots and this ledge not existing. But me sitting on it?

The mind's powers are enormous, but thinking about ceasing to exist slams into a cognitive roadblock. How can I think about not thinking? How simulate nonexistence? Mine or anyone else's? Or, as philosopher Miguel de Unamuno has observed: "Try to fill your consciousness with the representation of no-consciousness, and you will see the impossibility of it…we cannot conceive of ourselves not existing."

How much more comprehensible is our yearning to believe that when we die and the body incontrovertibly disintegrates, we nevertheless continue to exist. That somewhere we are able to laugh or cry, speak or listen. But such belief requires, Antran declares, that we take "what is materially false to be true" and "what is materially true to be false." Our eyes may tell us the person whose ashes fill a brass urn or have been cast to the wind is gone, but our minds assure us that somewhere in physicality he exists. We choose to persist in believing this, not just because we wish to live forever, but because we want to be again with the person we love even if in a different way than we'd been with him on earth.

Some years ago, as a visiting writer at a middle school, I spent a few weeks working on poetry with a sixth-grade class. One morning, I brought in Pablo Neruda's *Book of Questions*. In it, each poem is a series of questions. The world at its most trivial and essential is Neruda's subject, his language infused with color and vivid imagery, his way of looking provocative. He asks, "What did the tree learn of the earth to confide to the sky? Have you wondered what color April is to the sick?" The students and I first spent a lot of time talking about questions—our discussion ranging from how essential questions are to whether it's the answer or the question that's more important, more powerful. Students were asked to write their own poems. One virtue of this exercise is that no one can really fail. Everyone has questions. As expected, those the students ultimately posed were wide-ranging, surprising, and revealing. Some spoke to adolescence: "Who decided 'opposites attract'?" "Why is sadness always pushing like a runner to overtake happiness?" Some asked out of wonder: "Does every living thing have a way of communicating?" "Is pine-scented insecticide a good idea?" Some queried: "Who decided to call this Earth?" "Does rain fall because God cries when a young person dies for no reason at all?" And from a boy who seldom spoke out in class and wrote even less, this: "What happens if Heaven gets too crowded?"

Whether deriving from lyrical wonder or a genuine unease, such a question is not unreasonable. Just counting human deaths from a long history of wars, plagues, starvations, genocides, any number of diseases, a panoply of natural disasters from Vesuvius and Pompeii to the world's latest tsunamis and earthquakes, and Heaven, as pictured by a sixth grader, must be a packed and teeming place. How, he might wonder, can another one of us or our loved ones possibly squeeze in? Even with imaginations stoked, it's hard to grasp a place so vast, so elastic as to expand and accommodate us all.

Long ago, Descartes helped pave the way for the separation of the material body and the immaterial mind. And from there, suggests Paul Bloom in *Descartes' Baby*, it was a short step toward the acceptance that our roaming minds don't stay anchored in the body. And from there, he asks, how much of a leap is required to land at the doorstep of the immaterial soul that, when coupled with the belief in our continued existence in some other noncorporeal form, helps some of us accept death's certainty? Thinking of ourselves not thinking might be an impossible task, but accepting life's brevity is hard work, too. For a sixth grader worried over Heaven's capacity, the idea of a disembodied soul might offer some consolation. Without the corporeal aspect of things, gone, too, are the considerations of what form the body takes in Heaven. Returned to youthful vigor and beauty? Absent the scars and wounds? Restored to it the lost arm, the ruptured heart?

Sprawled on this little island, and though its granite is much less hospitable to back and limbs than my yard's lawn, I'm reminded of a clear August night last summer when I similarly reclined, anticipating a promised Perseid meteor shower.

Above me, the sky stunned with its staggering abundance, its uncountable stars the ancients believed were pinholes in the sky's vault through which light of another outer world shone. But it offered me none of the movement or dazzle of what I'd read could be numerous meteors hurtling into view. Of what I'd pictured as a storm of stars dropping from the sky. Streams of blazing light.

For a long time, a bit disappointed, I looked. I searched. And then in that vastness, off to the right, a bright arc, so brief and quick I almost missed it. And then, a short time later, another, again almost missed, in another direction. I soon understood I had to scan the sky, turn my head, look hard. I'd anticipated that a falling star would announce its passing in a scream of glitter and light, a trail of fire. Which these were, but with a fire so distant, a transit so brief, I had to search, train my eyes, be ready.

Since then, I've learned a meteor shower is linked to the trajectories of a distant comet and the estimated one million tons of particulate matter spread throughout a comet's orbit. What I had been watching were actually bits of stone and grit, cometary particles streaking 150,000 miles per hour toward Earth. When heated by friction entering our atmosphere, they sizzle, vaporize. In a final fiery plunge, they seem to disappear. But according to astronomer-writer Chet Raymo, such particulate matter is continually adding to Earth's bulk. Cosmic dust that survives a dive into our atmosphere settles onto the planet's surface. Raymo claims that scientists can dig into Arctic and Antarctic ice and collect bits of Perseid dust that plummeted toward Earth a thousand years ago. Sky dust unseen by a pair of eyes on an August night is an indisputable part of our planet's surface, its atmospheric mix. Particles smaller than ash.

Recently I read that in Hebrew scriptures, everyone is a sojourner. We're all passing through, never completely at home on the earth or in our bodies. Each of us a passing guest. Plato put forth the concept of *metaxu*, which speaks, poet Adam Zagajewski writes, of our being "in between"—in between the concrete, comprehensible earth and a larger, transcendent mystery. We're forever "en route." In constant movement. Indeed, as I sit in my chair at my desk writing this, the ground firm beneath my feet, I'm on a journey. Thanks to continental drift and tectonic plate shifts, North America and Europe are, centimeter by centimeter, slipping farther apart in the sea like bobbing dumplings in an immense vat of wondrous soup.

Last night while I slept, our entire planet whirled on its axis, hurtled along its circular orbit. I lay in my familiar bed as still as on a barred islet while the entire planet traveled half a million miles across the Perseids, raced toward the sun at more than 10,000 miles per hour. Every moment, the earth moves at such a terrifying speed it's almost surprising I'm not flung from bed or granite ledge. Our beloved planet, spinning in a universe sometimes seemingly chaotic or random, but with an order, a logic that we neither created nor have yet to fully comprehend.

Not that we haven't developed new ways of seeing. With its Deep Field capabilities, the Hubble has revealed vast empires of countless galaxies, has beamed back images of expanding light halos and illuminated stellar dust that, to my amateur eyes, bear eerie resemblance to van Gogh's masterpiece, "Starry Night." What resemble grains of sand are really individual points of light millions of light-years away. Yet even Deep Field capacities can't probe far enough. The late Edwin Hubble was said to have observed: "With increasing distance, our knowledge fades." We glimpse "mere shadows."

Some cloudless nights, I step out onto the deck or lawn, tilt my head back and gaze at the sky above the island blessedly free of any ambient light. In all that staggering, bright abundance overhead, space in all its immensity seems somehow compressed, as though, by simply reaching out, I might touch a star, close my fingers around something tangible. Other nights, in awe, I feel only the enormity of my individual puniness.

The cosmic galaxy, something so vast, so far beyond the boundaries of earth by which my life is defined and supported, is beyond my imagination's grasp. The scale of our hurtling planetary home, itself nothing more than a grain of dust in the galaxy, a speck like a Perseid meteor against the sky, makes one individual being on a small nubbin of rock in the ocean something so infinitesimal, words fail. Only the soul, I've been asked to believe, can make each of us limitless, an infinitude.

*I*t's time to leave. If I stay, the incoming tide will prevent my return. I stand, stretch, climb down from the ledge, and, scrambling over the rimming boulders, circle back to the cove and harbor side of Barred Island. I pick my way along the shore pocked with stones. "What heaven do stones have?" Neruda asked, to which my attempt at response has always been, "This one."

I poke my walking stick here and there, beneath rocks, into crevices and a tangle of driftwood. I overturn emptied periwinkles, mussels, the spiny, picked-clean domes of sea urchins, a green crab's brittle carapace. This beach a morgue of vessels, of death's empty remains.

Last year about this time, on a blue-and-gold day much like this one, I walked another favorite island place that possesses, too, at its furthermost tip, a sandbar. As I approached it, I saw what looked to be a piece of weathered timber the waves had pitched ashore. But it was the corpse of a harbor seal. This was no youngster who'd gotten separated and lost, nor was it, judging by size, a particularly old seal like those I've watched haul their bulk onto the safety of a sea-encircled ledge. A young adult in its prime, my guess, large in life but now in decay shrunk down into itself. To my novice eye, no wound suggested it had been shot, caught in a trap or ripped by a boat propeller, but there was no mistaking that the sodden lump over which flies nattered and buzzed was lifeless, absent all vitality, without clue of a former fluidity and grace beneath waves. Gone too were the eyes, always the first to go, those soft and vulnerable places no crow or gull has to work very hard to get at.

The eyes: portals through which the world is taken in, where, in humans, mind and world meet. But are the eyes also, perhaps, outlets? That when the heart stops, it's through them that an essence flees? An imperishable energy and force that, after death, leaps out of the body into the life of the world?

Long before Joe's body was lifted from the shower, was it as if tiles loosened and that small enclosure ruptured with his essence breaking— leaping—free? At what speed does the soul travel? Meteoric? Or like breath dispersed on the wind?

I will never know what my brother last saw. Or heard. On that workday afternoon in an air-conditioned house sealed against Arizona heat. But it seems somehow fitting—even just?—to imagine that whenever or however fast Joe's essence departed, and especially because he was alone, some sort of sound should have accompanied those moments, a final pronouncement—"I was here," "I mattered"—if only by way of a hum or vibration or the thrumming in one final exhalation. Hard to accept that it was as silent as a distant meteor's final transit to the earth-bound on a mid-August night. Or that with Joe's collapse, the earth, if only for a nanosecond, didn't pause in its orbit.

Leaving Barred Island, I reach the sandbar to discover the tidal transit has indeed given way to flood. The transcript of the birds' scribblings in the sand has disappeared. Parts of the narrow track along which I can still make my way back have already been subsumed by the incoming sea. A boundary is dissolving. A border that may have earlier invited me to cross over is now, if I want to return, demanding it.

In their clarity and opacity, with their constant yet mercurial persistence, the tides have long been for me a source of assurance. The way in which, with a certainty I can rely on, they alter and transform, claim and fix. Endless repeatings that dissolve again and again the boundaries between disparate elements, between one world and another, though each remains suffused with the other.

Many mornings, I wake early and watch light enter the sky. From my western-facing windows, I can't witness the sun's actual ascent. But looking out at the water, I see its climb in the way, after washing the sky with an initial backdrop of silver and rose, it brightens first the distant islands, plashes bleached rocky outcroppings with a coppery sheen, gilds spruce tops, and often, as if they were torch-lit, sets them ablaze with color. Sometimes, in all that shimmer and gleam, a shaft of light from behind a bank of clouds erupts, illuminates with molten brilliance one particular island or stand of trees. A sudden luminosity, an unexpected—is there any other word for it?—radiance. It doesn't last long but is all I need. Transparency bumps aside translucence, and, if only for a short time, banishes the persistence of doubt and the not-knowing that wrenches small the heart.

Stepping across the last remnants of the exposed bar, I'm surprised by how cold the water is sloshing over my ankles as my feet, making small sucking sounds, press into sand. But on the other side, the footing becomes firmer, more certain. I pause before climbing up over the rocks to the wooded trail that leads me home. Turning back, I linger, watching as the water from either side of the sandbar, as though in no particular hurry, on no predetermined schedule, slowly nudges forward, meets, laps, and mingles, covers the last of my—a sojourner's—footprints. As the minutes begin to tick past in the flood tide's reclamation, its own narrow window, the water deepens. The bar disappears from sight. Seamless now, that transformation. And in it the reminder once again. Water always departs. And returns.

THE LONG GOOD-BYE

*T*here's little chance of misinterpreting today's chill, its gray and brooding sky. Weather and time don't lie. Just as tides ebb and flow, just as lobsters shed, come in to feed then head back into deep water, and ospreys return in spring to reclaim their warp-and-stick nests then leave them as reliably as the calendar tells me it's now October, summer ticks away and autumn arrives. Primitive and ancestral, such cycles are beyond our clocks or barometers, or our wishes.

So far, we've had no hard frost, but surely, and soon enough, one will come. Perhaps we won't mind as much if it arrives on a clear night, the stars staggering in their plenitude. That frost followed by another, and another, each stealthily working its way into the ground not to budge until spring's mud season, whenever—forget any predictions—it may come. In advance, as the trees in their slow burn are undressing, there seems to be a kind of pause now, a waiting, though of a different sort than spring's expectancy and surely the opposite of the timelessness June at summer's threshold suggests.

I'm not fooled. I know what waits even if this morning I crank up the heat and with a cup of coffee am tempted to sink into a comfortable chair and watch the captain of *Frayed Knot* haul out the last of his traps just off our shore. In the last several days, I've had to resemble more the fabled catch-up grasshopper than the slower, persevering ant because, as September was winding down with its abundant warm and clear days, I heeded the end-of-summer siren call: "Come out. Come out. Wait, and it will be too late." I chose to walk the shore or read and indulge in the view from one of our yard's Adirondack chairs, or, while driving the island, to be mindful of but not persuaded by my neighbors' stacked fire wood, tarp-covered yard furniture, and shrink-wrapped boats. I wasn't yet ready to ask: Is it time to assess summer? A season that at its cusp always seems so full of promise, that suggests this time I will be able to deliver on all my seasonal plans—in the garden, the house, at my desk. All those new walks I've yet to take, books to read, recipes to try, people to meet, a manuscript to finish, the new volunteer assignments I swore to take on. What of my commitment to learn, really learn, how to sea kayak? Or to spend more afternoon hours sprawled in the hammock with no other place to be? All in a season, if measured from solstice to equinox, of just 91 days.

Now, weeks past the day in late August when we wake and discover sunlight has suddenly and undeniably shifted and the air possesses a new and brittle clarity, past evenings when the sun retreats behind the Camden Hills long before dinner guests move on to dessert, I feel an inner restlessness tug at me. An urge to make ready. Something more than the wisdom in and necessity of preparing for a long Maine winter. Is such a seasonal tug inherent? Some vestige of a once nomadic life? Some internal knowing similar to the inner synchronization of migrant birds? Their recognition of days shrinking with less light and for which they need no calendar?

I've not yet decided on the day of my seasonal departure from the island, but soon "I'll know in my bones," as I like to say. As though it's an intuitive, in-the-body knowing. Some interior signal that instructs: *Now.*

Weeks ago, the ospreys heeded their internal urging and emptied our skies of their music. The massive nest at Mill Pond on the trail to Sheephead Island is now such a forlorn-looking thing with its few long branches trailing down, the whole left side of it in a downward tilt as though the juvenile offspring had slid from it rather than taken to the air on their first-ever journey to a place they've never seen and, unfortunately, with the odds stacked against them, likely never will. The chattering flocks of passing-through waxwings have already continued on. The island's frogs and turtles are, I suspect, settling into the mud. Maybe, too, that salamander I rescued from our cellar in July. But bees are still buzzing in my garden even if, in the morning's chill and waiting for the sun to move above the trees, they cling, unmoving, as though in drugged sleep to the snakeroot's still blossom-packed spikes. Any honeybees among them will surely soon have to tightly pack themselves together, a buzzing sphere that heats the whole hive, each bee occasionally attempting to switch positions from the cold outer to the cozy inner. And thus survive. This year our house's western-facing wall has not been plastered with ladybugs on the move, suggesting what, I wonder, about aphids on my roses? And though there is less evidence here than in Illinois of honking geese V-ing their way south, I do still try to imagine what, if any, urges they create passing over a barnyard of domesticated fowl. The deer are, of course, still busy, now more boldly stepping from the woods for apple windfall, but given the unmistakable signs at Joyce Hardware that next month's color of choice is blaze-orange, they'd do well, if they could, to book their departure.

*T*he signs we humans make that we've arrived at the season of Almost Winter are no less obvious. Along with the "Closed" signs appearing like mushrooms after rain on restaurants, galleries, and certain access roads, there are the hauled-ashore boats and tarped lawn furniture. Also sheets of plastic taped to the windows of old drafty Capes and hay bales piled against the cellar doors of the island's earliest farmhouses. More folks now park at the causeway and pitchfork the shoreline's mineral-rich wrack into their pickup beds to mulch and protect their overwintering garden beds. And Burnt Cove Market offers more proof that it's never too early to talk about snow and ice. As abundant with boxes of cereals and cans of soup, the aisles fill with predictions about impending weather, though the dire choices, it seems, boil down to just two: "Snow, lots of snow" or, in its absence, the "Worse than last year" prolonged spell of subzero days. There is to all this speculation a submission to the inevitable. But isn't it also a way for islanders to remind one another we've been through this before and, properly prepared, we'll get through it again? Elsewhere and less obvious, but no less an imperative, is the final fling of canning and preserving taking place in numerous island kitchens. And all done at such a pace, it's as if winter is a tangible being lurking in the wings, some cruel foreman on an assembly line who's about to flick a switch and hurtle the whole process forward at an unmanageable speed.

My end-of-season tasks, though many, seem so much simpler. Now, with the flowerpots emptied, the furniture stowed, the wood stacked, I make calls: to suspend the phone service, to ask Lewis to come and bleed the pipes and disconnect the appliances, to remind Ron we need to erect the deer fencing. There are still runs to the dump to be made, mothballs to be sprinkled into closets.

Outside, I've yet to tag the last of the trees or do my ritualistic culling of a summer's worth of "finds"—all the myriad shells, sand dollars, bits of bones and wishing rocks our houseguests and grandchildren hauled up from shore but then left behind, piled on deck railings and windowsills like miniature middens. My garden, though, having gotten my keenest attention, is close to being tucked in.

Little says as much about time passing, of another summer's falling away, as a garden in October. Spent blooms, bare stalks, dried seed pods and tattered crowns, stakes holding up nothing—all speak to a garden's past, but not truly its end. That isn't known yet. Unless you're talking about a vegetable garden where little that grows is perennial, and for which, come each mid-September, an end is in sight. A perennial and shrub garden speaks to an assumed continuity, but it, too, can end in the mortal sense. Starved by drought. Fungus-blighted by record rain. Killed by cycles of freeze-and-thaw or a snowless, desiccating cold. Who can predict what the bugs will savor, the deer or rabbits or gnawing voles, or what, in their springtime plunder, the squirrels will unearth? All those unseen eyes now watching me from the woods. To where the fence goes up and the spring bulbs are planted, to what is transplanted and where, and if, on my countless trips to the garage, I carry from it a roll of protective gnaw-proof tape to wrap the young Japanese maple's tender trunk.

There is an end, though, to what the garden this past summer looked like. Never again will it look the same. Next summer, if they survive, the roses will climb further up the deck railing. If we get enough early rain, the liatris will likely double, but a drier spring will surely keep the lushness out of the lungwort and lady's mantle. With Chris's removal this winter of some of the dying spruce in the adjacent woods, one of my perennial beds will get more sun—a gift surely to the hydrangea, an unwelcome adjustment for the aruncus.

This afternoon, as I cut back the last of the spent perennials, the weight of the sun falling more lightly on my back than just a few days ago, I join the vast family of gardeners who foster delusions of grandeur in January when garden catalogues first appear in mailboxes and through the spring thaw that never arrives fast enough. As winter winds blow, in the absence of any actual clearing or digging, any need to amend or transplant, we lean back in our armchairs and dream big. Suddenly, our narrow cultivated borders have the immensity of the beds at Sissinghurst. Our native lean cover of topsoil becomes hospitable and forgiving. We may, for a time, thumbing those catalogue pages, forget we're in Zone 5. And just barely.

July of course tells another story. We'll know then whether spring disappointed. Rain will have delivered either too much or not enough. Whatever the conditions responsible for it, there may be an army of slugs decimating the seedlings we encouraged for weeks beneath grow lights. And time, we'll wonder in midsummer—where did it go? We'll scratch our heads, look around at the yet-to-be-painted garden shed, the ravaged lettuce and peas a testament to the deer fence that never went up. What happened to the trellises planned for the clematis and the New Dawn rose, the painterly vision of abundant pink blooms climbing the house's south-facing wall? Just look at the weeds taking hold where what was planted refused to grow. So much for the campanula being strangled by the mallow that didn't get yanked, the monarda that wasn't thinned. In the woods bordering the lawn, touch-me-not, unchecked, still goes berserk.

And yet now, in early October with imminent frost threatening, with the wind-alert forecast of tonight's "leaf-stripping gusts," I stake out a new expanded bed facing the bay. I transition into the future, thinking about beginnings, armed with a garden's truest gift: its promise of hope and renewal.

*S*till with us today are remnants of rain and the big winds that blew through last night—and yes, stripped away leaves, even the oak's, plastering them against the window panes and deck planks. Suddenly, there's more barrenness overhead, although, oddly, the shadows the trees now cast seem deeper, darker.

Walking through our woods in my ongoing forest management efforts, among the newly fallen deciduous leaves yet to dry and obligingly crunch beneath my feet, I tag a few more dead and dying spruce for Chris to cull this winter. The orange plastic tape I tie around the trunks dance in the wind like ribbon streamers. They almost look festive, as if the wind as harbinger of colder days ahead is being offered as a gaily wrapped gift. Trying to see beyond the ribbons to what this familiar landscape will look like when I return is nearly impossible. Months from now, I'll be surprised when I drive down our lane and see at first only empty spaces and not the healthier spruce seedlings taking hold or the oak and birch saplings long hungry for more light and, newly exposed, reaching for it.

This morning, walking these woods I've come to know, I'm reminded of how a place and a person can come to belong to each other, or rather, as Wendell Berry asserts, how a person can come to belong to a place, "for places really belong to nobody." We are, he says, the belongings of the world, not its owners. Indeed, a place outlives us. But it also bears the results of our ownership, all the ways we deeply affect a place for good or ill.

Again, I can't help but ask myself how I will go about leaving a mark on this land. What traces will I leave? It's what we all do, isn't it?—leave our traces. Make our mark.

"No one is making any more waterfront property," I've heard said by many people here, often by those who already possess their own shore-front and aren't griping about rising prices and taxes. And from the conservationists' camp: "When it's gone, it's gone." All of which makes the responsibility particularly keen. I hold as fact that if you're lucky enough to own land, especially in a beautiful place, even if a few bony acres, you have a responsibility in most decisions you make—what kind of house to build, how many trees to clear, how close to the shore to build, and, after, where or if to erect a fence. Where to cultivate, manicure, let grow wild. Traces of all such decisions last for years and years to come.

And over time, claims writer and rural landowner Verlyn Klinkenborg, a "self-portrait" emerges that, like it or not, bares the subtleties of our character.

The way the land is developed or not, how a house is sited, how and of what materials it is built reveal our sense of or lack of stewardship, as well as, among other things, our preference for order over disorder, for how much we need to hide and how big or little we've made our ambitions. What no one else notices, the land and homeowner readily sees. As hidden from the view of others as our secrets or dreams is the ideal home or landscape that exists only in our minds. A landscape, for example, without the tangle of raspberry canes threatening to strangle the new spruce seedlings. A shoreline without erosion or the woods without a boggy bowl of low-lying land where even skunk cabbage refuses to thrive. A house minus windows so improperly situated you can't take in what's considered the best view. Intentions coexist with reality. The garage workbench that for all your love of order and neatness is a nearly hopeless clutter of unused tools, paint cans, pipes, and tangled rope. At the woods' edge, the heaped granite blocks with jewelweed and hay-scented ferns now growing among them look almost picturesque but were meant years ago to be the makings of a walkway to the side door.

This time of year, a kind of accounting takes place. The fulfillment, perhaps, of our intentions. For many folks, it's about toting up a harvest—the bushels of apples, pounds of lobsters, cords of wood. The number of jars of stewed tomatoes and wild blueberry jam. Maybe it's the new roof on the garage or the rebuilt stone wall. It is, as Klinkenborg notes, an ancestral satisfaction.

I'm surrounded by so many people, some of them true jacks-of-all-trades, who possess an abiding resourcefulness, approach an enviable self-reliance. Who know how to make and fix. Who, even deep into winter, miles out in the dark and in stinging spray, with frozen lines and on ice-slick decks, trap and haul and drag. Folks who keep chickens for eggs, goats for cheese and yogurt and soap. Whose bees provide honey, and who, with well-tended orchards and kitchen vegetable gardens, coupled with abilities to preserve and stew, keep larders full. I admire such talents. I wish I had more of them. At times, I cast my eyes beyond my perennial beds, my cutting and herb gardens and pots on my deck, and wonder where I might put in a few rows of tomatoes and beans. Maybe some apple trees.

Unlike other islanders, I'm unlikely to do more than tinker in any of what they do with such competence and, to my observer's eye, natural ease. I do rejoice, though, in the abundance of those who grow, tend, card, and weave. I gladly take part in the cornucopia of the Friday mornings' farmers' market. For years, I was gratified to see the Chapins' wooden sign hung out on Route 15 to alert us to their first fall harvesting of Gravensteins and Paula Reds. All winter, I use Jon and Jen's amber maple syrup and dream of late-summer pancakes with Nicholas's hand-raked wild blueberries. For years, I vowed that were I here for Thanksgiving, I'd surely order a turkey from Island Acres, even though I'd grown to love the sight of them dumbly flocking atop an old wooden boat that for so long occupied the field where they ranged. My spirits are still raised by the mere sight of Neva's bright braided rugs and colorful skeins of local wool she shelves in Periwinkle all summer, even though I have no intention to knit or braid rugs.

But who knows? If I were to become a year-rounder, who can say what unlikely path I'd wander down? Klinkenborg, in describing his interest in getting a few pigs, wrote: "I'm giving into the logic of where I live and the land I live on."

I doubt pigs are in my future. (No doubt good news for my next-door neighbors.) I'm happy to buy my sausage, bacon and ham steaks from Sunset Acres or Old Ackley Farm. And any windfall from any apple trees I'd nurture would surely not go to pigs but be left for the browsing deer, if only to turn their attention away from my rhododendrons.

I may not have many of the admirable talents of my neighbors, but I have a leg up on two women down the road who, when moving here year-round from the city, didn't know how to properly stack their firewood and had four cords' worth topple over three times. And when stuffing the stove before going to bed, they didn't know enough to open the flues. *Red hot* does, under certain circumstances, take on serious meaning.

"The work of belonging to a place is never finished," asserts Sanders in *Staying Put*, suggesting that even with several years under my belt, I've not come close to knowing this island. But numerous fragments, like a mosaic's grouted shards or a quilt's stitched pattern, continue to be pieced together into something whole. These many summers I've spent here are still slowly revealing to me the kind of life I might live here, were I to stay year-round. I think of winter's long dark months, the wind beating against the window, pushing under the eaves, the coves and bays locked in ice, and I imagine what new projects I could take up here. Preserving or bread baking? Maybe weaving? Might I become more involved at the school? Take a workshop at Haystack and learn how to throw pots or twist wires into something resembling a basket? Audition for a part in the annual Cabin Fever Players production or for one of the play readings at Opera House Arts? Rather than closing things down in October, might I one day be asking in anticipation, "What next?"

Surely, when deep winter arrives and spring and summer's "outside concerns," as Berry calls them, lessen, I would, as I do back in Illinois, more seriously and joyously settle back into my writing, hunker down at my desk by the window, light falling across the inviting empty page, snow drifting up on the other side of the glass, puffed chickadees busily flitting at the feeder, sea smoke rising over the bay. When what in the future had been bearing down is now present.

Confronting winter, such an act of going inward seems as necessary as the need for other species to hibernate in burrow or mud bank. Winter demands its own pace. Requires elemental concerns. Asks of us the basics. To live here year-round requires a certain withdrawal. And for some islanders, an extraordinary effort not to tip into the darkness of depression or drink, or to sink into desperation as prices of heating oil rise and incomes stay fixed, or worse, decline. Maybe that's partly why, before spring, there are numerous intervening holidays and community events, some surely created for the sole purpose of physical connection, for communing with fellow islanders and feeding, often with potlucks or pancake breakfasts, our emotional well-being. Without a choice, people must submit to winter but are conjoined by the memories of other winters faced down, rooted to landscape and the social topography of community. To the central human act of inhabiting, connecting with a place that, for a time, belongs to us and we to it.

I wake up this morning to a gift—another dawn above freezing. Not that it's not cold or the air not obligatorily brittling in its march toward a raw, bitter bite.

Already, two days ago, on a mid-40s afternoon when I couldn't chase the chill from the house's bones, I relented and built the first fire. How much easier, isn't it, remembering the exact day of the woodstove's first blaze than its last in late spring when so many beginnings crowd out what ends? I'm sure then it was one of those weeks I can't help but wish now to have back, when the daylight hours were longer, the garden mere promising shoots, the summer commitment calendar blank. When our resident crows still quizzically pondered the peanuts I'd begun to put out for them each morning.

As more seasonal folks have packed up their cars and driven off, caretakers and other hired help descend. This morning's quiet is sliced open by the sound of chain saws somewhere near. Soon they'll cease and another kind of noise will shatter the morning's quiet, when anyone walking the woods will need an orange vest. Not long after that, mornings will succumb to a deep wintry stillness.

Before then, though, and fast approaching, is the day we make the pilgrimage from alarm clock to coffeemaker to microwave and adjust the time. "Fall back," we're reminded, as we adjust our clocks and gain the hour we lost in April's "Spring forward." All of that hour—every minute and second of it retrieved. In so little else do we get such a full refund, making Daylight Saving Time seem like a great deal. So much so, we might almost think we control time. Or that we can adequately name it. Recently I learned that Greenwich Mean Time has been bumped aside by what's presumptuously known as Coordinated Universal Time, as if it were capable of taking in the whole cosmos. Soon, with the clocks reset, I'll again lament the earlier, darker afternoons but welcome the brighter hint of early morning light, all the better to make sure the socks I'm pulling on match.

But still, for me, the time here seems most appropriately measured by *already* and *all ready*.

All summer I measure. Fourth of July *already*. Though maybe cool and wet and foggy in a summer that's still elusive, August almost over *already*. Labor Day, that other bookend of summer, here *already*. And now October, time to close things up, *already*. With each comes a kind of surprise—the rapidity of its arrival, the compression between each benchmark.

And with each *already* I ask: Am I *all ready*? Ready for our annual Fourth of July barbeque, our August houseguests? Ready for the onslaught of friends leaving the island over Labor Day weekend? *All ready* for the autumn crimsons and the yellow, *already* called-back-into-action school buses once too far in the distance to contemplate? But no time here asks, Am I *all ready*? as do these final weeks in October.

Beyond the physical acts of my becoming all ready in my necessary and ritualistic closing of the house is an overriding question: Am I all ready to assign to the past another season? Has another season here refreshed, renewed, engaged, fed me? I cannot measure it in terms of a squirrel's horde or a bear's girth of new fat. I do not mark the season by burrowing into a pond's mud or a den in the bank. Nor will I, soon, like the islanders hunkering down for the months ahead, pull closer to stove and hearth as smoke spirals rise and coves begin to skim over with ice.

The year-rounders and I do share a common direction though. We each travel into the unknown, whatever the time zone, however measured. There, nothing is guaranteed. Yes, come next summer, Heart Island will certainly remain off our shore, as will the Camden Hills on the horizon, and, closer in, the Nubbins and Gull Ledge. Most of the trees will likely remain, the bunchberries, mussel shoals, the squadrons of squabbling gulls. But who of us will not be here to witness?

Like others who pack up and drive off, I go into winter, planning that I will return, throw open windows and doors, plant a garden, walk the shore. Most days, I'm not even conscious of it as the days click past. But not so in October. Facing a long winter's uncertainty, whether here or away, requires confidence, a dose of hubris, a leap of faith. A belief, in whatever form it takes, that allows us to observe with incredulity, "Already?" even if, about the unknown, we may never be able to say with complete conviction, "I am all ready."

*T*oday at last, last tasks. I shelve bed linens and towels, cover furniture, drop the blinds, empty pantry and fridge, squeeze in a last walk on the shore before packing the car. Tomorrow, in advance of the militant frosts, I'll load my cooler and thermos into the front seat, and, for the first time in weeks, lock the garage. In predawn darkness, the wrens in their early nattering will sound perplexed at my unusual busy-ness. Our three crows up in the oak will undoubtedly engage in their imitation of a philosophical discussion. In the final act of my long good-bye, I'll drive down our lane more slowly than the way, months ago, I arrived. And so begin the drive away.

ACKNOWLEDGMENTS

*F*irst and foremost, I need to thank my husband Bob for his unflagging love, support, and tolerance, for his willingness to appear in these pages, and for the many ways he continues to open his heart to me. He is my one true partner in the journey, my safe harbor when seas are rough. If there is any failure here to reflect his generosity of spirit or good humor, the fault is solely mine.

I owe the deepest gratitude to Andrea Hollander Budy, extraordinary writer, editor, and dear friend of more than twenty-two years without whom this book would not have come into being. Her encouragement, insights, and critical suggestions are evident on every page.

I am blessed by the love and support of family, most particularly my sister, Christina Roberts, fellow keeper of old stories, whose hand on the tiller is often more steady than mine. I owe special thanks to Michael, Jimmy, Micaela, Annie, Sam, Sarah, Carolyn, and Daniel, the children of our family who, in visiting the island with youthful eyes, helped open my eyes to new wonders.

I couldn't have come close to understanding the importance of place without the community of friends with whom I share it. For their laughter and shared stories, their fine meals and long hikes, for their comfort and support in grieving times, for their ongoing interest in and encouragement of my work, I would be remiss not to acknowledge in particular several women: Deb DeWitt, Lydia Cassatt Osgood, Charlotte Podolsky, Joan Sorensen, Linda Powell, Mary Kay Ricks, and Chick White. And thank you as well to the many finest kind "local guides," my neighbors, friends, and fellow islanders who have contributed to my Deer Isle life over the years by way of their archival knowledge, individual talent, good example, and commitment to place and community. Though unnamed here, hopefully you know who you are. Chief among those folks who early on helped me secure my footing, maintain its balance, and who continue still to guide me toward my holding ground, I must acknowledge Linda Stratton, Neva Beck, Loring and Claudette Kydd, and Lew Ellis. Many—too many island friends—have died in recent years. I continue to mourn their passing and to celebrate their lives, among them Lael Stegall, Ingrid Mencken, Norma Hensslear, and Mary Talbot.

I am grateful to Marcia Aldrich, former editor of *Fourth Genre*, for first publishing "Ebb & Flow." Likewise, big thanks to Heidemarie Weidner of *Under The Sun*, in whose pages "Names" first appeared. Much appreciation goes to Maine Writers & Publishers Alliance for honoring "Ebb and Flow" as the winner in the Short Works of Nonfiction category of the 2012 Maine Literary Awards.

For providing the space and time and a nurturing, supportive environment in which several of these essays were first hatched or in later versions polished, I must thank the Virginia Center for the Creative Arts.

I also need to acknowledge Jane Karker and the good folks at Maine Authors Publishing, particularly Cheryl McKeary, David Allen and Lindy Gifford for their able assistance and patience, and Genie Daley for her keen eye. Thanks, too, to artist Alison Goodwin for her permission to use "House Island" for this book's cover. And to John Roberts for the authors photo.

As I make clear in numerous references and attributions in these pages, I had good company on this journey. In the words of writer Mary Rose O'Reilly, "I am not the first woman trying to form 'home' on a stuttering tongue." To the many fine writers who have inspired me with their insights, examples, and knowledge of their home ground, of digging in and staying put, I am deeply grateful. Good companions, their books have played a big role in my journey of discovery. I return to them still. Hopefully they've each been referenced and attributed with full accuracy in these pages and without omission in the Selected Bibliography, including James Galvin whose opening pages of *The Meadow* helped guide me in writing mine.

I must also acknowledge my gratitude for this island itself, and for the serendipitous confluence of factors, many of them bewildering to me still, that first brought me here and continue to enable my return.

Finally a tip of the cap to local lobsterman Dick Bridges, who, visiting us at our house for the first time, said, "So this is where you drop anchor." Indeed.

SELECTED BIBLIOGRAPHY

Gaston Bachelard. *The Poetics of Space*, Beacon Press, Boston,1969.
Wendell Berry. *The Long-Legged House*, Shoemaker and Hoard, Washington, D.C., 1965.
Henry Beston. *The Outermost House*, Henry Holt & Co., New York, 1955.
Philip Conkling. *Islands in Time*, Downeast Books, Rockport, ME, 198l.
Alain deBotton. *The Architecture of Happiness*, Pantheon Books, New York, 2006
Annie Dillard. *Pilgrim at Tinker Creek*, Harper & Row, New York, 1974.
Robert Finch. *The Primal Place*, The Countryman Press, Woodstock, VT, 1983.
———. *Death of a Hornet*, Counterpoint, Washington, D.C., 2000.
Winifred Gallagher. *The Power of Place*, Harper Perennial, New York, 1993.
James Galvin. *The Meadow*, Henry Holt & Co., New York, 1992.
David Gessner. *A Wild, Rank Place*, University Press of New England, Hanover, NH, 1997.
———. *Return of the Osprey*, Ballantine Books, New York, 2001.
Bernd Heinrich. A Year in the Maine Woods, Da Capo Press, New York, 1994.
Hannah Holmes. *Suburban Safari*, Bloomsbury, New York, 2005.
Barbara Hurd. *Stirring the Mud*, Mariner Books, Boston, 2001.
———. *Walking the Wrack Line*, The University of Georgia Press, Athens, GA, 2008.
Verlyn Klinkenborg. *Rural Life*, Back Bay Books, Boston, 2002.
Lisa Knopp. *The Nature of Home*, University of Nebraska Press, Lincoln, NE, 2002.

———. *Interior Places,* University of Nebraska Press, Lincoln, NE, 2008.

Ted Kooser. *Local Wonders,* University of Nebraska Press, Lincoln, NE, 2002.

John Lane. *Circling Home,* The University of Georgia Press, Athens, GA, 2007.

Thomas Lynch. *The Undertaking,* W.W. Norton & Co., New York, 1997.

Wesley McNair. *Mapping the Heart: Reflections on Place and Poetry,* Carnegie Mellon Press, Pittsburgh, 2002.

Kathleen Deane Moore. *The Pine Island Paradox,* Milkweed Editions, Minneapolis, 2004.

Kathleen Norris. *Dakota,* Houghton Mifflin, New York,1993.

Sherwin B. Nuland. *How We Die,* Alfred A. Knopf, New York, 1994.

Mary Rose O'Reilly. *The Love of Impermanent Things,* Milkweed Editions, Minneapolis, 2006

Juhani Pallasmaa. *The Thinking Hand,* John Wiley & Sons, West Sussex, United Kingdom, 2009

Chet Raymo. *Honey From Stone,* Cowley Publications, Cambridge, MA, 1987

PattiAnn Rogers. *The Dream of the Marsh Wren,* Milkweed Editions, Minneapolis, 1999.

Robert Root, editor. *Landscapes with Figures,* University of Nebraska Press, Lincoln, NE, 2007.

Bill Roorbach. *Temple Stream,* Dial Press, New York, 2005.

Scott Russell Sanders. *Staying Put,* Beacon Press, Boston, 1993.

Le Anne Schreiber. *Light Years,* Lyons & Burford, New York, 1996.

Tracy Seeley. *My Ruby Slippers,* University of Nebraska Press, Lincoln, NE, 2011.

Carolyn Servid. *Of Landscape and Longing.* Milkweed Editions, Minneapolis, 2000.

Alix Kates Shulman. *Drinking the Rain,* North Point Press, New York, 1995.

Deborah Tall. *From Where We Stand,* The Johns Hopkins University Press, Baltimore, 1993.

Yi-Fu Tuan. *Space and Place.* University of Minnesota Press, Minneapolis, 1977.

Terry Tempest Williams. *Refuge.* Vintage Books, New York, 1991.

Ann Haymond Zwinger. *Shaped by Wind & Water,* Milkweed Editions, Minneapolis, 2000.

ABOUT THE AUTHOR

*D*eborah Cummins is the author of two collections of poetry, *Beyond the Reach* and *Counting the Waves,* and a poetry chapbook, *From the Road It Looks Like Paradise.* Her work has appeared in numerous literary journals and magazines and has been featured often on Garrison Keillor's *The Writers' Almanac* and in the *American Life in Poetry* syndicated newspaper column edited by former U.S. Poet Laureate Ted Kooser. A former board member of the Poetry Foundation, Cummins served as its Board Chair in 2001–2005. She currently resides in Chicago, Illinois, and Deer Isle, Maine. Her website is: www.deborahcummins.com.